To Ladera—
all my best,

Pebble
in the
Water

BOB WELCH

AO CREATIVE
Eugene, Oregon

Published by AO CREATIVE
P.O. Box 41794
Eugene, OR 97404
www.aocreative.com

Back cover photo by Sally Welch

ISBN: 978-1-60643-576-2
Printed in Canada

Author information:

www.bobwelch.net
info@bobwelch.net

Cover image from Fotosearch,
licensed by Publitek, Inc.

Also by Bob Welch

Easy Company Soldier *
My Seasons
My Oregon
American Nightingale
The Things That Matter Most
Stories from the Game of Life
Where Roots Grow Deep
A Father for All Seasons
More to Life Than Having It All
Bellevue and the New East Side

* In collaboration with Don Malarkey

To Nathan Fendrich,
whose passion to remember the past
started it all

Drop a pebble in the water;
  just a splash and it is gone;
But there's a half-a-hundred ripples
  circling on and on,
Spreading, spreading, from the center,
  flowing on out to the sea
And there's no way of telling
  where the end is going to be.

  —James W. Foley
  Found in Frances Slanger's scrapbook

Author's note

This book was born of a passion far beyond my own, a passion rooted in Frances Slanger, a Polish Jew who immigrated to America, grew up the daughter of a Boston fruit peddler, and became a World War II nurse. Despite those who told her otherwise, Slanger believed she could change the world in some small but significant way. And she did.

Nearly sixty years after her body had been lowered into the snow-dusted soil of Belgium on October 24, 1944, I learned of her story. That discovery was either an amazing coincidence or, as British author G.K. Chesterson said of uncanny occurrences, a "spiritual pun."

"You didn't find this story," Jane Kirkpatrick, a novelist and friend, told me. "This story found you."

More than three years after I jotted ideas on a Wendy's Hamburgers napkin, *American Nightingale: The Story of Frances Slanger, Forgotten Heroine of Normandy*, was published by Simon & Schuster's Atria Books in May 2004. Nothing I've done in my three decades of journalism has been as difficult; at times I felt like a literary Indiana Jones, trying to outrun a giant bowling ball while searching for the Lost Ark of the Covenant. Meanwhile, nothing I've done has been as rewarding; at times I felt blessed just to be hacking through the jungle on this adventure. In retrospect, I must have realized from the beginning that I was in for something special because from Day One I kept a detailed journal of the journey on my laptop computer.

When it was over, I could never shake the idea that the larger story—the finding and telling of *American Nightingale*—needed to be told. Not because I helped breathe life into the original story, but because I learned lessons along the way, lessons worth sharing. The book-on-a-book approach, then, becomes, in the words of Philip Lopate in *The Art of the Personal Essay*, "the reverse of that set of Chinese boxes that you keep opening, only to find a smaller one within." I began with a single box, Frances Slanger. And each person who came alongside me in reviving her legacy thus added a slightly larger box to the collection, building stories upon stories, lessons upon lessons.

What I learned is that amazing things happen when people— even obscure, untested, and, in my case, obsessed people—catch a common vision and dare to invest in it. And that the treasure you find at adventure's end may not be the treasure you originally sought. Indeed, it may be far more valuable.

When *Nightingale* was published in 2004 and I spoke about it from Bellingham, Washington, to Boston—to 300 people in hotel ballrooms and to seven-person book clubs in living rooms— I discovered something else: People were intrigued not only by Slanger's story, but also by my story; not only by the "where, when, and why" of a Word War II nurse, but also in the "how" of an author. How do you resurrect a story that's been lying dormant since 1944 and happened thousands of miles from where you live?

In regard to books, I realized, some people are like a young boy I met at a Eugene Barnes & Noble autograph session. "I think I'd like to be an author," he said. "You sign autographs and people give you money." I laughed inside, unable to fault his limited perspective. He was no different from the diner who enjoys a restaurant meal but doesn't stop to think, from soil to kitchen to plate, all that was involved in creating that meal. We seldom consider what we cannot see for ourselves. And most of the research and writing of a book—surprisingly, most of the promoting and marketing of a book—are done in obscurity.

In the case of *American Nightingale*, the unseen stuff was my 5 A.M. research and writing sessions before heading off to my day job as a newspaper columnist; the three-hour, ten-phone-call research sessions that produces absolutely nothing; and the monthly four-digit Visa card bills.

But the unseen stuff was also the inspirational stuff: the strangers who, even as I was stymied in putting the Slanger puzzle together, would step forward with just the right-shaped piece of information at just the right time. The serendipitous stuff: how, in simply checking the spelling of a man's name, I came across a World War II expert who volunteered two years of his life to help unravel the mystery of Frances Slanger. The uncanny stuff: how my wife and I wound up in Normandy, France, on 9/11. Even the funny stuff: me madly racing around Eugene, Oregon, at three o'clock in the morning, desperately seeking an ink cartridge so I could get a 300-page manuscript printed in time for a 10 A.M. appointment with an agent.

Pebble in the Water, then, is for readers who might be interested in the seldom-told story of an author's journey, an emotional Mr. Toad's Wild Ride that includes side stories such as the complexities of a son dealing with a long-gone father and the craziness of a lukewarm baseball fan falling in love with a faraway team.

It is also for people looking for hope. While giving talks across the country about Slanger, I realized how hungry people are for something to believe in. Like *American Nightingale, Pebble in the Water* is rooted in hope, the belief that the Davids of the world can overcome the Goliaths. That the truest honor goes far beyond fame, beauty, power, and money, to the giving of ourselves to something greater than ourselves. And that each one of us is somehow *necessary*.

Finally, I've written this book for writers like those I've taught in my Beachside Writers Workshops—the ones who kept reminding me how, even as I encouraged them to take risks, I kept postponing "that Pebble book" I had promised to write. Part of my reluctance was feeling that I didn't deserve to write this book, that perhaps it was just my way of not letting go of Slanger, a case of literary postpartum blues. But then a writer friend reminded me that I'd had two books published since *American Nightingale*. "You're over it, Welch," she said. "So write the book."

But there was more. Another part of my reluctance was a sense that writing a book about, well, writing a book was somehow cheating, like in fourth grade when I wrote a paper on how I couldn't think of anything to write about. Or if not cheating, then at least self-serving, as if to say, in a time when 195,000 books were published the year *Nightingale* was: *Look at me. I wrote a book!*

As I resisted the urge to begin, my Beachside students kept holding my hypocritical feet to the fire. One reminded me how I was forever preaching that writers need two things: the confidence to believe they have something to say to the the world and the humility to allow others to help them say it better. So where was my confidence? And what about that quote from Pulitzer Prize-winning author Annie Dillard I often shared with students: "What would you begin writing if you knew you would die soon?"

I realized, assuming that hypothetical circumstance, I would begin writing the book you're reading. And what I would say is this: Writers or not, we all make more of a difference in the world than we possibly know.

It's a lesson I learned from a fruit peddler's daughter.

Bob Welch
Eugene, Oregon
June 2008

Chapter 1

April 2004
Boston, Massachusetts

I felt fear's echo, and along with that I felt the unhinged,
uncontrollable joy which had been its accompaniment and
opposite face, joy which had broke out sometimes in those days
like Northern Lights across the black sky.
  —John Knowles, *A Separate Peace*

The voices of the subterranean river in the shadows were
different from the voices of the sunlit river ahead. In the
shadows against the cliff the river was deep and engaged in
profundities .... But the river ahead came out in the sunny
world like a chatterbox, doing its best to be friendly.
  —Norman Maclean, *A River Runs Through It*

I AWOKE a block from Boston's Fenway Park in a century-old hotel so strange that my room not only contained a locked door labeled "Mechanical Room No. 3" but also a list on the wall of what I'd be charged for every item I stole: "Lamp $50, Blow Dryer $35, Towel $10," etc.

A night clerk once told me that Babe Ruth—the great "Bambino" himself—had stayed in this hotel when he'd played baseball for the Red Sox from 1915 to 1919. But if you could picture the Hotel Buckminster having had a certain nobility to it, by April 2004 the place was like the corpse of Hemingway's great marlin in *The Old Man and the Sea,* a mere shell of what it had been, picked clean by the hands of time. And, given the price list on the wall, apparently not expecting a particularly noble clientele either.

It was, thanks to some of Boston's spoke-like street layouts, triangular in shape, like a giant slice of mud pie: five stories tall, brick, with narrow hallways jutting this way and that. My tempo-

1

rary abode was the size of a pregnant college dorm room, walls done in salmon pink, the decor sort of "European craigslist." In the bathroom, you could towel-off only north-south, lest your elbows punch holes in the walls. No mints on the bed. No terry cloth bath-robes in the closet. Just a coupon for a free continental breakfast at the Sushi bar next door—and whatever lay behind the door saying "Mechanical Room No. 3."

I noted "5:12" on the alarm clock, one of two I had set, and said a prayer. Nothing fancy, and probably more selfishly des-perate than God would have preferred in a world of war, hunger, and disease, but at least honest. Something, I recall, about staying calm. In about three hours, I expected my life to change big-time: I was going to be interviewed for *Good Morning America* about my forthcoming book, *American Nightingale: The Story of Frances Slanger, Forgotten Heroine of Normandy.*

Forget butterflies. My stomach was aflutter with thousands of those winged creatures in Jurrasic Park. Part of me couldn't wait for this opportunity. And part of me dreaded it. Anticipation and fear. The story of my life.

The anticipation: I was to be interviewed by ABC Medical Edi-tor Dr. Timothy Johnson for a show that, when aired six week's hence, might send my book into marketing orbit. I'd somehow won the authors' equivalent of a state lottery, certainly not *Oprah!* but a show on which *American Nightingale* would be exposed to more people than even live in my home state of Oregon.

The fear: I'd oversleep. Or because of a language barrier, my cabbie would misunderstand my destination and take me to Quincy or Sharon or Cleveland. Or, if I did somehow make the interview, some catastrophic event—say, the death of a president—would blow us off the air at the last minute. Somehow, the clock would strike midnight.

It was a fear probably born of similar experiences I'd had as a Kidsports baseball coach and nurtured by my having fallen in love with the Red Sox since coming to Boston for book research three years before. As if, like the Sox, I were under some sort of close-but-no-cigar curse. Since trading Babe Ruth to the Yankees in 1920, Boston was thought to have been under the "curse of the Bambino." Even if the team had its hands wrapped tightly around a pennant, something would happen and another championship would slip away. Yankees World Series titles since the Babe Ruth trade? Twenty-five. Red Sox? Zero.

No fewer than eleven times the Sox had been the bride who got to the altar—or at least began climbing the steps—only to have some self-imposed catastrophe scrub the wedding, fans running out of the church in teeth-gnashing anguish.

Among the more notable chokes came in 1986, when the Sox led the New York Mets 5-3 in the top of the tenth and were within one out of winning the World Series. But a Kidsports grounder—a sure out—rolled beneath first baseman Bill Buckner's legs like a well-struck croquet ball through a wicket. The Sox went on to lose the game and the Series.

I could relate. I was the guy whose Kidsports baseball team made it to the championship game one year, only to have it can-celed because of the first rainfall of the summer. (Both teams were declared co-champions.) The guy whose team worked its way into the championship game two years later only to lose by a single run. Whose father had once made a movie, *Trout in the High Country*, that was going to hit the big-time but never got beyond being shown in a junior high auditorium.

I lay awake, reminded that it was just after 2 A.M. back home in Oregon and my wife, Sally, would be fast asleep. Reminded that I was in a Boston hotel that, in an odd way, I'd come to like because of its quirkiness. And in a room that, though lacking size and splendor, was saving me $100 to $200 a night compared to what I'd be paying in downtown's more austere blocks.

The price, I imagined, was largely what attracted other Buck-minster guests, though in two years of coming to Boston to do book research, I seldom had seen them. In fact, because I could go days without spotting another guest, at times I imagined I was the only person staying at the Buckminster, as if part of some weird *Twilight Zone* episode in which Rod Serling were going to sud-denly appear in the darkened lobby, take a drag on his cigarette, exhale, and say: "Bob Welch, an unknown Oregon author battling the demons of credit-card debt, thought he had discovered a cheap hotel in Boston that would keep Uncle Visa happy. What he didn't know was that this was no ordinary hotel. Because behind Mechanical Room No. 3 lay a sixth dimension beyond that which is known to man, a world where some say lurked the Ghost of the Great Bambino himself, Babe Ruth, all part of something known as the Buckminster Twilight Zone."

Indeed, if readers of my newspaper column back in Oregon imagined me enjoying the rarefied air of an "author's tour" for my forthcoming book, they didn't understand the wider context. Didn't understand that such rarefied air was imbued with the slight smell of a breakfast burrito wrapper from McDonald's, just across the street. And air which, in the 5:30 A.M. darkness, I could hear myself softly breathing, each breath an inhalation of anticipation and an exhalation of fear. For now, forget whatever lay beyond that odd door in my room. The chains of other ghosts were clinking from my past.

MY FATHER, Warren, who had died unexpectedly at seventy-two, had been a commercial photographer. More importantly, a dreamer. A tinkerer. An inventor. I remember him filming something for a state-funded "teaching research" program that involved a local thespian reading Longfellow's "The Wreck of the Hesperus" poem. Meanwhile, the film showed a ship being battered by huge waves. The waves were actually only two inches high, my father having turned our bathtub into the Atlantic Ocean, using a fan to buffet the scale-model ship with gale-force winds.

Long before you could buy an underwater camera with a click of a computer mouse, my father had built an underwater housing box so he could film rainbow trout beneath the surfaces of pack-in lakes high in the Cascade Mountains. After I received a Tudor Tru-Action Electric Football set for my fifth birthday, he made me a set of NFL-style goal posts out of coat hangers, complete with electrical tape padding at their base to protect my two-inch-tall players from injury.

A few years later, he launched his ultimate dream: to make a movie about fishing the high lakes of Oregon and, ultimately, to have some Hollywood mogul buy the rights to it and have it shown all over the world on the big screen. The mantra from my "Wonder Years" childhood was " ... when the movie sells ... ." It was seared into our family history, a promise of great things to come.

I'd say, "Mom, the Woodmans got a new Cadillac. Are we ever gonna get a new car?" And she'd say, "When the movie sells."

Meanwhile, my father spent years on *Trout in the High Country* during the pre-video days of the sixties. At night, I'd lie in bed while he did narration for the film with a reel-to-reel tape recorder in the family "rec room" next to my bedroom. Just as I was about to drift off to sleep I'd hear it: "Dammit!" He had garbled a sentence. Or the music that was supposed to start when a trout broke the surface of a lake began late. Or the film itself, like a derailed train, had slid off the tracks of the projector sprockets and was coiling up like a twenty-foot cobra.

The movie never sold. It was shown at our local junior high to an audience far smaller than we had anticipated. But though we managed to buy a 1962 Impala and even took a trip to Disneyland, *Trout in the High Country* died a quiet death somewhere in my childhood.

I grew up and become a newspaper reporter. Wrote some magazine articles and a few books. And always felt my father was proud of me. But if I was happy to have him as my father, in the years after he died in 1996 I was also quietly disappointed that he had given up on his dream. That, in his later years, instead of sharing his talents with others—even teaching a photography class at a local community college when asked—he had retreated inward. That, when he'd died of congestive heart failure, he had left some unfinished business.

At his memorial service, I had held up a tuna fish can in which a paint brush was permanently encased in dried fiberglass. He was better at creating things than cleaning up after the creation. "My father," I told the people gathered at First Presbyterian Church in Corvallis, "was a good man." But, I good-naturedly added, "his forte was not follow-through." I'll never know how such failures as the movie wounded him; I can only surmise that part of his sullenness in his later years was due to a sense that he'd taken a few leaps of faith and, in his estimation, landed on his face.

In 1986, the year Buckner made the error that Red Sox fans cannot forgive him for, I, too, decided to take a leap. At thirty-two, I bought a computer to do freelance writing in an attempt to supplement my newspaper income. At the time, my wife Sally and I had two young boys, Ryan, seven, and Jason, four. We lived in a house with pea-green carpet in Bellevue, Washington, sure we were the only renters in a wealthy community that was to the Welches what Beverly Hills was to the Clampets.

Over the next fifteen years, my freelance career climbed and dipped like a volatile stock market. In 1992, I had the good fortune of having a book published, *More to Life Than Having it All*, in which I decried the allure of materialism. But it sold so poorly— why couldn't people be more materialistic and buy it?—that the publisher called me a year after it was out to tell me it was being "remaindered." In essence, the plug was being pulled on it. "But we have five thousand copies here in the warehouse that we'll sell you for only seventy-five cents each," he said.

I thought of the year I had invested in that book. The late nights. The great hopes. The day I'd first seen it on the book shelf.

"So, what happens to those five thousand books if I don't buy them?"

"We'll have them recycled," he said.

Recycled? A few days later, I was having breakfast with a friend from Grace Community Fellowship, the church we both attended in Eugene, Oregon. He worked for a local company that did recycling.

"So, Steve, if they recycle my books, what might they make them into?"

"Oh, paper towels, tissues—uh, toilet paper."

"Toilet paper?"

As an author, my submarine of pride had just hit rock bottom, the Mariana Trench.

"Really? They could turn my book into toilet paper?"

" 'Fraid so, Bob," he said, trying to muffle his laughter lest he spew scrambled eggs in my face.

I mulled the scenario. "Man, when I started that book, I remember thinking: I want to write a book that will touch people's lives in a special place. That's not quite what I had in mind."

Authors, like animals, learn survival skills. Like clowns, we laugh so we don't cry. Thus, when people asked how my book was doing, I'd simply say, "Hey, I'm on a roll."

Ultimately, I would buy those 5,000 books and sell them at

talks I gave. Give them away to friends. Donate them to churches and other nonprofits. Once, for a "tacky party" Sally and I had, we lined the entire living room—every nook, shelf, and mantle—with dozens of copies of *More to Life Than Having It All*.

But laughing about one's failure is easier if you're the one who starts the joke. At a white-elephant Christmas party, we were laughing as we opened an array of stuff that people had either picked up at garage sales or gotten as gifts from taste-free aunts. Suddenly, my gut lurched. As someone unwrapped a present, there it was: a copy of *More to Life*. People howled. I didn't. I forced a smile—I didn't want to embarrass the gift-opener—but I hadn't been the giver of this gift. Someone else had thought that a book I'd poured my heart into was, in essence, a joke. Or, at least, had underestimated the staying power of failure.

I was reminded of that a few months after my father died and I'd gone to visit my mother. When I was about to leave, she took me out to the garage, still sprinkled with the stuff of the man we'd both loved. "I've got something here of your father's," she said. "I'm not sure whether you want it or not, but it's yours if you do."

She then handed me a dusty spool of movie film. It was *Trout in the High Country*.

TAKING NO chances, I showed up at Boston's Fairmont Copley Plaza more than an hour before I needed to be there. The hotel was even grander than I had imagined. A pair of regal gold lions welcomed guests on either side of the entry. Burgundy awnings cascaded off the sculpted exterior of the 1912 hotel. Attendants in well-starched uniforms welcomed me as if I were royalty instead of a guy who, while researching *American Nightingale*, had spent a night on the skywalk between Logan International Airport and a Hilton Hotel to save a hundred bucks on a night's lodging.

After being seated in the restaurant to grab a bite, I nearly spit out my water when seeing the prices on the menu. I looked around at business types in four-digit suits. I ordered fruit, a croissant, and orange juice, which was going to run me $18.50, not counting tip. I read the *Boston Globe*. It was April 21, 2004. In Colorado, Columbine High had just observed the five-year anniversary of its tragic shootings. CIA Director George Tenet was losing favor after his recent acknowledgment of intelligence failures prior to the 9/11 terrorist attack. Ronald Reagan was nearing death. And the Red Sox were heading into a three-game series against the New York Yankees, the team Boston fans had hated since the day Babe Ruth first put on pinstripes in 1920.

As I waited for my moment in the sun, the harpies in my mind were working overtime. I was hoping this interview was going to be my writing career's tipping point, a reversal of past failures, my *Trout in the High Country* with a happier ending, my "… grounder-to-Buckner-who-fields-it-and-steps-on-first-base-and-the-Red-Sox-win-the-Series!" moment.

Alas, the harpies had me right where they wanted me: hopeful. That's what makes curses so vexing: they tease us with hope. Just as Charlie Brown swings his leg, Lucy, with that innocent look on her face, pulls back the football. Just as I'm getting in the car to leave for that championship Kidsports baseball game, the skies open up and we don't get to play.

It was now five minutes to nine. I paid my bill—ouch—and headed for the elevator, the oddest of inspirations suddenly coming to mind. I'd seen it on my cab ride to the hotel earlier, a billboard featuring a giant photo of Red Sox left fielder Manny Ramirez, the kind of billboard you'd only find in a baseball city that had been haunted by eighty-six years of coming close but not getting to the top. "Keep the Faith," it said.

I had been on this journey for more than three years and when it was over would learn an array of lessons, one of which was this: nobody is changed more by a book than the one who writes it. For now, a slow grounder was dribbling toward me at first base. I stood in front of the suite where the *Good Morning America* interview would be. I breathed deeply, knocked on the door, and waited for whatever was to be.

Chapter 2

December 2000
Eugene, Oregon

*Every journey has a secret destination of which the traveler
is unaware.*
   —Martin Bube

A rocket won't fly unless someone lights the fuse.
   —Homer Hickam, Jr., *October Sky*

THERE ALMOST was no beginning. That's because, at first,
I was going to ignore the phone number on a yellow sticky
note. It was one of a dozen that, by a Friday afternoon like this one
in early December 2000, would wind up scattered on my desk at
The Register-Guard newspaper in Eugene, Oregon. At that point,
having just finished my third column for the week—Sunday's—
my mind had automatically switched to "weekend" mode. Perhaps
I'd watch a video at home that night with Sally and put up the
outside Christmas lights the next day with a few breaks to catch
Army-Navy on TV.

It had been an exhausting week. Eugene, a city of about
125,000 people at the time, is known as Berkeley North, a place in
the southern Willamette Valley—100 miles south of Portland and
sixty-five miles east of the Pacific Ocean—with a hippy hangover
dating back to the sixties. A place where political fervor is like valley rain: if someone isn't protesting something, wait five minutes.
A place where, in late 2000, political correctness was wrapping
itself around our civic leaders like ivy twining Eugene's riverside

maples. And so it was that our city manager heralded the coming of the Christmas season by taking a page from The Grinch's playbook. He banned Christmas trees on public property.

Left-leaning as Eugene was, the announcement had gone over like a ban on the blues in Memphis. I'd spent the week researching the issue, writing about it—political correctness gone mad, I said—and discussing it with dozens of readers, most of whom wanted to banish the city manager to the Grinch's Mount Crumpit.

I was whipped. It was 5 P.M. I made a few calls, tossed a few sticky notes, then picked up the final one. It said "Nathan Fendrich" with a phone number scrawled next to the name.

Who was Nathan Fendrich and why had he called? That question rose from the nobler side of me. The other side said: *who gives a rip?* I picked up the note to pitch it in the trash can, then felt a tinge of guilt; if people call me and aren't yelling at me, I try to call them back. I punched in the numbers.

Nathan Fendrich, I soon realized, was a retired man I'd read about before in our paper for being something of an expert on European cuisine. He was in his mid-sixties, a small man who also had a big interest in World War II and the Holocaust. Passionate. Driven. And a tad pushy. Beyond his culinary expertise, the paper had done a feature about the slide shows he'd present to local high schools to enlighten students on historical stuff he thought they needed to know and weren't getting in their regular curriculum.

"Bob, I've stumbled across an amazing World War II letter from an army nurse," he said.

"OK." *Was there popcorn at home to go with the video or should I pick some up?*

"I found it in a book on Jewish women in the military, written by a World War II nurse named Frances Slanger. She wrote it from her field hospital tent one night with rain falling and shells pounding in the distance. It honors the soldiers she and the other nurses were taking care of."

"Uh huh. Yeah, right." *Maybe, to be safe, I should call Sally and see what she's in the mood for. Nothing worse than getting some heavy flick like* Gladiator *when she'd have preferred* When Harry Met Sally.

Fendrich's passion shifted into a higher gear. "Bob, she captures the American GI—the citizen soldier, the government issue—in a way I've never seen. And I've read everything there is to read about World War II."

"Interesting." I glanced at my watch.

"But what happened after she sent the letter to the *Stars and Stripes* newspaper that next day—well, you read lots of stories about guys falling on grenades, and that's heroic. This is a different kind of heroic. Bob, you've got to write a column about Frances Slanger."

Even if I were interested in the idea, it would be dead on arrival when my editor, Margaret Haberman, saw it. No local connection. An event that happened back in—when?—the forties. And didn't even have a Veteran's or Memorial Day peg. Sounded like three-strikes-and-yer-out to me.

"She wasn't from around here, right?" I said.

"Not that I know of. But, Bob, there's more."

Lucky me.

"After she writes the letter, she's killed by a German sniper."

My journalistic instincts snapped to attention. Actually, now that the tree controversy was dying down, the column-idea cupboard was getting a bit bare.

"This letter needs to be inscribed on the new World War II Memorial they're building in Washington, D.C.," said Fendrich. "And I'm hoping to make that happen."

A nurse dying in battle? Maybe this column did have some legs.

"And you have a copy of this letter, Mr. Fendrich?"

"Yes," he said. "I live ten minutes from your office."

He arrived in what seemed like five, out of breath, holding a briefcase. He wore gloves, a huge winter coat, and a black fur hat, looking like some sort of Russian spy from decades past. We went into a conference room, and Fendrich—with the air of an undercover agent preparing to show me, say, $500,000 in small, unmarked bills—clicked open the briefcase. He took out a thin book, *Women in the Military: A Jewish Perspective*.

He opened the book to a single page on the nurse, Frances Slanger, that included a photo of a ship named in her honor and a photo of her grave site.

"If anything deserves to be on that memorial, it's this," he said.

I began reading the selections from the letter.

It is 0200 and I have been lying awake for one hour, listening to the steady, even breathing of the other three nurses in the tent. Thinking about some of the things we had discussed during the day. The rain is beating down on the tent with a torrential force. The wind is on a mad rampage and its main objective seems to be to lift the tent off its poles and fling it about our heads.

The fire is burning low and just a few live coals are on the bottom. With the slow feeding of wood, and finally coal, a roaring fire is started. I couldn't help thinking how similar to a human being a fire is; if it is allowed to run down too low and if there is a spark of life left in it, it can be nursed back … . So can a human being. It is slow, it is gradual, it is done all the time in these Field Hospitals and others hospitals in the ETO.

I liked her fire metaphor. Clearly, she was a thinker, someone who noticed the nuances that others might not have.

We had read several articles in different magazines and papers sent in by grateful GIs, praising the work of the nurses around the combat areas. Praising us—for what?

We wade ankle deep in mud. You have to lie in it. We are restricted to our immediate area, a cow pasture or hay field, but then, who is not restricted?

We have a stove and coal. We even have a laundry line in the tent … .

The wind (is) howling, the tent waving precariously, the rain beating down, the guns firing, and me with a flashlight, writing. It all adds up to a feeling of unrealness. Sure, we rough it, but in comparison to the way you men are taking it, we can't complain, nor do we feel that bouquets are due us. But you, the men behind the guns, the men driving our tanks, flying our planes, sailing our ships, building bridges and to the men who pave the way and to the men who are left behind—it is to you we doff our helmets. To every GI wearing the American uniform, for you we have the greatest admiration and respect.

She was selfless, a rare human commodity then, rarer now.

> Yes, this time we are handing out the bouquets ... but after taking care of some of your buddies; seeing them when they are brought in bloody, dirty, with the earth, mud and grime, and most of them so tired. Somebody's brothers, somebody's fathers and somebody's sons. Seeing them gradually brought back to life, to consciousness and to see their lips separate into a grin when they first welcome you. Usually they kid, hurt as they are. It doesn't amaze us to hear one of them say, "How'ya, babe," or "Holy Mackerel, an American woman!" or most indiscreetly, "How about a kiss?"
>
> These soldiers stay with us but a short time, from 10 days to possibly two weeks. We have learned a great deal about our American boy, and the stuff he is made of. The wounded do not cry. Their buddies come first. The patience and determination they show, the courage and fortitude they have is sometimes awesome to behold. It is we who are proud of you, a great distinction to see you open your eyes and with that swell American grin, say, "Hi-ya babe!"

In moments, I was taken back from Eugene in the year 2000 to a field hospital tent in Belgium on a rainy night in October 1944. The letter wasn't great literature, but genuine and well written, especially for someone who'd penned it by flashlight in a field hospital tent during a storm. So deeply rooted in this woman's heart. So compassionate. And yet dusted with a sort of real-war grit.

One particular section convinced me that I needed to write about Frances Slanger: " ... this time we are handing out the bouquets ... but after taking care of some of your buddies; seeing them when they are brought in bloody, dirty, with the earth, mud and grime, and most of them so tired. Somebody's brothers, somebody's fathers and somebody's sons."

This woman had an amazing ability to see war not from afar, but from the rare perspective of someone up close, looking it in the eye.

"You're right," I said. "It's a great letter."

Fendrich leaned toward me, fingers clasped and lips pursed. His eyes glistened. "Will you write the column, Bob?" he asked.

"There's still no local tie," I said, "but I'll run it by editor."

The following Monday, I e-mailed Haberman, having, over the

weekend, come up with a peg I thought might make the idea an easier sell. The fathers of two friends had recently died. So had a friend of my mother's. We were, in essence, losing an entire generation. More than a thousand World War II vets were dying every day, I'd learned. And they must be remembered. In fact, I told Haberman, a Eugene man—a local man—wants to get the words from this army nurse's letter on the new World War II Memorial in D.C. that Tom Hanks and others had been raising money for.

Haberman OK'd the idea; no discussion. So I wrote the column, ending it with Slanger's reference to how "the wounded do not cry. Their buddies come first. The patience and determination they show, the courage and fortitude they have is something awesome to behold."

"As is the courage and fortitude of Slanger, whose letter— perhaps framed by the bouquets due her—deserves a wider audience," I wrote.

> Not just because she defined so well the American GI. Not just because she represents the best of an honorable generation. But also because she understood too well the price that freedom asks.
> An hour after writing the letter, Slanger was killed by a German sniper.

THE COLUMN appeared on December 14. Judging by phone and e-mail response, it moved some to tears, called some readers to action ("you need to get the Women in Military Service for America involved in getting Slanger's words on that memorial"), and flat-out stunned one.

Her name was Sallylou Bonzer, an eighty-two-year-old Eugene woman who, when reading the name in the fourth paragraph— "Lt. Frances Slanger"—thought: *Could it be? It must be. Goodness, he's written about my old friend, Frances.*

Sallylou Bonzer had been a nurse with the Forty-fifth Field Hospital Unit in World War II. "John, come here!" Sallylou said to her husband, a retired doctor whom she'd met in England before the invasion of France. "You won't believe this, but Bob Welch has written about Frances Slanger in his column this morning."

"Slanger? Wasn't she in our unit?"

"Yes," Sallylou said. "She was the Jewish nurse. Short. From Boston."

"The one who died."

"Yes, the one who wrote the letter to *Stars and Stripes* and then was killed."

John, also part of the Forty-fifth, had been a doctor in Slanger's Second Platoon. He'd watched her die. Within minutes, the Bonzers had found the old scrapbooks and were poring over photos they hadn't looked at in decades. Sallylou reached for a phone book and looked up the name "Nathan Fendrich." She called him and told him about the connection. Fendrich, stunned and stoked, called me.

"Bob, you're not going to believe what I'm going to tell you," he said.

Had the column already gotten the wheels turning in D.C. for Slanger's words to be put on the memorial?

"I just heard from a woman here in Eugene who served with Slanger in France. And her husband was a doctor in the same platoon. Bob, this is unbelievable!"

I didn't even try to comprehend the odds of this geographic coincidence. "Did you get a phone number?" I asked.

He had. Within minutes, I was on the phone to Sallylou Bonzer. She and John lived in Eugene's south hills, a ten-minute drive from my house, twenty from the newspaper. I asked if I might come meet the two of them and see the scrapbooks. They eagerly obliged.

The Bonzers lived in a late-forties, one-story house perched near a golf course, the kind of house that you could imagine being a cutting-edge doctor's house when it was built but was now nice but nothing fancy. Sallylou, with auburn hair, was a young-looking eighty-two. She played golf at the Eugene Country Club and hit the spa twice a week. John, white-haired and rosy-cheeked, wasn't as spry, though he'd been a club champ in the past.

As I started leafing through the scrapbooks, photos of a twenty-five-year-old Sallylou reminded me of a young Katharine Hepburn. "Here's the letter Slanger wrote," she said. "We clipped it from the *Stars and Stripes* after it was published. She did such a beautiful job on it."

And there it was, nearly six decades later, a copy of the same letter that was in the book on Jewish women in the military Fendrich had shown me. On the next page appeared the *Stars and Stripes'* story of her death. Slanger, the story said, was from Roxbury, Massachusetts.

"Says here she was killed in a shelling," I said, "but that book Nathan showed me said it was sniper fire."

"The book's wrong," John said. "It was night, just after dinner. Out of the blue, we were attacked. Forty-five minutes worth of shelling. Three people died. A major, a private, and Frances. It was terrible."

I turned another page: photos of Sallylou and John. Of women in army fatigues training in the pine forests of North Carolina. Crouching in fox holes. Debarking from a landing craft, wearing steel helmets, musette bags strapped to their upper bodies.

"You were on this boat?" I asked Sallylou.

"We all were," she said. "We waded ashore at Utah Beach just like the men. Among the first nurses to step ashore in France."

I'd had no idea. When Fendrich had first mentioned a "nurse in France during World War II," I'd pictured women in white dresses, white shoes, and white nurses' hats walking down the well-polished floor of some French hospital. Not women in fatigues jumping out of landing crafts. Not women wearing helmets. Not women working, as Sallylou informed me, twelve-hour shifts, seven days a week, for nearly a year.

"Frances almost drowned coming ashore," Sallylou said. "She was only about five-feet tall and jumped in a spot where there was a shell hole."

I turned each page like a man climbing higher on a ladder above a landscape that he'd never seen before, each step broadening the context. A newspaper headline: "1st ETO Nurse Killed in Action." Beneath it: a story about, and a photo of, Slanger, the first time I'd seen what she'd looked like. She was no Sallylou Bonzer. Roundish face. Medium black hair. But a smile that, you could see, would bring comfort to any wounded soldier, as if that warmth were the essence of who she was.

Another page showed a photo of the ship that had been named in her honor. "The soldiers who read her letter in *Stars and Stripes* insisted something be done so she wouldn't be forgotten," Sally-lou said, "so that's what they did. We took this shot when we were in England, after the war, just before we returned to the states. It was a hospital ship, used to bring the wounded back home."

I slowly shook my head. This was all so much bigger, deeper, and more profound than I'd originally thought. After an hour with the Bonzers, I drove away wondering a single thought: could I possibly write a book about this woman?

But before I could consider the question too deeply, I had another column to write about this nurse. And I knew Haberman would green-light this one without thinking twice. Never mind that Frances Slanger was from Boston and died in Belgium. We now had the two words city editors longed to hear: local angle.

I wrote about the Bonzer-Slanger connection. About how Slanger had actually died. And about Fendrich's reaction to news that two people right here in Eugene had served with this woman. "I practically fell over," he said. "Coincidences like this only happen in Hollywood movies."

LIKE A RIVER funneling into rapids, the Christmas season intensified—despite the grinches at City Hall—and Frances Slanger was lost in the swirl of presents, parties, and travel. Now it was December 31, the last day of 2000, and Sally and I were en route to her sister and brother-in-law's house in Shelton, Washington, on the Olympic Peninsula, for New Year's.

Just over halfway through the five-hour drive, we started talking about the year ahead. I asked Sally about her resolutions, and she said the same thing she usually says: No resolutions. No disappointment. I'm the opposite. Lots of resolutions. Lots of disappointment. I'll be sifting through some old files and find goals I set five years before—and they're roughly the same goals I'm setting for the year ahead. But that doesn't deter me from setting the bar high. Better to have loved and lost—and all that stuff.

I'd had three books published in the previous four years—*A Father for All Seasons* (1998), *Where Roots Grow Deep* (1999), and *Stories from the Game of Life* (2000). A fourth, *The Things That Matter Most*, would be out soon. All had been personal in nature. About relationships. The lure of materialism. Faith and family. All had been fairly easy to write. Basically, I would mine my memory for stories with a message—things readers could relate to in their own lives—and tell those stories: about being a son, being a father, being a long-haired, overall-wearing hippie wanna-be back in the 1970s and how Sally's Baptist grandparents—the kind of folks whom the stereotype would suggest would give me all the respect of a barn cat—had accepted me unconditionally.

And yet, somehow, my zeal to write the Slanger book had, like day-old soda, lost its fizz over the holidays. Maybe that was a sign this project wasn't to be. Maybe I was growing weary of the book business. Maybe the better-to-have-loved adage was wearing thin.

After all, none of the books had sold particularly well. Not that they were particularly difficult to write; done on top of my *Register-Guard* job, they each took roughly six months. They were nice complements to my 675-word, three-times-a-week columns that I wrote by day, making me feel like both sprinter and marathoner. Still, something was keeping me from saying yes to Frances Slanger. Was it me—the idea of embarking on a book journey where, unlike my others, I'd be plying untested waters? Or the idea of not wanting to become my father, the guy with all the spools of film and nowhere to go?

"So," said Sally, who was driving at the time, "what about writing a book on that nurse?"

It caught me off guard. "Not sure there's enough information."

"But you think there's a story there, right?" she asked.

"Oh, sure there's a story," I said. "Nurse writes inspiring letter from a field hospital tent. Sends it to *Stars and Stripes*. Is killed the next night. Paper runs letter, not knowing she's dead. Ship named in her honor. It's a good story."

"So," she said, "why don't you write it?"

"It's not that simple."

At the moment, I was thinking about the lack of information there was on Slanger. And, I suppose, about the abundance of time and distance between when and where her story had occurred: six decades ago and thousands of miles from my home in Oregon. The information trail was stone cold, long obscured by the years and the deaths, I assumed, of many whom were there and whom

I would need as my "eyes." I'd just recently heard it on the news: three in four World War II veterans were dead—and the rate of their dying was, naturally, accelerating. In retrospect, I believe I was subconsciously thinking far beyond the whole time, distance, and information obstacles. I think I meant "not that simple" in a deeper sense. In a "setting-myself-up-for-failure-again" sense. In a "when-the-movie-sells" sense.

"I didn't say it would be simple," Sally said. "But you've got this nurse and doctor right in Eugene. It's a start."

"Yeah," I said. "The Bonzers do have those scrapbooks."

And yet what did I know about World War II? Nurses? The Jewish culture? The forties? I was a recovering sportswriter who'd found his comfort in stories about games, family relationships, and humor, close-to-home stuff that didn't require much of a stretch; books whose informational "digging" might mean pulling a few photo albums or old letters off a shelf. This nurse book would be far different.

"Have the Bonzers kept in touch with any others in this field hospital unit?" Sally asked.

Gee, I thought, this woman would have made a good court attorney. (Though she was quite content working in a quilt shop that played to her passion of handcrafts.)

"Uh, it's been more than fifty years, but, yeah, I think Sallylou mentioned they still trade Christmas cards with a few of them."

Then it happened: the thought of trying to find these other eighty-something people sparked my journalistic intrigue. I'd always been fascinated with the where-are-they-now story: say, the family of the first soldier in Bellevue, Washington, to die in Vietnam, after I'd found a newspaper clipping reporting his death. I was always intrigued by stories about the past and how they related to the present. I did like history.

What would these people remember about coming ashore at Normandy? About Slanger? About the night she died? My mind began pumping with the fuel that makes journalists journalists: questions looking for answers.

I opened the glove compartment, took out a Wendy's napkin and jotted: *Sources: Other nurses. Still alive?*

"The World Wide Web might have info on her," I said, though

I'd hardly tested this new Internet stuff that everybody was talking about. I jotted on the napkin: *Web. Other Slanger stories?* My imagination was on the loose.

"Was she married?" Sally asked.

"I don't think so, but there was some article in the scrapbook about her having had a sister."

"How old was Frances when she died?"

"Maybe thirty." I did some quick math. "She died in forty-four, meaning she'd be—what?—eighty-six if she were alive. So we'd be looking for a really old sister—"

"Or, more likely, younger nieces and nephews."

"Exactly. They'd be a little older than me, maybe fifty, fifty-five, sixty."

I scribbled more notes. Dusk was setting in but I hardly noticed. It was as if something were pulling me into this story and I was suddenly happy to be pulled. On paper—more specifically, on a Wendy's napkin—it made no sense. I was a 675-word column guy. This would need to be close to 100,000 words. I was a journalist. Frances Slanger had been a nurse. Had been dead for fifty-six years. I did the math. A book would be the equivalent of writing 150 columns, which, of course, would need to be written while I continued kicking out three columns a week. What's more, when it was finished, what hope did I have of finding an agent, much less a publisher? Something whispered: *don't go there, Bob.*

"I could get up early, make calls before work," I said, almost surprised at my own boldness. "Maybe get in some long weekends at the beach cabin."

Then I was blindsided by an obstacle far more ominous than the possibility of there not being enough information—the thought of there being too much. More precisely, the thought of someone else already having written this book, meaning it had become their story and would never be mine. I felt an odd twang of jealousy of nearly losing something that wasn't even mine to lose, an echo of a twang I'd felt nearly thirty years before when, just before leaving for college, I'd considered asking out a girl up the street, a girl I knew casually. I kept putting it off and putting it off until late one August night, I was standing in our kitchen window when the car of a friend zipped up our street—and pulled into the girl's driveway. *My gosh, he's bringing her home from a date. I've waited and lost.*

The only way to be sure was to take the plunge. The next day I called and asked if she wanted to play tennis. She did; turns out she hadn't gone on a date with the guy but to a drive-in movie with a girlfriend of hers on whom he had his sights. He'd dropped his girlfriend off first because she lived out of the way.

When, during our tennis game, she whacked three balls over the fence and rocketed a net shot that hit me below the belt—me rolling around in pain and laughter, she in laughter alone—I knew this relationship had potential. I loved her spirit. How easily we could talk about virtually anything. We were married three summers later. In fact, she was the one sitting next to me in the car on this New Year's Eve.

The lesson was clear. I'd met Sally, and fallen in love with her, because I'd dared to take one step toward getting to know her with a simple game of tennis. And look what had become of it: twenty-five years of marriage, two children, dozens of photo albums of memories and, thanks to our first date, an easy answer to that "most-embarrassing-moment" question that you'd sometimes get asked in small-group settings. Take that step and, yes, you risk failure. But don't take that step and failure is a certainty.

"What if I just took a week off from work, right away, and just went all out—phone calls, e-mails, the works?" I said. "See what's there?"

"Go for it."

"You think I should?"

"I think you should."

By the time we arrived in Shelton, the front and back of six Wendy's napkins were covered with words and phrases that only I could translate. And yet even if those words could never be deciphered by anyone else, like Native American hieroglyphics, they had deep meaning to me. They were, in essence, sources from which ultimately I might find answers that, pieced together, would someday create a book.

To wit: Who was Frances Slanger? Why had she bothered to write this letter? How had she died? And, in the end, how had her life made the world any different than if she had never lived?

After a night of raucous bowl-game watching with my brother-in-law, Greg, I awoke on New Year's morning 2001. Before anybody else was up, I went to Greg's computer and navigated to the Web. I then typed in two words—"Frances Slanger"—and waited to see where the response would take me.

Chapter 3

January 2001
Eugene, Oregon

The secret of telling a story of influence is not found by asking the question, "How do I tell a story even though I don't believe it will make a difference?" but "How do I begin to believe I can make a difference?"
—Annette Simmons, *The Story Factor*

Only a small crack ... but cracks make caves collapse.
— Alexsndr Solzhenitsyn

NOBODY HAD written a book on Frances Slanger. In fact, nobody had written much about Frances Slanger, period. That was the good news. The bad news: on the Web that New Year's Day, I found only a dozen references to Slanger. Little of the information was new; instead, it was references to her letter, her death, and her having a ship named for her. The one exception was a trail I picked up in Boston, Massachusetts, where it appeared some state representative was trying to have a plaque placed in the State House in Slanger's honor.

I took a vacation week from work to jump-start the research. I was giving myself until February 1 to prove there was sufficient information to keep going; otherwise, I'd call off the search. At the University of Oregon's Knight Library I sifted through fifty-four volumes of *Reader's Guide to Periodical Literature* to see what, if any, magazine articles had been written about Slanger. I found only a handful of references to her, none after 1945.

At home, a 1939 house in which Sally and I had turned a spare

bedroom into my office and her crafting quarters, I began searching every Web site that had anything to do with women or medical
teams serving in World War II. If a site had some sort of contact
e-mail address, I sent a copy-and-pasted note—thirty-one that first
week alone, explaining I was seeking information on Slanger and
could they help. I sent e-mails—in some cases, hard-copy letters—to about three dozen college libraries and archives in Massachusetts. I talked to Joanne Tierney, administrative assistant to
Rep. Joe Manning in Boston, who was trying to get a bill through
the Massachusetts political thresher to have Slanger honored. For
some reason, an earlier bill to honor her had been signed by then-
Governor Michael Dukakis in 1986 but apparently had died of
neglect.

Tierney offered some morsels of Slanger info from articles she
had, the most helpful of which was that Slanger's lone sister—
with the married name of Sidman—had lived in Boston's Cam-
bridge area before her death. Tierney said she could send copies of
a few newspaper clippings she had. Meanwhile, the Boston University library e-mailed me back to say it had found eleven articles
regarding Slanger. Encouraging.

At the Bonzers, I gathered scrapbooks, photo albums, and
names and phone numbers of other nurses in the unit. Among the
two most helpful items the Bonzers offered were Sallylou's list of
each place the Forty-fifth Field Hospital's First Platoon pitched
its tents as the unit moved from the beaches of Normandy to Germany and, ultimately, to Czechoslovakia, in 1944-45. (Slanger,
along with John Bonzer, was in the Second, but the two platoons
generally leapfrogged each other on similar routes.) Sallylou also
had a list of all eighteen nurses in the Forty-fifth. Though it was a
fifty-five-year-old list and included only names, ranks, and serial
numbers—and though most nurses had presumably changed their
names when marrying and some had died—it was a start.

"Ah, Tex!" Sallylou said, looking at one card. "Her real name
was Carolea Roe but she was from Texas and so we called her Tex.
Tall. Everybody liked her. Became Mrs. Allen Dunbar after the
war. Last known address 690 Covington Road, Los Altos, California ... ."

By week's end, I felt a little like the farmer who'd sowed hundreds of acres of seed and had little to show for it. Beyond Sally-lou, I had made contact with only three nurses from the Forty-fifth who were still alive: Mae "Monty" Montague (Bowen) of Dover, Delaware; Betty Belanger (Quinn) of Manchester, New Hampshire; and Dorothy "Dottie" Richter (Lewis), of Rehoboth Beach, Delaware. None had been particularly close to Slanger and, thus, could offer little in the way of stories, insight, or other sources to contact.

"Frances," Belanger said, "was a quiet girl. Hard to get to know."

At the National Archives in Washington, D.C., a researcher named Richard Boylan, who clearly knew his World War II stuff, responded to an e-mail, offering a few citations I might check out if I were to get to Washington, D.C. He said to let him know if he could help more.

Judith Bellfaire, the curator at the Women in Military Service for America Memorial in Washington, D.C., checked and could find nothing specifically on Slanger or the Forty-fifth Field Hospital. After contacting *Stars and Stripes*, the army newspaper, to request anything Slanger had written from June 1944 when she arrived in France until shortly after her death in October 1944, I was told the task could take up to three months.

I did connect with a man who had been a dentist/cook in the Forty-fifth and remembered Slanger well. Joseph Shoham, eighty-six and living in Latham, New York, showed promise as a source. Nevertheless, that Saturday night, my journal reflected my sense of wheel-spinning:

> I lay there and said to myself: I'm fooling myself. There's no way I can possibly write this book. I don't have enough info. I wasn't in Europe with those nurses. I can't possibly re-create that. Then, for some reason, I thought of a book I'd recently read called *The Perfect Storm* by Sebastian Junger. And thought: here's a guy who wrote a No. 1 best-seller about a boat sinking and he never saw that boat or talked to a single man aboard that boat, and yet he not only told us what was happening on that boat, but on a nearby boat, on a nearby sailboat, in the U.S. Coast Guard helicopter, etc. I CAN DO THIS!

The next day, the last day of my "immerse-myself-for-a-week" plan, I planned an all-out phone assault to find a Slanger relative. If she had nephews or nieces still alive, the odds suggested Boston would be the place to start. So on Sunday, January 14, I came home from church, grabbed a bottle of water for my throat, and began cold-calling every "Sidman" in the Boston phone directory. There were forty.

I found Boston Sidmans to be friendly people who seemed genuinely interested in me finding someone related to Frances. And, of course, they had those wonderful *Bawston* accents. But after nineteen calls, none of the Sidmans I'd contacted was a match. It was late afternoon; I'd been calling for about four hours. *Please, God, I whispered, one connection.*

On the twentieth call, I went through my spiel and—ye of little faith—waited for the usual "sorry." Instead the woman who'd answered paused. "Just a moment," she said with a sense of urgency in her voice.

"Stanley," I heard her say to someone else, "there's a man on the phone who says he's writing a book about Frances!"

"My husband," she said back to me, "is a cousin of Frances's nephews."

"How many nephews of Frances Slanger's are there?" I asked. "And are there any nieces?"

"No nieces. Three nephews. Here, I'll put my husband on the line."

Stanley Sidman told me one nephew lived in Sharon, a Boston suburb, one south in Attleboro, Massachusetts, and one in Lakeland, Florida. Within ten minutes, I'd punched the number of Irwin Sidman, the eldest of the nephews and, based on Stanley's age estimates, about nine or ten years old when Frances had died. It was about 4 P.M. in Eugene, 7 P.M. in Boston.

My anticipation notched up with each ring of the phone. *Come on, please answer, please answer.*

"Hello," came a deep voice.

"Irwin Sidman?"

"Yes."

"Mr. Sidman, this is Bob Welch. I'm a newspaper columnist out here in Oregon and, well, I'm hoping to write a book about your

Aunt Frances."

"Oh, my God. Really?"

"Yes. Nobody's written a book about her, right?"

"No, huh-uh."

I explained how this had all started: The phone call from Fendrich. The discovery of a nurse and doctor from Frances's unit who lived ten minutes from me. The decision to see, in a month, if there was enough information to write a book.

"Oh, there are a couple of suitcases of information!" he said.

"Suitcases, huh?" I said, my journalistic glands salivating. "And you have them?"

"Uh, no, we don't know where they are."

Huh? It was as if someone pulled the plug on a jukebox.

I'd heard him right. He remembered there being two suitcases of letters, newspaper stories, scrapbooks and more, but wasn't sure where they were.

"Frances's parents—my grandparents—died decades ago. Her sister, Sally, and James—my parents—are gone, too. I'm thinking that the suitcases might have been given to, say, the Jewish War Veterans Museum in Washington, D.C."

I asked about his brothers, Jerry and Frank, and whether they could be of help. "I was the oldest," Irwin said. "Eight when she died. Jerry was four. Mom was pregnant with Franky when the Western Union telegram man showed up at our door with the news about Frances. I don't think either of them can tell you much. But I remember that day as if it were yesterday."

He knew of another aunt of his—a cousin of Frances's—who was still alive and might have memories of Frances: Sylvia Fine, who lived in New Jersey. Other than that, he said, he knew of no one who had information. Slanger's immediate family had immigrated to the United States from Poland, he told me. With the exception of one person, the rest had been killed in Adolf Hitler's death camps during World War II.

This story was getting more intriguing with every morsel of information. "Frances was like nobody else," Irwin said. "Unbelievable. Sensitive. Caring. A woman who'd give you the shirt off her back. She died the way she lived."

"So even though you were a little boy you knew her well?"

"Very well. I was very close to her. She'd make a wonderful book."

"I'm sure she would," I said. "Now, if we can only find those suitcases."

The next day, I contacted the National Museum of American Jewish Military History in Washington, D.C. A woman said she knew nothing of such information. I pressed her. Could she ask around?

I updated Irwin Sidman. Since we'd talked, he had contacted his brothers, Jerry and Frank. They believed their aunt's stuff had wound up at the Smithsonian Institute in Washington, D.C., not the museum. And Frank remembered that Frances was, as Irwin told me, "a published author and wrote a book of poetry." That sounded encouraging; writing is a window to the soul and, at the moment, I wasn't anywhere near understanding the soul of Frances Slanger.

I contacted the Smithsonian. Even though I had the museum search using "Slanger" and "Sidman," nothing turned up. Meanwhile, I'd learned that two of Slanger's three tent mates—whose arms were wrapped around her as the shells rained down on her that final night—were dead: Elizabeth Powers of West Roxbury and Margaret Bowler of Springfield, Massachusetts. After Web and phone searches that included the Library of Congress and Boston bookstores, I could find no references to poetry books written by Slanger.

"I'm at rock bottom," I wrote in my journal. "Two of three nurses who, presumably, would know Slanger better than all the others, are dead and the letters that were going to carry this book are nowhere to be found."

Then, out of nowhere, one of those e-mail seeds I'd planted two weeks before sprouted. I got an e-mail back from The Howard Gotlieb Archival Research Center at Boston University. According to their index, wrote Alex Rankin, assistant director for manuscripts, the center had five boxes of information on Frances Slanger.

I pumped a fist in the air. Presumably this represented the "two suitcases" Irwin had referred to. But how was I to know? It was too early in the search to fly back to Boston; beyond assessing what the archives had, I didn't have enough of a source base to do much in the way of interviewing. So instead of going myself, I went to Susan Honthumb, a news aide at *The Register-Guard* whom I knew had a niece in Boston. Would she, for some hamburger money, be willing to check what was in those five boxes?

Easier said than done, a four-word phrase that would become far more the norm on this search than I would imagine. February 1, my deadline, arrived. I extended it, one of the few perks of being a one-person operation being the power to make such calls without getting any flack. The "report" didn't arrive until February 11 and wasn't promising. The letters didn't appear to be to or from Slanger, Honthumb's niece said. There were some scrapbooks, she said, but certainly not enough for a book. I asked her to copy some samples and send them to me. I wouldn't get those for another three weeks.

Meanwhile, I tracked down three daughters of Christine Cox, the third tent mate of Slanger's. More bad news. The mother of ten, she had died at age forty-seven and apparently left no war letters or photos or other memories to anybody. My journal entry of February 10:

> I'm stumped as to whether to continue or not. I decide I will give it one last shot of fine-tooth-combing over all possible sources. At the coast for a breather, I drew up a list of twenty places I could try again or for the first time. Second wind. Renewed energy.

I'd made a few small but significant connections; Slanger's cousin, Syliva Fine, shared how Frances was serious, book-wormish, not at all interested in clothes and makeup like her sister Sally. Interestingly, Frances had been detained at Ellis Island in 1920 because of an eye infection. Good stuff. But I needed more from other sources.

I wracked my brain for other informational rocks to turn over. I bought a University of Oregon Knight Library card and started hauling out World War II books by the armload. For $146.20, I placed an ad in the *Boston Globe* seeking information on Slanger. Through the National Personnel Records Center in St. Louis, I made a request for the military records of all eighteen nurses, plus the major and private who were killed along with Slanger. I sent letters to the National Archives in D.C., seeking ship-passenger information on the Slanger family which, presumably, arrived at Ellis Island in New York Harbor. I asked John Greenwood, chief of the army's Office of Medical History, Office of the Surgeon General, for records of the Forty-fifth Field Hospital's daily action.

Meanwhile, in an e-mail, I vented my frustration with a friend and fellow writer, Jane Kirkpatrick, who knew plenty about taking risks. She and husband Jerry had pulled up stakes from a cozy life in Bend, Oregon, during the eighties to homestead on the John Day River. They called it their Seven-Eleven Ranch—seven miles from their mailbox and eleven miles from pavement. I admired them greatly.

"The story has found you and you must write it," Jane wrote back, "and the passion will absolutely make it happen and you'll find an agent and a publisher, absolutely."

I appreciated her confidence in me, but agent? Publisher? I was just trying to find enough information to write the book, much less get it sold. Not that I needed a second opinion, but I e-mailed another friend and author, Karen Zacharias, who lived in Hermiston, in north-central Oregon, near the Columbia River. "God has given you the vision, the resources, the ability," she wrote. "So exactly what is it that you think you need?"

It wasn't until later that I'd realize what I thought I needed: Courage. Faith. The willingness to believe what I couldn't see then—reams of information on Slanger—might yet come. By now, it was hard believing such manna would fall from the heavens. I was approaching two months of getting up at 5 A.M. and working the phone and sending e-mails before heading off to work at 9 A.M. My February 23 update on the glacial progress:

> Been a cold, cold week in terms of results. Neil Goldman called yesterday and said he'd have a Florence Lavine call me in regard to Slanger letters that were supposedly at the Jewish Military Museum in D.C. Today is the fourth day the classified ad has run in the *Boston Globe*; thus far, one response, from a nurse who knew who Slanger was, but didn't actually know her. E-mailed Irwin Sidman

on Feb. 17 and have gotten no response. Letters to archivists went out a week ago and six of the twelve have responded, none with the least bit of info. I feel like a man who's been tunneling and just knows he's only a foot from daylight but can't seem to reach it.

Slowly, I got double-whammy responses to my dozen-plus letters I'd sent seeking information from the National Personnel Records Center. A fire in 1973 had destroyed "the major portion of records of amy military personnel for the period 1912 through 1959 ... ." and the Privacy Act of 1974 prevented "the release of information without consent of the individual to whom the records pertain."

On February 25, on a walk, I expressed serious doubts to Sally about this plane getting off the ground. "I don't know whether to keep going or not," I said. She looked at me. "Keep going," she said, "You know you want to write this book and you'll regret if you don't."

She was right, of course. But as February inched toward March, the only promising news came from someone whom I hadn't contacted and would never have contacted—John Miller, a silver-haired greeter at church. Knowing I'm a writer, Miller, who regularly scours used book stores for good buys, occasionally brings me books he thinks I'll enjoy. This time it was Theodore H. White's *In Search of History: A Personal Adventure*.

That night, I was perusing the book when I realized White was writing about his boyhood in Roxbury, Massachusetts, which suddenly sounded familiar. Roxbury? Of course: the south Boston town where Frances Slanger had grown up! Thanks to Miller and White, my fuzzy vision of her childhood started to grow sharper as I understood the lay of the land—and of the times. Started to hear the sound of the peddlers barking to customers about their goods. Started to smell fresh herring, coal-fed fires, and Old World cooking of the twenties and thirties.

I had some context, now I needed specifics about Slanger herself. Who was this woman? By February 28, I had sent 231 e-mails, spent about $500, and used most of my non-working *Register-Guard* hours in search of this World War II nurse. Then, a letter arrived from a Boston man who'd seen my classified ad. It was handwritten on notebook paper by someone who clearly had some miles on his tires.

> To Bob Welch: I knew Frances Slanger when I was a young boy. My father and her father were fruit peddlers. She came from the South End area of Boston. Genesee St. Harrison Ave. Then moved to Angel St., Dorchester. She was my nurse at Boston City Hospital Jan. of 1942. We knew each other well enough to call ourselves by our Yiddish names. Her name was "Faigie." The Jewish War Vet. commemorated the corner of Angel St. and Blue Hill Ave. in her honor. Milton Zola, Canton, MA.

This was a huge breakthrough. Zola left a phone number that I began calling. Every. Single. Day. But each time I called, I got the emptiness of continual rings and no message. After a week, I started checking the *Boston Globe's* on-line obituaries, thinking Mr. Zola had written the letter, dropped it in the mailbox, and had promptly died. Or had gotten sick and gone to some assisted-living home.

After half a dozen phone calls, I tracked down one of the last few nurses I still thought might be alive, Mary Reynolds in Maine. But she had recently died, I discovered. I found a woman outside Boston who had been a classmate of Slanger's at Boston City Hospital—the first African-American in the nursing program—but she was ill and could barely talk. And where was Milton Zola, if even still alive? Each day I called; each day, no response. I began wondering if I'd dreamed that this link to Slanger's past had even written me. On March 9 I wrote in my journal:

> The low point of the whole process came about 7 A.M. today when trying to connect with someone from the Boston School District about Slanger's school records and I wound up talking to someone in the boiler room of a high school. The guy had no clue what I was talking about. Dead-ends are driving me crazy. I need someone to pull through for me. None of the nurses or docs from the Forty-fifth have returned the questionnaires I sent them nineteen days ago.

My hours of sleep were shrinking, my Visa bill growing, my

faith waning. From the start, I'd had this sense that I was meant to write this book, that there was some deeper purpose that I didn't fully understand now but would later. If so, God wasn't making the going easy.

Oddly, what didn't seem to be suffering was my newspaper column, mainly because good ideas kept rolling in from readers. In early March a man from Cottage Grove, a small community south of Eugene, called to tell me about leaving his beloved "Book of Psalms" on an airplane in New York. For nearly twenty years, he'd taken this book of biblical inspiration on trip after trip; he figured it had 150,000 miles on it. But now it was gone, the airlines no help in getting it back to him. He felt as if he'd lost an old friend.

Then, weeks later, he opened his mailbox and there it was in a tattered package: his book. But that's not what was so amazing; any Good Samaritan could have seen someone's address inside a book—his was there—and sent it to its owner. What was amazing was that the book had been sent to him from a woman in Israel, the birthplace of the Psalms. After New York, the plane had flown to Jerusalem, where a friend of Rivka Freudenstein had a relative who worked for the airlines. Speaking and reading only Hebrew, the airline worker passed it on to Rivka's friend, like her, an American. And she gave it to Rivka, who saw the name and address and sent it to Cottage Grove. An amazing story that I told *Register-Guard* readers about in a column.

Beyond a breakthrough, I simply needed a break. Some R&R. After getting an invitation for a weekend getaway, Sally and I drove over Oregon's Cascade Mountains to north-central Oregon, to spend a weekend with Jane and Jerry Kirkpatrick. I had known Jane for nearly twenty years, having been her first writing instructor when, in my mid-twenties, I'd taught a freelance class at Central Oregon Community College in Bend. Now, she'd had a handful of historical novels published and was building a solid following, especially in the Northwest.

At times, my books had led to speaking offers, and Jane wondered if I would talk at her hole-in-the-wall Presbyterian church. It was in Moro, a Sherman County town of 337 people that was one of the few structures interrupting rolling hills, sagebrush, and rimrock. I was glad to do so, knowing a weekend away would give me a chance to vent to someone other than Sally.

On Saturday, the four of us walked along the John Day River and gazed at a sky that seemed to go on forever. Jane and I talked here and there about my frustration with the book. "I have a quote from the German poet, Rainer Maria Rilke, I'm going to send you," she said. On Sunday morning, at Jane and Jerry's church, I shared a short message about living for the things that matter—God and people—instead of the material things that never satisfy, quoting from Matthew 6:19.

> Do not store up for yourselves treasure on earth, where moth and rust destroy, and where thieves break in and steal. But store up for yourselves treasures in heaven, where moth and rust do not destroy, and where thieves do not break in and steal. For where your treasure is, there you heart will be also.

Clearly, I was preaching to the choir, though they seemed to enjoy the message. These were salt-of-the-earth, good-hearted people. Ranchers, blue-collar, bake-your-own-bread folks straight from *Little House on the Prairie*. And their warmth and passion for the things of God helped ground me, the one who was supposedly there to enlighten them. The weekend was good for my perspective. After returning home—no response from Milton Zola—I e-mailed Jane with a thank-you. She wrote back:

> Hope your trip back was uneventful. We loved having you here. You're a big hit and everyone thinks I'm great because I brought you here. Hurrah! Here's that Rainer Maria Rilke quote about God's naming us, then walking out with us into the darkness whispering as we go these words: "You, sent out beyond your recall, go to the limits of your longing. Embody me."
> Go to the limits of your longing. Frances and the rest of us will be forever grateful. Hugs to Sally. Jane and Jerry

Go to the limits. Fine. But how did you know where those limits were? Two days later: light in the darkness. For the first time, my pick-ax broke a small hole through the rock wall. John Greenwood, chief of the army's Office of Medical History, Office of The Surgeon General, called. He said he had faxed me a chapter on the ship named for Slanger from a book about hospital ships of World War II.

By now, I knew plenty about the *Frances Y. Slanger* ship. What I needed to know about was Frances herself. What was she like as a little girl? When had she arrived in America from Poland? Why did she want to become a nurse?

I picked up the fax—twenty pages copied from Emory A. Massman's *Hospital Ships of World War II: An Illustrated Reference to 39 United States Military Vessels.* The first few pages contained specifics about the ship—*yawn*—but on the top of Page 5, my eyes widened.

> The ship's namesake, Frances Y. Slanger, was the daughter of David and Eva Slanger of 126 Homestead Street, Roxbury, Massachusetts. She was their second child and born in Lødz, Poland, on August 9, 1913. She and her older sister Sally accompanied their parents to the United States in 1919 when Frances was six years old … . Frances Y. Slanger entered the Abraham Lincoln School in the fourth grade. While she was there, a teacher making comments on her writing ability, said, "You must be Polish; brush up your grammar." The teacher then suggested some books on the subject for Frances to read and study. Frances must have at least considered the advice, since later in life she became a prolific and creative writer. She became the author of 21 poems, including "Effects of the Wind," "Repentance," "The Queen of Hate and Prince Sweetface," "The Flag," "Temptation," "About the Patient," "Mother," (and) "Chaste Lucy."

Intriguing. I flipped forward in the pages. There was a small piece Slanger had written on army drills for the *American Journal of Nursing*, details about the Forty-fifth Field Hospital's work in France, and specifics about the night she died.

> When Capt. Isadore Schwartz of Quincy, Massachusetts, arrived at Slanger's side, she was still conscious. She told him, "I am dying." He had her taken to another area of the field hospital where, in spite of his efforts, she did in fact die a half hour later. Second Lt. Christine Cox of Beverly, Massachusetts, was with Slanger when she died.

At first, I thought: wonderful information. But something on Page 6, a photo of the Western Union telegram announcing her death to the family, suggested the article was even more than that. It appeared to have come from the two suitcases Irwin had referred to. It had to be the "family" information.

That night, I searched the Web for Emory Massman's name and phone number; if I could get to him, I might be able to find where the mother lode of Slanger information was. Within ten minutes, I had his address and phone number in Palmetto, Florida. I called him for two days—that was nothing, I was now on Day Fourteen with calls to Milton Zola—and, finally, heard a "hello" from an older man, probably World War II-vintage.

I explained who I was and what I was seeking. "Can I ask where you got the bulk of your information for that chapter on Slanger?"

"Sure," he said. "I got it at Boston University's nursing archives."

"Boston University?"

"Yes."

"But I had someone search the Slanger files at BU and she said there wasn't much available, certainly not enough to jump-start a book."

"There's lots of information," he said. "Lots. I've seen it. Poetry and stories she wrote. School background. Photos. Newspaper clippings."

My heart rate was climbing stairs, two at a time. "And the letters," I said. "I was told they weren't even to or from Frances."

"I'm not sure that she wrote many of them herself, but there plenty written *to* her."

"Mr. Massman," I said, "just how many linear feet would you say the collection is?"

"Oh, maybe five."

"Five—uh, five feet of information just on Slanger?"

"Five or six. Lots of stuff."

"Thank you, sir. You've made my day."

I hung up the phone and bolted out of my office. "We found it! We found it!" I yelled as I clamored upstairs to tell Sally.

"Found what?" she said, looking up from a quilt she was working on.

"The two suitcases," I said. "The Lost Ark of the Covenant."

Chapter 4

May 2001
Eugene, Boston

There's gold, and it's haunting and haunting;
It's luring me on as of old;
Yet it isn't the gold that I'm wanting
So much as just finding the gold.
  — Robert Service, *The Spell of the Yukon*

The idea of proximity to someone from the place and time I
was interested in was almost too tantalizing, too powerful, to
bear; my leg was shaking ... .
  —Daniel Mendelsohn, *The Lost: The Search for Six of Six Million*

THE DISCOVERY OF the "suitcase" information breathed new life into the search. It was time. Time to head for Boston.

"I'll treat you to dinner," said Irwin Sidman, who, naturally, was thrilled at my tracking down what he, too, believed was the Slanger "family" collection. He surmised that Boston University, with a large and impressive archive on nurses, had probably arranged to get the stuff Frances left behind, either from her mother or her sister.

"And don't give up on Milton Zola," Irwin said. "You've never spent a winter in Boston, Bob. It's snowing here. He's probably vacationing in Florida"—or, as he pronounced it, *Flawida*.

"Right," I said, trying to picture a ninety-year-old guy sipping a beer at a Red Sox spring training game with palm trees swaying in the breeze.

Milton Zola had to be alive. For now, he was my only link to Slanger's childhood in Boston. How can you just write a letter and then disappear—or, at least, not answer your phone? Even as I started to plan for an early-May trip to the Northeast, each unanswered phone call drained my pool of hope, as did a letter from the National Archives saying its search of ship passenger arrival records at Ellis Island turned up nothing about the Slangers.

As spring arrived, I'd confirmed, through wild-goose chases ranging from relatives of nurses to the Social Security Death Index to newspaper obituaries, that eleven of the eighteen were dead. My only hopes beyond Bonzer, Belanger, Richter, and Montague were Carolea "Tex" Roe; Margaret Fielden; and Margaret Morrison, a nurse from Hyde Park, Massachusetts, whose current Arizona address—and married name, Margaret Morrison Ryan—I'd tracked down on a World War II nursing Web site.

Beyond eighteen nurses, the Forty-fifth Field Hospital consisted of 208 men, of whom a dozen or so were doctors and the rest were—as Sallylou Bonzer called them—"grunts." Privates. Guys who set up tents, drove water trucks, packed bandages, served food, and the like. Even with a few leads from the Bonzers, I'd been unable to find any doctors still alive. The Forty-fifth had no Web site and, the Bonzers said, had never held any sort of reunion for which there might be a data base of people.

Isadore Schwartz, in whose arms Slanger had died, had passed away in 1994 in Sarasota, Florida, after a long career as chief of surgery at Jewish Memorial Hospital in Boston and as a senior surgeon at nearby Quincy Hospital. It took me no fewer than two dozen e-mails and phone calls to determine Herman Hirsch—most of the Forty-fifth's doctors were Jewish—was dead, too.

Beyond John Bonzer, I'd been able to touch base with only two men from the Forty-fifth: Shoham, the upstate New York cook/dentist whose memory was sharp, and Fred Michalove, a Rhode Island man whose memory was not. And yet, Michalove's son, Jim, told me, his father teared up whenever the name "Frances Slanger" was mentioned. As with the others, I would interview him by phone for starters.

In mid-March, over dinner with our friends Jason and Ann Schar, Sally and I were discussing the book when Jason asked what I was calling it. "My working title is *Lieutenant Slanger's Letter*," I said.

He nodded his head unconvincingly. Ann wasn't exactly doing backflips. I'd had lukewarm reactions from others when floating that possibility. I cold take a hint; as we ate, I mulled the name and got an idea.

"There's that part in her letter where she talks about how these soldiers aren't just dog-tag serial numbers, they're 'somebody's brother, somebody's father, and somebody's son.' So, how about *Somebody's Daughter?*"

The Schars liked it. Sally liked it. I liked it. Not that by having a working title meant all our winds would suddenly be fair. I arrived home from work one evening to find a letter from a retired military nurse, Margaret Morrison Ryan. *Yes!* This could be a major find, another living, breathing person who knew Slanger. But there were at least two Margaret Morrisons who served the United States as nurses during World War II. This one had been with the navy, not the army.

I BEGAN WRITING the book about four months into the research, even though I had only the basic outline for the story and a smidgen of necessary information. The risk of starting to write before you've completed your research is trying to stretch a quart of paint to cover a whole bedroom: to make it stretch, you paint too thinly. The reward is discovering what questions still needed answering.

I began the book with Slanger and the nurses coming ashore from their landing craft at Utah Beach on June 10, 1944, four days after D-Day. Slanger, Sallylou had told me, had nearly drowned because she was short to begin with and, while weighted down with gear and a three-pound helmet, had stepped into a shell hole. Imagining her flailing underwater conjured up an almost womb-like image to me. At that point, I decided, why not flash back to 1913 and her birth in Poland? From there, I'd just tell the story of her life chronologically.

Though my introduction and first chapter went smoothly, I soon realized I was painting with quarts and I needed gallons to cover. Thanks to my trips to the University of Oregon's Knight Library and a $200 afternoon at Powell's Books in Portland, I had an abundance of contextual information. But because of my being 3,000 miles from where the bulk of my sources were—the Northeast—I had a decided lack of Slanger information.

This house had little more than a foundation to it. Now, it was time to give it shape and style and soul. To talk face-to-face with those who'd known Slanger. To immerse myself in whatever clues to Frances Slanger lay in those "five or six" linear feet of information at the Boston Archives. And to try and answer a nagging question upon which much of the book depended:

What proof, really, did I have that Frances Slanger had made any difference in the world? Yes, she'd written a moving letter. She'd had a ship named for her. But where was the evidence that her words had really made a difference? How had she touched those around her? How was the world different because she lived? If I couldn't answer those questions, I didn't have a book.

Over the next week, I roughed out a seven-day trip that, the more I thought about, became an eleven-day trip. It would take me to Massachusetts, New Hampshire, Rhode Island, New York, Washington, D.C., and Delaware. It would take me to people who'd known Slanger; places, such as Ellis Island, where she had apparently been; and to the cemetery, outside Boston, where she was buried. My hope was that when I headed back to Oregon, the trip would have taken me to Frances Slanger herself.

My annual tax refund would be the economic fuel for the journey, though I would try to cut corners whenever possible to keep costs down. To save a night's hotel fare, I would leave on a red-eye flight from Portland on a Friday night and start my interviews soon after touching down. In Washington, D.C., I would stay in the house of a former *Register-Guard* photographer who was now skipping around the world shooting pictures for *The Christian Science Monitor* while his wife was off saving chimpanzees somewhere. I would eat at restaurants whose hosts greeted patrons with that austere welcome, "Is this for here or to go?" And, of course, after looking at the $200-to-$350-a-night Boston hotels on-line, I would take the recommendation of some voice at the end of a 1-800-GOCHEAP phone call and stay at someplace called the Hotel Buckminster.

My tickets were bought, rooms reserved, appointments confirmed. I'd even gone so far as to arrange assistance from the Boston Police. Irwin Sidman had warned me that Slanger's old neighborhood, in Roxbury, was a dangerous place. "I wouldn't go there without a police escort," he said. "Honestly." I mulled his advice for a few moments, called the only contact I had in the Eugene Police Department, and asked if he had any buddies on the Boston Police force. Within two days, I'd arranged to tour Roxbury with one of Boston's finest, a detective who, weirdly enough, worked out of the Roxbury station and, not incidentally, suggested that Irwin was exaggerating. Roxbury, he told my Eugene contact, was on its way back. "He said they haven't had a shooting, let alone a homicide, in days," said my Eugene police pal. "Stop the presses!"

Shortly before I left, I set a lunch meeting with Nathan Fendrich, the man whose phone call had started all this. It was May 1. I had not talked to him since December, when he'd called to tell me about the Bonzer-Slanger connection. Fendrich, in his mid-sixties, was an intriguing man with deep respect for his Jewish heritage, for those who had been killed in the death camps, and for those who put their lives on the line to keep our country free. If I'd caught the spirit of Frances Slanger, it was only because Fendrich had introduced me to it.

We were only a few slurps into our soup at the Giant Grinder, a Eugene soup and sandwich place, when I said, "Nathan, I'm going to write a book on Frances Slanger."

He didn't say a word. He didn't need to. His eyes, growing moist, said it all.

"I leave Friday for Boston to interview her nephew, nurses who knew her, and guys who served in the Forty-fifth."

He shook his head in disbelief. "In my wildest dreams I never imagined ... ."

"Hey, you started it all. This is your journey, too."

"A book, all about Frances Slanger?"

"It's not an inscription on the World War II Memorial," I said. "But, who knows, maybe it'll be even better."

He finally took another sip of soup, which seemed to trigger another thought. "Say, might I be mentioned in this book of yours?"

"Prominently. I've written the introduction. 'Nathan Fendrich' is the first name I use."

He smiled. At the time, I had no idea that Fendrich would be one of dozens of people who would come alongside me, put some piece in the Slanger puzzle, or point me toward someone who would. In so doing, they would become part of the story itself.

Among the others would be Milton Zola, who, on the thirty-second day of my calling, my journal shows, answered his phone.

"Hello," he said. "Milton Zola."

Like a dog scratching all night outside a door, I didn't quite know what to do once someone finally let me in.

"Uh, this is Bob Welch, the guy who's doing the book on Frances Slanger," I said. "I mean, you're alive, Mr. Zola!"

"So, you got my letter, huh?"

"Yes, long ago. I'm coming to Boston and would love to talk to you about Slanger."

"Glad to talk to you."

"Great. But do you mind my asking why you didn't answer the phone for an entire month?"

"Couldn't," he said. "I was gone. Me and the missus, we always go to *Flawida* every year—to watch the Red Sox play in spring training."

UNITED FLIGHT 556 climbed into the night above Portland, Oregon, and headed east, 11,239-foot Mount Hood somewhere out there in the darkness. It was just before midnight on May 4. Beyond a trip to Haiti to serve as photographer/pill-distributor/flat-tire-changer on a church-related medical team, this eleven-day venture would be the longest I'd been away from my family.

Sally's support for this book-writing project had never wavered, even if, at times, she needed a break from it. By now, much of our conversation was Slanger-related: Where was that book of poetry Frances supposedly published? What would I find in that "five or six" linear feet of information at Boston University? Was Slanger discriminated against because of her Jewishness?

One night, as I prattled on about my subject, Sally said, "Why do I feel like we've become a threesome?"

"Huh?"

"Me, you, and Frances." In retrospect, it was an appropriate shot across the bow, and I reminded myself that as compulsive as I'd become about all this, Sally needed to be my priority. So did the whole family.

The approaching summer was to be a banner season for the Welches: Ryan, now twenty-one and a senior at Linfield College in McMinnville, Oregon, would graduate later in May and, in July, be married to a young woman of whom Sally and I heartily approved, Susan Anderson. Jason, nineteen, would graduate from Sheldon High in June. For now, his world was baseball; the state playoffs would begin soon.

"My hotel," I had told him before leaving, "is a block from Fenway Park. I'll touch the Green Monster in your honor, kid."

"Sweet," he said.

The first thirty hours after my arrival would be the most challenging: three interviews in two states on whatever shut-eye I could get on a plane, which usually wasn't much in my case. But since starting this project, I'd already learned this: You did what you had to do. Years before, I'd done an extensive feature story on a guy who'd been a bombardier on an A6 Intruder during the Gulf War. He was driven like nobody I'd met. Once, in a swimming class at the University of Oregon, his teacher announced they were going to have a contest to see who could swim the farthest underwater. "I looked around at the other guys in the class and assessed the competition," he told me. "I then determined that to win, I'd need to go 'x' far—and, by the way, go unconscious. So that's what I did. And I won."

I was hoping to avoid blacking out, but completing this Slanger book was becoming my underwater swim. You did what you had to do.

MILTON ZOLA—small, tanned from watching baseball in Florida and, at seventy-seven, not nearly as old as his handwriting suggested—half-listened to my story about getting the police escort for a look at Roxbury. He then flipped a hand at me to pooh-pooh my plan. "Ya don't need no police escort to see where Frances Slanger grew up," he said. "You just need me. Get in the *caw*, Bob."

And so there I was, being driven around Roxbury with a World War II vet who I'd known for forty-five minutes. The scariest thing wasn't Roxbury, but Mr. Zola's driving. Beyond that, I found him open to my questions, eager to help, salty with the tongue, a guy who would spit out lines in staccato bursts, as if fired from a machine gun.

As we drove around Roxbury and Boston's South End, it hit home: though seven to eight decades after she'd left, I was in the place where Frances Slanger once walked to school, played at Franklin Park, read at the library. Zola showed me her three-decker row house that sill stood on Oneida Street. I got out and started taking photographs. This, I thought, is where Slanger would have heard the Boston & Albany Railroad Company's car rumble to the east. And two blocks away, from the west, the clack of the Boston Elevated Railway. Nearly all flats such as the Slanger's had, back then, been filled with Jewish immigrants who had escaped Eastern Europe beginning with the Russian pogroms against the Jews in 1881. They were survivors welcomed by relatives as if shipwrecked sailors clinging to the same life raft.

If it was emotional for me, it was for Milton as well. "Jeez, I haven't been down here in a long time," he said.

Mentally, he alternated between now and then, one minute watching a traffic signal, the next minute seemingly sitting beside his father on a horse-drawn fruit cart during the Depression years. "Three to five miles a day. Up at 4 A.M. to sell fruit. Same with Frances and her father. My father worked one side of Harrison Avenue and her father worked the other. I'd see Frances riding with her father. We went to the same school, Abraham Lincoln, but she was way older than me. I knew her best in 1933 and 1934. She was eighteen. I was nine."

He pointed to a church. "That, my friend, used to be a synagogue, the Crawford Street Synagogue."

"Where Slanger's funeral was at, right?" I said.

"Yes, hundreds of people came. More to the burial."

I wished I could see it the way it had been back then instead of the way it was now. But this, I suppose, was the next best thing.

"We used to use a public bathhouse," Zola said. "Our houses were too cold, so we'd come down here to shower. Two cents for soap and a towel."

We drove down Blue Hill Avenue, past a vast park. "The politicians loved to come here to Franklin Park because there were 17,000 votes in this little neighborhood. People just packed in. I can still smell the cooking on the streets: cabbage soup, beet soup, delis. You'd go watch the Red Sox at Fenway. Twenty-five cents to be in the Knothole Gang, and you'd be watching guys like Ted Williams and Bobby Doerr … ."

We continued down Blue Hill Avenue. "I got beat up here when I was 12. Why? Because I was a Jew. The east side of Blue Hill was Irish, west was Jewish." Now, it was cars and stores and iron-barred windows and graffiti on both. The lights of three police cars flashed a block away.

"After Slanger died, they named this corner in her honor," Zola said. "Had a sign and everything. But it's long gone."

We drove to what was once Boston City Hospital, the old brick portion now dwarfed by sleek glass-and-steel additions, and called Boston Medical Center. "In January forty-one, I had my appendix out and when I awoke I saw Frances Slanger. She was doing special nursing with one patient but wound up take caring of me. Nursed me back to health. She was sneaky that way. Couldn't believe it. It wasn't because I was a friend of hers or because I was Jewish. That was just the way Frances Slanger operated."

He was drafted and found himself in an anti-aircraft unit that hit Normandy a week after the invasion and pushed through to Germany. That's where he was when he heard about Slanger's death. He read it in the *Stars and Stripes*. "1ST ETO NURSE KILLED IN ACTION." "I was upset. Couldn't believe it. She was such a caring person."

In spring 1945, his unit had come across one of Hitler's concentration camps in German, full of dead and dying Jews. "We wanted to give them food but they couldn't handle it because they'd been starved so long," he said. "We just tried to give them a little soup. The smell, the bodies, the stench. It burned your nose. I couldn't handle it. I walked away."

I said goodbye to Zola after three hours. The thirty-two-day wait had proven worth it. I would fill in many holes by finding photos and maps of 1930s Boston at the city library, but Milton Zola had done something no photo could do: unlocked Slanger's childhood for me.

AS I HEADED for Irwin Sidman's house—ironically, only minutes away—the sight and smell of Boston's spring blossoms diffused the images of Jewish concentration camps in Germany a tad, but not much. Had the Forty-fifth, I wondered, encountered these barbed-wired corrals of hell?

Sidman, a man who'd lost numerous relatives at worse camps in Poland, lived in a wooded area similar to Zola's. When we shook hands and looked each other in the eye, it seemed to be with a sense of mutual respect—me, for him, because of his obvious affection for, and understanding of, Frances; him, for me, because I wanted to tell her story to the world.

As a source of information, Sidman was like the spinster farm wife who saved pieces of string here and there, knowing someday that ball of string would come in handy. He didn't have much to work with, having been only eight years old when his aunt died, but he had held on to an amazing number of memories from those eight years, as if knowing they were going to be needed someday. He handed me a family photo album—"take it with you"—that had dozens of photos of Frances, each a source of information and a catalyst for more. His attention to detail was a journalist's delight. "When the Western Union telegram man arrived, I was listening to *The Green Hornet* on our radio," he said. "It starred 'The Shadow.'"

He remembered his grandparents, David and Eva—Frances's parents—and snippets of pained conversation about relatives back in Poland; the only one who survived Adolf Hitler's war against the Jews had been a cousin of Frances's, Franya, who had fled to Israel. He remembered the day Frances, while going to nursing school, burst into the Oneida Street apartment in tears, having been reprimanded by a supervisor for spending too much time with patients. How Frances would take him to Franklin Park and let him ride the ponies. And what it was like the day he last saw her in Hull, a town on land jutting into Massachusetts Bay and the southern point of Boston Harbor.

As with all my in-person interviews, I kept notes with a personalized shorthand system that basically involved writing only key words and abbreviating others. For example, "w wt t g t food b t cnt hd it bec thd b starved s long" was shorthand for Zola's statement that "we wanted to get them food but they couldn't handle it because they'd been starved for so long." I backed up my interviews with a tape recorder.

"When Frances Slanger came down the street," Irwin told me, "the world lit up."

I asked him if I could see the place where she'd said goodbye in Hull. "Of course," he said.

Already, I was slack-jawed at Boston's history. Not far from Sidman's house was a still-standing house where Paul Revere once lived. Hull, a beachy village that's like a fingernail on a long finger, was founded in 1644, a full century and a half before Lewis and Clark reached the Pacific Ocean near what's now Astoria. In Oregon, which was occupied by only Native Americans until the Oregon Trail in the mid-1840s, our sense of "history" was so skewed that you half-expected pre-seventies modular homes to be nominated for national historic designation.

Now, about as far from Astoria as you can get in the mainland U.S., Irwin and I looked east to the Atlantic Ocean. We later pulled into a park called Pemberton Point and stepped out. The ocean breeze was invigorating but the adrenaline I'd been running on waning. On the drive out, despite seeing a new place and hearing new stories, I'd realized the red-eye flight had caught up with me; I hadn't slept in nearly thirty-six hours.

Across the bay, you could see Boston. "In the evening, guys would bring their girls out here to neck or to tell them goodbye, sometimes both," Sidman said. "There was a war on. You could look across the bay and see the Quincy shipyards all lit up."

We drove to a spot just east of the corner of Warren and Nantucket and parked. We started walking across a curbless street in a neighborhood with an eclectic mix of laid-back houses, mainly summer homes. Irwin pointed to a three-story bungalow. "Our family would rent that cottage out here in the summer," he said.

In early August 1943, Frances showed up for reasons Irwin didn't understand at the time. To say goodbye. To go to war. They walked on the beach. Came back to the off-white, Cape-style home with the open porch on front, and sat on a swing. "Then," he said, "she began singing me a lullaby." His face reddened, his eyes moistened. He swallowed. "It was ... the last time ... I ever saw her." In that moment, I understood, for the first time, how much she had meant to him.

We walked to the car. We had one more task, one that would be no easier for him than reliving the last goodbye. En route, I asked for a postponement on dinner until the next night, after my return from New Hampshire. I'd decided that, after our last stop, it was wiser for me to head for Manchester and get a good night's sleep instead of having to get up early again. Irwin understood.

We drove up a hill southwest of Boston, in West Roxbury, to the Pride of Independence Cemetery.

"I remember they brought her body to the cemetery on the same horse-drawn caisson that had carried Roosevelt's body," he said as we parked on a narrow road amid grave markers as far as you could see. "Imagine 1,500 people here," he said. "That's how many attended her graveside service."

Frances's grave was next to her father's and mother's. The lower part of the headstone said:

LT. FRANCES Y. SLANGER
BELOVED DAUGHTER AND SISTER
KILLED IN BELGIUM OCT. 21, 1944

Below, her name had been inscribed in Yiddish—*Freidel Yachet Slanger.* It was, of course, impossible for me to read; Irwin translated it for me.

"And the Hebrew inscription below it?" I asked.

" 'May her soul be bound in everlasting life.' "

The headstone was etched in a pattern of flowers on both sides, framing the symbol of the Army Nurse Corps. The upper part of it included a line from Frances's letter to *Stars and Stripes:*

U.S. ARMY NURSE CORPS
"THE WOUNDED DO NOT CRY,
THEIR BUDDIES COME FIRST."

Irwin picked up small rock the size of a bottle cap, walked to the headstone, and placed it on top.

"It's a Jewish custom," he said.

"Meaning?"

"Meaning 'I was here.' "

I nodded. "May I?"

"Sure."

I picked up a rock and did the same. *I was here.*

As the journey continued, I began sensing there was a reason I was here, as if Jane Kirkpatrick's insight—"you didn't find this story, this story found you"—was becoming clearer and clearer with each stop along the way.

That night, after a two-hour drive to a New Hampshire Holiday Inn, I was exhausted. But I had to flip through that pre-World War II family photo album. There she was: A twenty-something Frances in her Boston City Hospital nurses uniform; a teenage Frances reading a book at a Cape Cod cottage; a 12-year-old Frances, unsmiling, her dark-socketed eyes seemingly boring into mine from seventy-five years ago. The look led to my last thought before closing the book and falling asleep: *Frances Slanger, who were you?*

Chapter 5

May 2001
Manchester, New Hampshire, and Boston

*All knowledge of the past which is not just supposition derives
ultimately from people who can say "I was there."*
—John Carey, *Eyewitness to History*

*(Many of us) decide that just because we've found the courage
to show up at the page and jot down a few words, we will be
published. It takes more than that. It takes dedication, commitment
to craft, and in some rash cases, tens of thousands of dollars of
credit card debt. Is that enough? I wish.*
—Elaura Niles, *Some Writers Deserve to Starve!*

BETTY BELANGER Quinn lived in Manchester, a city of 107,000 that reminded me of my home city of Eugene, a hybrid of city and town, sprinkled liberally with trees. Belanger and her husband Charlie, a retired high school principal, lived in a pleasant, two-story house whose muted tones were accented with an American flag. She had spent most of her life, predictably, as a nurse, retiring in 1980.

I'd seen World War II photos of Betty. In fact, I'd shown up at her doorstep half-expecting her to be in her upper twenties and wearing army fatigues. Instead, she was trim with short, gray hair, and a can-do Yankee disposition. Friendly, but blunt about how war can sully the soul.

"I started writing a journal during the war," she said soon after we'd sat down at her kitchen table, "but it was too painful so I stopped. After the war I had terrible nightmares. I'd wake up screaming. I kept thinking I was being chased by enemy soldiers."

After we talked for about an hour, she pulled out some photo

albums. "I should have written the names on the backs of the photos but at the time I never thought I'd grow old and forget who was
who. Guess what?"

She started looking at the photos and talking. "Morrison was
nice; she'd always volunteer to change dressings, do colostomies,
which wasn't a fun job. The worst job was changing dressing;
it smelled awful. Dottie Richter: I remember her, in Normandy,
shooing away cows because she'd been brought up on a farm and
knew how to do it. If you came to a field with live cows, you had to
be careful; there could be mines in the field. If you found a bunch
of dead cows, it was usually because the mines had already been
triggered."

She turned another page. "Roe. She was a good sport. Liked to
party. The party people were Roe, Bonzer, Bowen, Richter—and
me."

"And Frances Slanger?" I asked

"Oh, no, no, no. She'd be off writing somewhere. She'd have
that pen in her hand."

She told me about the fear of climbing down the side of a ship,
on a rope ladder, and into a landing craft. About a young soldier
who'd lost a leg; the doctors couldn't get him anesthetized for
surgery. "He was so frightened. I just held him, the poor kid. So
many of them lied about their ages so they could get in." About
being at Bastogne, Belgium, three months after they'd landed at
Utah Beach and how doctors were recognizing casualties because
they had done surgeries on the same soldiers back in Normandy.
And, in December, during the Battle of the Bulge, about keeping
blood warm by putting the bottles of it next to the potbelly stoves
in their tents.

She served in the First Platoon, Slanger in the Second. So, once
the nurses hit the Normandy beach, she didn't see a lot of Frances.
But in England, only weeks before the invasion, Betty and Frances
found themselves eye-to-eye in a moment that could have explod-
ed. A handful of nurses were bathing the only way they could—
out of their helmets—when Betty laughed at the experiment in
primitive cleansing.

"Where I'm from, we used to call these 'Jewish baths,' " she
said. Her words had barely left her mouth when she realized who

else was in the room: Frances, the lone Jewish nurse. Betty was mortified at her lack of tact. But how do you un-ring a bell?

There was a moment of awkwardness. Talking stopped. All eyes subtly turned to Frances. "Well," Frances said, considering Belanger's French name. "My people call it a French bath." There was a split second of uncertainty, then Frances burst out laughing and the others followed, none more enthusiastically than Betty.

My time with Belanger hadn't been fantastic, but fruitful. She hadn't known Slanger particularly well. I stayed all morning, then said goodbye, though it wouldn't be the last time I would see her. I would learn, as this adventure continued, that these sources, because of our common link to Slanger, were now forever connected to me, some in ho-hum ways, others in deeply significant ways.

In time, a gesture of Belanger's would prove to be one of the most inspirational moments of the journey. But, like Slanger's, her life would end tragically.

EN ROUTE BACK to Boston, I stopped at a Holiday Inn along Interstate-95 and used its lobby—and an electrical outlet—to transcribe my interview notes onto my laptop; it was too early to check into my room at the Hotel Buckminster. When I did, I immediately got a taste of the big city.

"And the parking is where?" I asked the desk clerk.

"There is no hotel parking," she said. "But there's a covered lot next door. It's $20 a day. There's a code you press to have the gate open. You've got to be there by 8 tomorrow morning or you won't get a spot."

For a guy on a budget, this was not good news; as a hotel welcome, I preferred Doubletrees' warm chocolate-chip cookies. But what balanced the bad news was that, from my room, if I stood on my tip toes and tilted my head just right, I could see the back of Fenway Park's Green Monster left-field wall. And, really, what price can you put on that?

As I waited for Irwin to pick me up for dinner, I did two things I knew I needed to do above all else: call Sally to update her—and to hear how life was going for her back home. And, with a phone call to the ticket office, secure a ticket for a Red Sox game Tuesday night. I was a lukewarm baseball fan, but I loved sports and history, and Fenway was to baseball what St. Andrews was to golf. I had no particular interest in the Red Sox; I had grown up a Dodgers fan, then became a lukewarm Mariners fan during my years near Seattle. But after a hard day in the archives and knowing only two people in Boston, Irwin and Milton, relaxing at a ball game sounded perfect.

I parked the rental car just opposite the Green Monster, set my alarm for 5 A.M.—no way was I going to oversleep and get towed—and waited in the dark and mysterious Buckminster lobby for Irwin to pick me up. This was not your typical vast, well-lighted lobby with comfy chairs where people in business suits met and, over drinks, talked about seven-digit deals. This was the marble-floored entry that, I would learn over time, was almost always being remodeled; the place that led to the two elevators, one of which almost never worked; the lobby in which I always seemed to be the hotel's lone guest coming or going.

But it did have some history. Babe Ruth had stayed here. And built in 1897, it was the site of the world's first network radio broadcast. WNAC Radio had moved into new studios in the Buckminster in July of 1929 and later that year, arranged the first network broadcast with station WEAF in New York City, using a 100-foot antennae connected to the building's roof with clothesline.

When learning something like this, I would always put the information into perspective with Slanger. Let's see, she would have been sixteen at the time, living about five miles south of here. Did she listen to that first broadcast? Did she ever see a game at Fenway? Ever think someone would write a book about her?

I joined Irwin and his wife Joan at Jimmy's Chowder House on Boston Harbor for a fish-and-chips dinner. After forty-eight hours on the go, it was nice to relax, sip a glass of white Zinfandel, and get to know people who, in the next few years, would become almost like East Coast relatives. But, I confess, even as we ate, my mind kept fast-forwarding to the next morning. It was almost time to see what was in the proverbial "two suitcases."

BOSTON UNIVERSITY lined both sides of Commonwealth Avenue more like a business district than a campus, though the Charles River did flow past its backyard. I awoke at 5 A.M. to move the rental car into the parking garage and to take a run along the river. As I huffed and puffed, I watched the crew shells ply the smoothness and thought of Meryl Streep rowing on the same waters in that opening scene of *A River Wild*. Beautiful.

When I arrived on the fifth floor of Mugar Memorial Library, home of the archives, Irwin was already there. We were led to a high-ceilinged room with lots of tables. Shortly after 9 A.M., Alex Rankin, the assistant director for manuscripts and a man with whom I'd exchanged numerous e-mails, wheeled in a cart with five boxes that said "Frances Y. Slanger Collection."

"You'll need these," Rankin said. He handed Irwin and me white gloves. "And no pens please."

My belongings had to be locked in a box; the archive folks valued this information and didn't want people stealing it.

"But the laptop is OK, right?" I asked.

"Yes."

"And a camera?"

"Sure. For what?"

"I just want to take a picture of this. The room, the files. I've waited a long time to see what's in here."

He laughed. I clicked. And clicked. Then, I looked at the index of material. It listed easily more than a hundred items. I knew in a glance this was what I'd been after, the clue-clincher being Slanger's Purple Heart award, given to her mother posthumously. Nothing said "family collection" like that. I handed the index to Irwin.

"This is it, right," I said, "the suitcase stuff?"

He scanned the list. His head started nodding, slowly at first, then faster. "Yes, yes, definitely. This is it, Bob."

"Good. That's a good thing. A very good thing." We exchanged quiet smiles.

Irwin stayed a couple hours, then headed back to work. I could have stayed for a week. And almost did. I was a detective who'd been working a case for five months without much success, then suddenly had a table of juicy evidence spread before him. Where to even start?

I would, ultimately, order copies of ninety-five items. But I'd already decided, with the foresight of a shopping-spree veteran working against a clock, to copy onto my laptop as much pertinent information as possible in the three days I'd scheduled myself for the archives. I powered up my Macintosh G3 laptop, opened a scrapbook and, beneath a header saying "BOX 1," started typing notes.

Every clipping, every photograph, every letter became a pixel of evidence that would ultimately create a picture of who Frances Slanger was. And the picture would constantly be changing, given that the evidence—once sparse and simple—was suddenly flowing like Oregon's snow-fed rivers after a spring thaw.

Rivers, given the forces of nature, sometimes redefine their banks. "We are glad to have severed those ties that held us down and are proud to be members of the United States Army," I discovered Slanger had written in a newspaper published at a training camp in 1943. On May 7, 2001, when I first read that line at the Boston University archives, I thought: *Proud to serve her country.*

But months later, after learning she had, because of a father's illness, become the family breadwinner and after reading a short story she had written about a burned-out nurse who takes a cruise and falls in love with a doctor, I would think: *Happy to be free of clinging family. Thirsting for adventure.*

As a journalist, you follow the truth. But once you think you know the essence of your subject, once you've established a "framing" for who somebody is, you subconsciously root for data or anecdotes to support your supposition. You still seek the truth, but while being willing to shift your point of view should the evidence demand it, you hope that truth will help you color in the sketch you've already drawn.

Given what I knew, I sensed Slanger was a courageous woman whom time had forgotten. But was that true or was that simply what I wanted to be true? As morning became afternoon—I stopped only once, for a quick bowl of crab chowder at the student union—I found my hunch repeatedly affirmed. Slanger had been lauded by Charles Sawyer, the U.S. ambassador to Belgium, in a speech whose audience included General Douglas McArthur at the Henri-Chapelle Cemetery in Belgium where she'd been buried. She had been featured on a New York radio program starring actress Joan Fontaine. She'd been written up in *Newsweek* magazine and in the *Boston Evening American:*

BY KENT HUNTER
Boston Evening American Washington Bureau
Washington, Oct. 14—One day the name of 2nd Lt. Frances Y. Slanger will be linked in the annals of the Army Nurse Corps with the same reverence universally accorded Florence Nightingale.

First Army men remember the story that appeared in the *Stars and Stripes*, the army overseas paper, about the nurse who pleaded for an assignment further forward than the base hospital where she worked. She wanted to be further forward to share the dangers of the men instead of the nerve-taking job of patching up those sent back to base hospitals.

The collection included dozens of poems and stories Slanger had written as a teenager and woman in her twenties. As I copied them, I began realizing she was a passionate, if not polished, writer who wrote from the heart. An optimist. A patriot. A young woman who looked at the world and saw nuances others did not—the stuff of the physical world (weather, flowers, sunsets, etc.), the stuff of the inner world (feelings, fears, temptations, etc.), and the stuff of the cultural world (politics, religion, social change, etc.)

Most stunning were newspaper and magazine clippings she'd saved about the Jews being systematically murdered: a newspaper clipping about the Russians invasion of Poland, another about a rabbi in 1938 warning America about the dangers of Hitler, and a poem by Edna St. Vincent Millay, "The Murder of Lidice." It was about the Germans' attack on a Czechoslovakian village on June 10, 1942, in which they killed 246 adults and deported dozens of women and children to concentration camps.

Midway through the morning, I found, in a giant scrapbook that Frances had obviously created and maintained, page after page of inspirational quotes. Quotes from people such as Abraham Lincoln, Seneca, and Ella Wheeler Wilcox. They were clipped from magazines and pasted in a book, which told me: *this nugget of truth was somehow meaningful to her.*

That's the easy part, realizing something that's saved or displayed had special meaning. The hard part is answering the "why" question. Why did Slanger clip the "Mrs. A.J. Stanley" quote about how "he has achieved success who has lived well, laughed often and loved much?" Why the anonymous quote about how "you cannot dream yourself into a character—you must hammer and forge yourself one?" Why the reference, in Box 4, to a biblical quote that would prove amazingly prophetic for her own life: "Greater love had no man than this, that a man lay down his life for his friend."—St. John, Ch. XV, Verse 13?"

Writers start their research with the presupposition that everything means something. Not that you can hope to answer every question that the evidence triggers. But you look for themes, patterns, tendencies, then connect the dots, taking into account not only what the information suggests but from whom it came. The closer the source was to Slanger, the more weight the information should carry.

I got through about half the collection on my first day. I took twenty-seven pages of notes and requested thirty copies. Back at the Buckminster, a friend in Oregon gave me the play-by-play of the last inning of my son Jason's game, an 8-7 thriller that his Sheldon High team had won. As I'd promised, I raced outside, to Fenway's Green Monster wall, and touched the fence in his honor. It had been a great day for the Welches.

ON MY NEXT day in the archives, I came across a guest book that Frances called "Buddies: My Record of Friends in Service." Just before Slanger was transferring to another of her four stateside training camps, others she'd served with would write their names, home towns, and a few words to Frances. Those words, though sparse, offered all sorts of clues about her: "A place for everything and everything in its place," wrote Catherine B. Sheehand of Rowley, Massachusetts. (So, Slanger was a neatnik, huh?) "Pounding away at her typewriter with a heart of gold—she'd give you the shirt off her back," wrote Florence M. Sayer of Haverhill, Massachusetts. (Confirms exactly what Irwin had told me: she was a writer and a giver.) "Please tell me when you complete your first bestseller. You will make it if you are as good a writer as you are a nurse," wrote Margaret Morrison. (She was respected by her colleagues, and thought highly of by some, one of whom, Frances

C. Ryder of Canada, suggested in a poem—more than a year before Slanger's death—that camp wouldn't be the same after she'd left):

> *The days of the skipping rope, now are past*
> *The voice of high opera gone at last*
> *The clang of the typewriter heard no more*
> *It's not like home since you closed the door*

   The information at the archives wasn't only gold in terms of helping me better understand Slanger, it was gold in terms of leading me to other sources who might enlighten me even more. I found lists of nurses at the training camps she was at before heading for Europe, lists of women who had gone to school with her at Boston City Hospital's School of Nursing, and letters to her and her mother from dozens of people. How many of these dozens of other people named in the book were still alive? Could they be found? If so, would they remember her? If they remembered her, would they offer anything that would help me understand her?

   As I approached my fifteenth hour in the archives over two days, I was still coming across interesting stuff: a letter, for example, suggesting that after expressing interest in joining the U.S. Army Nurse Corps in 1941—before the United States had been attacked by Japan and entered World War II—Slanger had rescinded her enlistment to take care of her ailing father; a letter, two years later, after she'd joined the Corps, saying that, because of "defective vision, bilateral," she would be limited to state-side service; and a poem she hadn't written, but obviously was important to her:

> *Drop a pebble in the water; just a splash and it is gone;*
> *But there's a half-a-hundred ripples circling on and on,*
> *Spreading, spreading, from the center, flowing on out to the sea*
> *And there's no way of telling where the end is going to be.*
>   —James W. Foley

   The poem would, in time, become something of an anthem to the book and to my experience of writing the book. When first seeing it, I didn't realize how deeply it would speak to me as Slanger's story unfolded.

I went back through all the material one final time, making sure I hadn't missed anything. I had transcribed forty-seven pages of notes and ordered nearly one hundred copies that would be sent to me in a few weeks. I was disappointed that I hadn't found anything about Slanger's life in Poland nor about when and where she arrived in America. And I'd found precious little that, beyond Slanger's death, enlightened me about her war experiences. It was as if once the nurses stepped on that beach at Normandy on June 10, 1944, the paper trail ended until the Germans inexplicably attacked the field hospital on October 21, 1944. Nevertheless, as I wrote in my journal: "The Boston University mission was a complete success." If I hadn't found everything I'd hoped for, I'd still found scores of clues into the life of Frances Slanger, and dozens of names of people who might help me answer the questions that remained.

That night at Fenway I watched the Red Sox beat the Seattle Mariners 12-4 to pull one game ahead in the American League East Division. Weirdly, I found myself rooting for the home team against my old Mariners. And I began wondering: *Could I learn to love these Red Sox?*

The next day, at Harvard's Schlesinger Library, I dug up some information about Massachusetts Congresswoman Edith Nourse Rogers visiting the Forty-fifth Field Hospital in Belgium. And skimmed through enough microfilm copies of 1940s *Boston Globes* to make me sick to my stomach.

Once finished, I walked across the street to the Boston University Barnes & Noble to treat myself to some book browsing before retiring for the evening. As I stood near the entry way, students came and went with a sense of urgency, cell phones seemingly surgically affixed to their ears. I didn't know them. They didn't know me. It was an odd sense of obscurity, being among so many people and yet being so totally anonymous.

Mentally, I made myself a promise that evening. Someday, I told myself, I'm going to come back to this store, and I won't be here to browse.

I'll be here for a book signing.

Chapter 6

May 9-16, 2001
Rhode Island, New York,
Washington, D.C., Delaware

As much as Civil War soldiers, the GIs believed in their cause.
They knew they were fighting for decency and democracy and they
were proud of it and motivated by it. They just didn't talk or write
about it. They speak with their own voices and in their own words.

—Stephen Ambrose, *Citizen Soldiers*

Eighty-six years is a long time to stew on the fated turmoil of a
loved one. Most Red Sox fans say they hate this whole Bambino
business but underneath the veneer, cannot help but wonder about
the pattern.

— Alex Rankin, The Howard Gotlieb Archival Research Center at
Boston University

ON INTERSTATE-93, headed south from Boston to Rhode
Island, I thought about all that I still didn't know about Frances Slanger. I knew nothing about her coming to America from
Poland. Little about her time in war. And little about her real impact on troops with the letter she wrote. For some reason, it was
the latter that worried me most.

Yes, I knew that a United States ambassador had honored her in
a speech. And that a ship had been named in her honor. But I needed more. More evidence that her words had touched these soldiers'
lives. More confirmation that, as that ambassador had suggested in
his speech, she'd given them hope when they were hopeless.

Near Westerly, Rhode Island, I stopped for the night. After re-
questing a room shift at the motel—chewing gum on the night-
stand and a makeup-splotched towel in the refrigerator—I caught
some sleep. In the morning, I met Fred Michalove and his son Jim
in Westerly, a Victorian-home-and-picket-fence community on the

ocean that Sally, I thought when seeing it, would drool over.

Michalove had been the Second Platoon's chief administrative officer, a former reporter who'd enlisted right after the bombing of Pearl Harbor. Now, at eighty-eight, he was in the early stages of Alzheimer's, though in my phone interview with him six weeks before he had offered a sprinkling of good, specific information about Slanger, including a wonderful story about an egg that I wondered if he would remember this time around. "At times he remembers things, at times he doesn't," Jim said.

As we talked in the plushest assisted-living dining area I'd ever seen, Michalove reminded me of a grandfather of mine who'd died a few years before: hands that barely worked, so twisted with arthritis. And a mind that faded in and out like a late-night radio station on a country drive.

"I'm trying to dig this up out of my mind," he said after one of my questions. "What the devil was their name?" He bowed his head in frustration.

"I've got all the time in the world," I said, thinking at how frustrated my grandfather would get.

"Sirmons, the Sirmons. We were billeted in England with the Sirmons. Me and—what was his name?"

"Isadore Schwartz? The doctor they called 'Tiny'?"

"Yes. Me and Tiny were billeted with the Sirmons in England."

I asked about the trip across the English Channel beginning two days after the D-Day Invasion. He remembered a little. I asked him about loading from the ships to the landing crafts, the harrowing climb down the rope ladders. He remembered a little.

"And then you're on this beach," I said. "Utah Beach. What do you see? What do you smell? What do you hear?"

He stared off to something only he could see, then swallowed. "We were billeted in England with the Sirmons."

I shuffled the deck and dealt again. Got him on the ship. Into the landing craft. Onto the beach. "And can you describe, Mr. Michalove, what you experienced when you hit the beach?"

Nothing. Just the stare. And once again he took me back to England, to where he and Tiny were billeted with the Sirmons.

I tried one last time to get him to tell me about Utah Beach.

Again, he had no trouble recounting the steps to get there, but, again, froze once he hit the beach. The Alzheimer's, I assumed, was jamming his memory. But why the same place each time? Why the beach, which was being tattered with enemy fire but was hardly the bloodbath Omaha Beach, of *Saving Private Ryan* fame, had been? Then, I discovered why. Just as I was about to concede this memory—it wasn't his fault he couldn't remember—he suddenly spoke.

"They were hanging from the trees."

That's all. *They were hanging from the trees*. And the stare into nothingness.

"Who?" I asked. "Who was hanging from the trees?"

"Our guys, paratroopers." Suddenly, I understood why it had been so hard to tell me what he'd seen. He'd been referring to paratroopers from the Eighty-Second or 101st Airborne Divisions who had jumped into the darkness of D-Day. Some had landed in trees and, yes, the Germans had used some for target practice. To recall that memory was to relive it and to relive it was painful and, at this point in his life, he didn't need any more pain. "The Germans shot them as they were dangling there, dead, with their parachutes on. Such a sad thing to me. I can't forget it."

His eyes, I realized, were growing moist. "I knew then that if it happened to them, it could happen to me."

He paused as if collecting himself for more. "Just up the way there was a guy burned in a tank. They brought him in, toward us, still alive. All he said was, 'Save my gun, save my gun.' "

Such morsels of detail, I would find on this trip, did not come easily for the men and women of the Forty-fifth. Part of that, I would discover, was simply the passage of time. It had been nearly sixty years since this war. I couldn't expect each person to remember every detail. As a *Register-Guard* colleague back in Eugene had once told me over lunch: "You don't need every conversation, every detail, every anecdote. You're not Van Gogh drawing a portrait. You're just trying to draw a composite sketch of this woman. The key to your whole book will be this: when she dies, does the reader know her well enough to care?"

Beyond the passage of time, what further impeded getting more details was that Michalove and the others were products of a self-effacing generation raised to *do*—to work hard, fight hard, raise a family—and not to analyze what they were doing. Here I was, a representative of the navel-gazing baby boom generation, asking Michalove, "What's the worst you saw in a field hospital tent?" His answer?

"We just did what we had to do. We had a job and we did it." Time and again, I heard that from World War II sources. Time and again, I heard from their adult children how they never spoke about the war. I came to realize that another reason they couldn't—or didn't want to—remember details was that they didn't think such details were particularly significant, didn't think they had done anything particularly profound.

But, often, they wouldn't remember because, like Michalove, they simply didn't want to. War is painful and though some might have a certain morbid fascination with the horror of it, there's nothing the least bit fascinating about it for people who have lived it, seen pals die in it, and, in some cases, been haunted by it.

That said, I was surprised at Michalove's reaction to my question about Slanger dying. I knew he'd been there. If he'd been so disturbed seeing the paratroopers in the trees, how would he handle the death of "one of his own," a nurse from his own platoon, a woman, and, like him, Jewish.

"She and the others—when the shells started falling, they were huddled on cots," he said. "Frances Slanger was in the middle."

He stopped. "And that's when she was wounded, right?" I asked.

"Right. Shrapnel caught her in the stomach. Bad. They brought her into a tent and she said, 'Sit me up, sit me up.' As a nurse, she knew she'd be better off that way than on her back. Fifteen minutes later, she was dead."

He paused. "She was deeply committed to the cause," he said.

"What cause?" I asked.

He acted as if he hadn't heard.

"She was such a nice girl. After the war, I tried to find her family, to phone them, but had no luck."

I mentioned that in our phone interview, he'd told me about a gift she'd given him.

"Oh, yes, the egg."

He went on to tell me about how eggs were delicacies in wartime France, highly coveted in the soldiers' K-ration culinary world. And how Slanger, in one of the darkest moments of his weeks in Normandy—the death count rising—had come up to him from behind and said, "Here, for you," and placed a still-warm egg in his hand.

"She was such a nice girl," he said. And then he teared up again.

After a bit more conversation, I said goodbye. Before the book that he'd helped me write would be on a bookshelf, Fred Michalove would be dead.

IT WAS NEARLY noon. I needed to be in Latham, New York, 181 miles away, for an interview with Joseph Shoham by 4 P.M. I would, in a four-hour drive, be in four states (Rhode Island, Connecticut, Massachusetts, and New York), a strange concept for someone from the West, where an east-to-west trip across Oregon alone was about 400 miles and, with two major mountain passes to climb, would take perhaps eight hours.

At mid-afternoon, I crested Massachusetts' Berkshire Mountains, remembering that wonderful James Taylor lines from his "Sweet Baby James" song:

> Now the first of December was covered with snow
> And so was the turnpike from Stockbridge to Boston
> Lord, the Berkshires seemed dreamlike
> On account of that frostin'
> With ten miles behind me, and ten thousand more to go

I could relate. I seemingly had ten thousand miles to go—Ellis Island in the morning, with Washington, D.C., and Delaware to follow, all in only four days.

Of those I'd interviewed, none was more eager to share his experiences, nor as adept at recall, as Joseph Shoham, who was the Forty-fifth's dentist and cook. Soon after my arrival in Latham, Joseph—his wife Ethel, sitting as an interested observer—broke out a photo album. Back then, he resembled a young William Shatner from *Star Trek*.

He'd grown up in the Bronx, fascinated by nature—the stars above Cortlandt Park, the monarch butterflies making their yearly pilgrimage across Staten Island. He was among the Forty-fifth's more whimsical characters, a collector of beetles, butterflies, German dental instruments, and teeth. On a post-liberation trip to Paris, he had brought back a wire-haired terrier he'd named Penny—short for the new lifesaving drug, penicillin—to the field hospital. It became the unit's unofficial mascot. "Strange, but we never saw Penny after the night Frances died," he said.

He was easily the most perceptive member of the Forty-fifth I would find. He remembered the pile of German dead near Utah Beach and the hand of one soldier having two rings on it, a tad surprised that an American soldier hadn't taken them for souvenirs or resale. He remembered the stench of death, from animals and humans. The sound of Isadore Schwartz's trumpet tugging people's hearts toward home. How deeply his tent mate, John Bonzer, had fallen for Sallylou. And the Jewish people in the outfit, himself among them, holding occasional Friday night sabbath services, non-Jewish soldiers often coming to "fill in the quorum."

He had kept a journal of every stop the Second Platoon—Slanger's platoon and his—had made on the trip. Now, at eighty-six, he not only remembered details, but could compare, contrast, and contextualize a person, place, or event amazingly well. He was to the Forty-fifth Field Hospital what Aubrey Montague was to *Chariots of Fire*—not the star, not the life of the party, but someone who, from the shadows, noticed all that was going on, and at a level deeper than the rest. He was, in many ways, a male counterpart to the person in the Forty-fifth he would come to admire the most: Frances Slanger.

Most people think visually but, when communicating that idea, grind the images into powdered verbiage. Not Shoham, who seemingly had a colorful story to spice every recollection.

Was Sallylou Bonzer really the life of the Forty-fifth's party? I asked. "Definitely," he said. "I remember the time she pieced together this Nazi flag into a two-piece bathing suit, with the swastika right where you sit down." He laughed. "Sallylou was always laughing, always smiling, and a bit of a flirt."

And Frances Slanger? "Frances was quiet, and probably the

best nurse in the whole damn outfit. I remember her giving me a back rub, complete with the karate chops, the works. That was Frances Slanger. It'd be the end of the day, she was tired, but she was always looking out for others."

"And the letter?" I asked.

"Oh, yes, the letter. She showed me the letter the morning she was to send it. I thought it was very good."

"It almost seemed as if the military was where Frances found her true calling," I said.

"It was like she was made for the military and it was made for her," he told me. "She was a doer. You might even call her a 'reformer.' You go through life thinking, 'What could I have possibly done for the world?' Well, she didn't just think it, she did it. That letter touched a lot of GIs."

I had plenty of people telling me that, but little evidence showing me. "All these nurses were special to the guys," he continued. "Imagine a guy who's just about dead and he opens his eyes and there she is: an American girl. It was heaven. They'd been out there for weeks, months, facing guys that wanted to kill them. Now they're staring at someone who wanted to make them better."

Like Michalove, Shoham had been there the night Slanger died. "The shells sounded like a railroad train when they were coming in. Louder and louder and louder." He remembered her saying, "I … am … dying," the desperate attempt to keep her alive. Finally, he remembered the stillness of death, and Isadore Schwartz bowing his head and whispering "shalom," then seeing him walk outside in the rain and dark, fall to his knees, and sob.

Shrapnel had caught Shoham in the arm during the attack, but he wasn't seriously wounded. He, like most of the Forty-fifth, survived to help treat soldiers through the frozen hell of the Battle of the Bulge and deeper into Germany. He remembered, if not actually coming across a Jewish concentration camp, seeing some who'd survived such camps. "Some looked like ghosts," he said.

"In the spring of 1945, we made it to Pilsen (Czechoslovakia). It was Passover and I was carrying matzo under my arm and I heard a Czech say to me, in Yiddish, '*Entshuldikt, wher bist du a Yid?*' "

" 'Yes,' I said. 'I am a Jew.' He and his wife hugged me and said: 'We are the only remaining Jews in Pilsen. All the others are dead.' "

AFTER WAKING at 4:30 A.M. and flying from Albany to Newark, New Jersey, by mid-morning I was on a ferry to Ellis Island. Having gotten about five hours sleep, I was far less chipper than the hundreds of school kids who bounced around the decks on this Friday morning like pin balls. I called my one source at the National Archives, Richard Boylan, and confirmed I'd be there Monday.

For a guy like me who lived in a city whose tallest building was eighteen stories, the site of New York City's downtown, crowned by the two World Trade Center towers, was mind-boggling: hundreds of high-rises packed together like an overcrowded elevator with a couple of seven-foot-four basketball centers squished in the middle. I'd never been to New York and this one-day, in-and-out trip to the harbor barely qualified as an official visit. But to understand Frances Slanger was to understand her past, and I had reason to believe this island had been a small, but significant, part of that past.

At this point in the search, the only evidence I had that Slanger had come through Ellis Island—as opposed to other immigrant portals such as Boston or Philadelphia—was her cousin, Sylvia Fine, whose letter said, "She was detained at Ellis Island because she had some kind of infection and it must have been a very traumatic experience for a young child." Having still not received ship-passenger manifestos back home, I immediately headed for the records room to beat the crowds.

It didn't take long to find a Slanger reference. On September 7, 1920, the passenger list of the *Nieuw Amsterdam*, which had sailed from Rotterdam, The Netherlands, included what appeared to be a mother and two daughters: Regina Slanger, 41, Chaja Slanger, 11, and Freidel Slanger, 7, of Lødz, Poland. The last name was right. The city and country were right. And Frances had had a sister who may well have been four years older. But their first names, at least in America, were Eva, Sally, and Frances. Could they have changed those names from Regina, Chaja, and Freidel? Or was this not them? And where was David Slanger, Frances's father?

The answers, like so many answers in this search, would have to wait. I ran a number of other searches, without discovering more. And yet as I stared at the handwritten ledger, specifically at the name "Freidel," it was mind-boggling. Quite possibly, this was Frances Slanger. These were words written by some clerk at Ellis Island in 1920, probably as Frances and her mother and sister waited anxiously in "The Great Registry Room" to be allowed into America.

Meanwhile, if the exhibits at Ellis Island helped me better appreciate why it was known as "the island of hope and island of tears," seeing the actual buildings did not. Eight decades after Slanger might have waited in one of the seemingly endless lines in this great room, the ventilation was good, the temperature pleasant, the floors scrubbed to a shine, the noise level nothing beyond the buzz of school children. Frankly, it was hard to imagine the reality of the 1920 Ellis Island. The room would have been hot; the air putrid with the smell of sweat, some people wearing layers and layers of clothes because they could not fit them in their baggage, and the stench of backed-up toilets and vomit; the lines snaking up and back; the chaotic chirping of thousands of people in dozens of languages, some conversations tinted with hope, others with desperation.

No, what moved me most at Ellis Island was not the building, far nicer than I'd imagined, but the huge photographs on the walls. The hungry looks of the waiting. The ethnic nuances in the faces. The touch of uncertainty in the eyes of young children, each holding an American flag—timidly hopeful, and yet, like flotsam and jetsam at slack tides, neither coming or going. Just waiting.

Had Frances Slanger once held one of those flags, a flag that, twenty-four years later, she would die for? Had she once looked up from a ship and seen the nearby Statue of Liberty? Once stepped here, where I had now stepped? I scribbled my last notes, took my last photographs, and headed back to the ferry to catch a plane for Washington, D.C.

AFTER AN EIGHTY-MINUTE flight, I arrived at Dulles International Airport and immediately called home. It was 6 P.M. Friday on the West Coast, meaning Jason, my younger son, was playing in his final regular-season baseball game. A friend at the game gave me periodic updates. Upon my landing, Jason's Sheldon High team was up by a run. By the time I rented my car, tied. And by the time I arrived to stay at a friend's house in Silver Springs, Maryland, had lost in extra innings.

I was tired. Feeling disconnected. And wishing I was home, wishing I could have been with Sally at Jason's game. But after catching up with my old newspaper colleague, Andy Nelson, I had to charge whatever was left in my emotional batteries for the next day: interviews in Delaware with the final two nurses I hadn't seen in person.

At dawn, I drove through a sleepy Washington, D.C., past the U.S. Naval Academy in nearby Annapolis, Maryland, and across the Chesapeake Bay Bridge, and into Delaware. The state had the feel of Oregon's Willamette Valley, though flat.

I found the first of the day's two World War II nurses, Mae Montague Bowen, at a pleasant, middle-of-the-road senior apartment complex in Dover. On the night before the Forty-fifth had shipped to England, she had become engaged to Ed Bowen, the administrator of the unit's First Platoon. (She was Third.) They were married on Thanksgiving day in Bastogne Belgium, she wearing paratrooper boots and an Eisenhower jacket. She got pregnant and, as army regulations required, sent home.

Of all the people I'd interviewed, none emphasized Slanger's "loneliness" more than Montague. "She was a fine, courteous, quiet individual," said Montague. "The only Jewish girl in the unit. She was billeted alone in England. That's why I have this picture up here." She pointed to a Monet painting of an English village. "It reminds me of where Slanger was billeted in England. When my daughter was helping me move here she wasn't going to pack this. I insisted it be moved. 'That,' I told her, 'was where your father and I would walk to see Frances Slanger.' "

"Did her staying alone have anything to do with her being the lone Jewish nurse?" I asked.

"No, I don't believe so," she said.

Montague, now seventy-nine and a widow since 1976, helped me understand the grit of army nurse life. She described being shelled on one of the first few nights in Normandy. Having to go to the bathroom while privates, on guard, watched for German snipers. And the wounds of soldiers being not only physical, but mental.

"When we landed, so many of the men who'd been fighting had just lost it. At night they'd be trembling. Some just couldn't go on, mentally. The war was a great experience; nothing can take its place. But the human body is very fragile, and it's amazing how many healthy young boys could, in just a second's time, be gone. One guy who only had one arm left kept saying he wanted to go back and finish the job because, the way he was, he had nothing to come home to."

After an hour's drive, I found Dottie Richter Lewis in a roomy old ranch house beneath the pine trees of Rehoboth Beach. Before this trip, I'd written only here and there about war; for example, I had written recently about a Eugene World War II vet who was dying and wanted to find a home for the pen-and-ink sketches that a long-dead buddy of his had drawn of Belgian castles and of bridges their engineering unit had built across Germany's Rhine River. But, as my interviews continued, I was understanding World War II better and appreciating more those who fought it and patched its wounded.

Dottie was, I would find, a little like Madonna's character in *A League of Their Own*, a movie about the women's baseball league during World War II: a bit of a fun-loving rebel. After a stint in the regular army in Puerto Rico, she had sauntered into Fort Bragg with golf clubs on one shoulder and a tennis racket in her hand. "My," Mae had said at the time, "what have we *here?*" But for Dottie, the landing at Utah Beach changed any notions that France was going to be another Puerto Rico. "When we waded ashore there were casualties as far as you could see," she said.

As we talked of the unit's landing at Normandy and moving across Europe, she mentioned that she occasionally would see a male cousin of hers who was with an Army engineering unit. "Quite the coincidences," she said.

"What exactly did the man do?" I asked.

"Oddly enough," she said, "he was an artist. He drew pictures for the Army."

Somewhere in my brain, two wires connected. How many art-

ists in engineering units could there have been? "Do you happen
to have any sketches of his?" I asked.

"Why, yes," said Richter, puzzled about my sudden interest in
her cousin. She led me to the dining room. There on the wall were
two large prints. One was of a castle, *Château Nodave*. The other
was of a pontoon bridge.

"Your cousin," I said, "was Rudy Wedow, right?"

Richter was stunned. "Well, yes, but how could you have possibly known that?" I told her about the Eugene World War II vet,
Guy Parker, who, at war's end, had been given some lithographs
from an artist buddy in the unit. On my laptop computer, I showed
her the column I'd written. She then told me about how her mother
and Wedow's mother were sisters in upstate New York. "He was
drawing, even as a boy," she remembered.

While an amazing coincidence, the story was like much of what
I had discovered in my interviews with those in the Forty-fifth:
fool's gold. Great information, but not pertinent to the real focus
of my story, Frances Slanger. It was interesting, but nothing that
would wind up in the book.

Dottie remembered Frances as a "thoughtful, quiet person."
But, like Mae, hadn't been in Slanger's Second Platoon. I tried to
get her to tell me more about Slanger, but, as with the others, she
had little she could tell. Those who'd known Slanger best—her
three tent mates, Cox, Powers, and Bowler—were dead. With the
exception of Shoham and, to a lesser degree, Michalove, listening
to the others talk about Slanger was like watching a baseball game
from the upper deck in right field—yes, you saw the game, but not
the nuances you'd wished for.

Late that night, back at Andy's house in D.C., I typed in my
notes, trying not to accidentally lube my keyboard with the grease
from my Wendy's fries. "So frustrating," I wrote, "that there are
people who knew of (Slanger) but didn't really know her. All the
people who knew her are dead. Where's that person who knew
her?"

And where was the evidence that Slanger was something more
than just another do-good army nurse? That she'd really deserved
having a ship named in her honor? It was fine to have people such
as Joseph Shoham and her nephew, Irwin Sidman, say she was one

of a kind, but what about the soldiers she apparently had served so well? Where were the voices of these GIs who'd read her letter in the *Stars and Stripes*?

"For now," I told Sally in a cell-call home, "my only hope for that kind of thing on this trip is the National Archives. But that's needle-in-a-haystack stuff."

IT WAS SUNDAY. The archives were closed until Monday. Thus, I spent part of the day at the Women in Military Service For America memorial—great contextual information but nothing specific to Frances or the Forty-fifth—and part of the day at the United States Holocaust Memorial Museum.

It proved to be among the more chilling three hours I've experienced in my life. It is one thing to read of the horror of Germany's murder of about six million Jews, another to see a cattle car stacked with the shoes of the dead. To step on a "street" paved with gravestones from a Jewish cemetery. To hear the recorded voices of Auschwitz survivors telling their stories. And amid this, to realize that even with this "you-are-there" experience, you *weren't* there. You are clueless about what it was like to be there—can't even begin to imagine the pain a father felt watching his family lined up on the edge of a mass grave and shot in the backs of their heads or a mother whose child is ripped from her arms and slammed against a wall. After three hours, I walked out into the sunshine feeling an unsettling blend of survivor's guilt, anger, and grace.

Later, I went to the Library of Congress and searched back issues of *Stars and Stripes*, looking for anything else that may have been written after Slanger's death. Nothing. Before it closed, I popped into the Library of Congress bookstore. That's when I saw it: a hardback, taupe-colored book with a cover photo of a woman working on an airplane propeller: *American Women and the U.S. Armed Forces: A Guide to the Records of Military Agencies in the National Archives Relating to American Women.*

Who knew? I began flipping through it and realized this entire 355-page book was devoted to helping people find information on military women at the archives where I'd be the next morning. I bought it on the spot. Outside, sitting on a bench, I began sifting through the index: *Sisk, Mildred Elizabeth, 338.6; Sisters of Char-*

ity, 112.43; Slacker raids (WWI), 165.38 ... . Come on, come on, list "Slanger." Nope. No Slanger reference.

That night, yellow highlighter and sticky notes in hand, I skimmed the entire book until 1 A.M., noting anything that sounded like it might get me to Slanger-related information. What I realized is that many of the index references pointed to the haystacks but I'd have to find the needles within. For example, Index 407.40 consisted of 8,035 linear feet—that's more than a mile!—of files on:

> Narrative reports and supporting documents relating to operations and activities of the Army during World War II and the postwar period, 1940-1948 ... are arranged by command level, so it is necessary to know the name and number of particular military units in order to make full use of this large-quantity of material. The series includes reference to a few reports concerning nurses, including one relating to operations during the invasion of Normandy .... Among records of nonorganic units (independent units not part of a hierarchy such as infantry or cavalry) filed at the end of the series are reports of hospital units and WAC units ...

It was the ultimate in good news/bad news. Yes, there was tons of information, but for a guy who had one day to spend in the archives, there wasn't much time to search. And nothing to suggest there was anything specifically about Slanger. But by the time I went to sleep that night, I had a dozen sticky notes, pages and pages of yellow underlining, and some guarded hope of success the next day.

The National Archives at College Park, Maryland, was nothing like what I expected, nothing like the original archives in D.C. The building itself, instead of being brick, stone, and venerable, was new, glassy, and boxy, like the corporate offices of some Fortune 500 company. The sign-in procedure alone was far more daunting than I expected; it took me about an hour simply to get registered. The index room was massive and lined with books that would tell more specifically what certain files offered. But by noon, my hopes of a major informational hit were dwindling, lost in a tangle of confusion.

All I knew was that dozens of us turned in index request slips and about an hour later someone retrieved the files for us. Information seekers weren't allowed in the archive rooms.

The doors would close at 5 P.M. By 1 P.M., I'd requested a few files and gotten them, but only three were particularly helpful: the annual reports for the Forty-fifth and Forty-second field hospitals, the latter which Slanger and the nurses were briefly attached to, and a similar report on the 128th Evacuation Hospital. The evac hospital had arrived at Utah Beach on the same *William N. Pendleton* ship that transported the Forty-fifth's nurses.

The Forty-fifth's report was fourteen pages long and helpful for context, though made only the briefest mention of Slanger's death: "Since being on the continent, one dental officer was wounded by an antipersonnel bomb on June 10; one nurse, one unit commander, and one enlisted man were killed by enemy artillery fire 21 October; one enlisted man was wounded by a mine; and 10 enlisted men lost from other causes ... ."

The Forty-second's report, ironically, was more helpful; the Forty-fifth's nurses had worked with that unit on their first day in Normandy. The hybrid surgical tent was, the report said, "the only functioning medical installation in the sector." OK, I thought, but where was any evidence that, as Sallylou Bonzer had told me, it was "chaos?" Or, as Mae Montague had told me only two days before, that "when we waded ashore there were casualties as far as you could see?" Where was the proof that these nurses weren't strolling through French hospitals in squeaky white shoes?

I scanned down the report, then saw it: "By 2200 hours, over 200 patients of all types of casualties had been admitted. Shortly thereafter, there was a concentrated bombing and strafing attack by enemy planes ... in the next two hours, the hospital facilities were taxed beyond capacity and by 2400 hours, nearly 300 more patients had been formally admitted, and 17 truckloads of wounded waited admittance."

I exhaled. "Seventeen truckloads of wounded" ... "only functioning medical installation" ... "bombing and strafing attack by enemy planes ... ." If anything, the nurses had understated the hell they stepped foot into on June 10, 1944, four days after D-Day.

Still, I still needed information specific to Slanger and the impact of her letter. It was 3:30 P.M. when his name came to mind: Richard Boylan. Of course! He was the archivist who had responded to my e-mail months ago and whom I had touched base with Friday. Maybe he could help. I headed for the office area, asked a receptionist if he were available and was directed to his hole-in-the-wall office.

I introduced myself—"Oh, yeah," he said, "the guy from Oregon"—and showed him an index number that I thought might have some promise for Slanger information. He looked at the number and did some cross-checking on his computers. I felt a little like I were handing the guy a single key and asking him to tell me which of a thousand doors it might open—without even having called ahead to schedule an appointment.

"Come with me," he said. Just like that. I followed. He punched an elevator button and we headed down. Where were we going? He wasn't saying. But when the door opened, I realized we were in the bowels of the archives, not another index room, but a massive area of files.

"There are twenty others this same size," he said. "The rows move electronically."

He looked at the index number, then pressed a button. A row of files parted as if it were an informational Red Sea. My eyes widened. Boylan walked down the row, stopped, looked up, looked down, reached out, and took hold of a file. "Here," he said, "try this."

I opened the nine-by-fourteen-inch envelope. On top was a handwritten letter that said "November 25, 1944" from "somewhere in France."

Amid the roar and thunder of war emerges at one time or another, the genuine, worth living for thoughts of a human being. Only few people can put it on paper, but all of us have that singular infinite thought deep in our minds and hearts. Frances Slanger put it on paper—so overwhelmingly beautiful—yet so much from her heart.

My attention ratcheted down a notch. I flipped to the next page. Another letter: "If ever a couple of doughboys were capable of tears … ." And another: "It is probably impossible to estimate how many service men and women were shocked at the fate which befell 2d Lt Frances Slanger … ." I was reading faster and faster. Letter after letter after letter: "I wish to pay homage to a true American woman, a true angel of mercy" … "It was the best editorial we've read to date" … "I was never so impressed by anything in my life as I was by France Slanger's article … ." " … helmets doffed, heads bowed in silent prayer to soldier Frances Slanger and her fellow nurses … ." " … there would be no finer way to honor this courageous woman than to name after her the best and finest hospital ship yet to come off the production-lines … ."

"Wow," I said, thumbing through a two-inch stack of letters that had been addressed to the *Stars and Stripes* newspaper.

"Good stuff?" Boylan asked.

"Great stuff," I said.

To this point, I'd known what Slanger had done; I'd read every word of her letter. But until then, I hadn't realize the depth of that letter's impact. There must have been close to a hundred letters in my hands. These soldiers, after four months of day-to-day fighting since the shores of Normandy, had lost more than buddies and limbs. They'd lost a sense of dignity, humanity, purpose. They had lost hope. And Slanger's letter had reaffirmed their worth, given them hope, melted their hearts. "Her letter," wrote Staff Sgt. Joe Chasin of the 602nd Engineers, "was enough to make a guy hold up his head, throw out his chest and step out with more pride and confidence than he ever had before."

I started sifting deeper and deeper into the stack.

"Hold on," Boylan said. "A bit of advice. We close in less than an hour and a half. Buy a card and start copying like crazy."

I thanked him profusely, then did as he suggested. Each page that spit out of that copy machine was a reminder that Frances Slanger had, indeed, made a difference in the world. Now, for the first time, I had proof. I had a book.

It wasn't until the next night, on a darkened flight home, that I fully appreciated what had happened that afternoon: a legacy from one generation had been passed across six decades to another generation. At the end of World War II, somebody, presumably a *Stars and Stripes* staffer, could have easily thrown out those soldiers' letters. But he or she had the foresight to think: *these soldiers' words need to be remembered.* Someone, somehow, amid the tangle of war and war's end, found a way to pass those letters on to the National Archives, which, thanks to Mr. Boylan, passed them on to me, which I hoped to pass on to thousands of readers.

I wondered if anyone, between war's end in 1945 and this March afternoon in 2001, had seen those letters but me. It was humbling to think perhaps not.

Chapter 7

May-September 2001
Eugene, Oregon

Writing a book is a horrible, exhausting struggle, like a long bout of some painful illness. One would never undertake such a thing if one were not driven on by some demon whom one can neither resist nor understand.

—George Orwell

I didn't realize how big the skeletons were until that happened. The skeletons here go back to grandmothers and grandfathers.

—Boston Red Sox Manager Rene Lachemann after the team's World Series collapse in 1986

OREGON'S schizophrenic spring—a rain-sun-hail spin cycle—gave way to the state's best-kept secret: another sunny, warm summer, the evenings of which would, in places, be touched with the scent of wild blackberries by August.

Jason's baseball team made it to the state semifinals. Two weeks later, he graduated from high school. Ryan graduated from Linfield College. Two months later he married Susan, whom he'd commuted two hours to see almost every weekend for the previous four years. Returning home after the wedding, Sally and I found it on our kitchen counter: a thank-you note and the kind of thing that makes parenting all worthwhile: a $10 gift certificate from Burrito Boy. I walked into the backyard and cried.

In some ways, authors live two lives: the nine-to-five life, the pay-the-mortgage life, the oh-that's-right-I-have-a-wife-and-two-kids life. And the life immersed in the subject of whatever book has drawn them in like that gooey black web in *Spiderman III*. Oh, sure, you never think of, say, Hemingway having another life beyond a bottle of merlot, a typewriter, and all those robust noun-verb constructions. But most writers aren't Hemingway. We're people trying to balance a book project and relationships. We're people who, too often, unfortunately, embody the question author Susanne Lipsett asks in *Surviving a Writer's Life*: "You mean life is more than material for books?"

The book became all-consuming, not that looking back, I'm particularly proud of that. After a fender-bender "totaled" my pickup, I bought another used pickup that I'd later regret buying because of its lack of air-conditioning, power steering, and a rear seat. Why didn't I look harder? Because I didn't have time. I had a book to write and allowed myself one Saturday morning to find a replacement. Given my self-imposed time constraints, that's the best I could do.

I was in church and our pastor, Steve Hill, was talking about the love of money—I Timothy, I believe—and I was thinking: What's a reasonable goal for first-year sales, perhaps 100,000 copies? Where can I find some World War II expert to help me with the book? Should I go to France?

"People who want to get rich fall into temptation and a trap and into many foolish and harmful desires that plunge men into ruin and destruction," said Pastor Steve, quoting the verse. "For the love of money is a root of all kinds of evil."

Oh, yes, right. Of course.

June 11. Letter from Shoham. "If I'm not on this planet when the book comes out, please send one copy to each of my two sons." Complete with addresses.

June 12. Letters to 40 Slangers across country go out.

June 15. Paul Neville, while we're on a run, asks if I've seen obits for David and Eva, Slanger's parents. Great idea that I'd overlooked. Mary, the Boston University librarian, happily agrees to look them up in the *Boston Globe* after she returns from vacation.

Though I was still light on post-Normandy Slanger stuff and insight from people who had known her well during the war years, I was awash in information by July. I had brought home about ten pounds of books from my travels to the Northeast, the most difficult part of the trip not being flight connections but closing my suitcase and making sure it was beneath the airlines' fifty-pound baggage limit. The books ranged from Paula Nassen Poulos's *A Woman's War, Too: U.S. Women in the Military in World II*, found at the National Archives' bookstore, to Dan Shaughnessy's *The Curse of the Bambino*, which enabled me to understand the Boston Red Sox and how the ghost of Babe Ruth had haunted the seemingly jinxed franchise since he departed Bean Town—and the Hotel Buckminster—in 1920.

By now, only weeks into my Red Sox infatuation, I was following daily box scores and, while trying to understand who Frances Slanger was, also trying to plumb the depths of Red Sox lore. I'd been back home only a short time when I began to understand how this "curse of the Bambino" was seemingly imbedded in some Red Sox faithful like tapeworms.

Five days after I returned from the East Coast, on May 23, a thirty-seven-year-old Boston fan named Paul Giorgio, on the advice of a Tibetan Buddhist holy man, placed a Red Sox baseball cap next to a stone altar at the base of Mount Everest, where climbers often burn juniper branches as an offering to the gods. He then carried the cap to the 29,028-foot summit, along with an American flag, in an attempt to "reverse the curse." Upon returning to the base camp, he completed one last ritual, as advised by the lama: he burned a Yankees cap.

Meanwhile, at the 400-foot elevation of Eugene, I continued my own trek toward the summit of Mount Slanger. At least once a week, I went on informational climbs to the University of Oregon's Knight Library. I'd rarely come home without at least half a dozen books: About the Jews—some undoubtedly Slanger's relatives—who'd been imprisoned in the Lødz ghetto when the Germans took control of the Polish city in 1939. About Ellis Island. About a war that books could only teach me so much about.

At night, before going to bed, I'd skim through those books, placing sticky notes on any paragraph that offered something I might want to incorporate into my story. Each weekday morning, I'd awaken at 5 A.M. to write, send e-mails, and make phone calls. At 8:30 A.M., I'd head for my job as a newspaper columnist, stopping at a Kinko's en route to copy the marked paragraphs. In the evening, after work, I'd funnel the copies into one of thirty-one notebooks I'd created for different subjects: "Slanger, Medics, Nurses, Jews, Forty-fifth Field Hospital (Individuals), Forty-fifth Field Hospital (Team), Ellis Island, Lødz, Boston," etc.

Thus did a new and unforeseen obstacle arise, an obstacle of my own making and, in a sense, a good obstacle to have: information overload. By the time the 120 pages of copies I'd ordered arrived from the Boston University nursing archives, I had easily more than a thousand pages of hard-copy information, a few dozen purchased books, and hundreds of photos, all stacked around me like pieces of a drum set. But I had no system so I could quickly get from, say, the snare drum to the tom-tom to the cymbals; at times, I didn't even know where each drum was.

I needed help. A sailing friend, Mike Thoele, who'd recently written a 647-page history on a local timber company, had once mentioned an index system he'd created to help him locate information. He was the most meticulous journalist I'd ever met, that rare blend of right-brain creativity and left-brain organization, the kind of guy who could make you understand the soul of an Eastern Oregon sheep rancher and yet design, and build, a pulley system to raise a mizzen mast on his sailboat.

As soon as I saw Thoele's computerized index system I knew I needed something similar. Using his model as a base, I took a week off from researching and created a computerized index system that ultimately would include 294 sources of information: every book, every interview, every trip to an archive had its own entry with specific notations of what type of information it contained. That way, if I needed something on, say, Lødz, Poland, where Slanger was born, I could type in the city's name in the index and quickly see what was available and where.

Meanwhile, using tab dividers, I broke the thirty-one notebooks into specific subjects. Under "Forty-fifth Field Hospital (Individuals)," for example, I had a section for each nurse, doctor, and enlisted man. I numbered each page within each section. Thus, if I searched the index for, say, Joseph Shoham and found an item that said "5-7-23," I knew to go to Notebook No. 5, Section 7, Page 23.

Beyond the notebooks, I organized systems for file folders to keep information that didn't fit neatly into a notebook, say a letter or a thick government document. And beyond file folders, I created systems for photos, audio tapes, and maps. These, too, were indexed on the computerized index system.

In addition to all this hard-copy information, much of my data lay in the computer itself. For example, I had a "Source List" file comprised of every person I'd contacted. By the end of the project, it would be 122 pages long and include contact information for more than 500 people, organizations, and companies. But thanks to my computer's search function, I could, in seconds, find any name and contact information I needed. As large as it was, this file was only one stream in an informational watershed that included hundreds of creeks, dozens of rivers, and a few major oceans, all a few keystrokes away.

By now, Sally's craft area of our office—and I wasn't particularly proud of this—had become Luxembourg to my France. Where fabric once was stacked, books were now stacked. Where once sat a sewing machine, boxes of Slanger file folders now sat. But if hunkered down for the long haul—and braced for my least-favorite time to write, summer—my sights were already far away: Europe.

"I think I need to go to France and Belgium," I told Sally one night in June 2001. "No, wait, *we* need to go to France and Belgium."

That's not the type of thing you expect to hear very often in the Welch household, where a more likely statement might be, "I think I need to go to Sears to get a new sparkplug for the lawn mower."

With the time, distance, and language barriers of Europe, I knew there wouldn't be much to get in terms of interviews with people. The Forty-fifth Field Hospital had camped-and-patched its way across France nearly sixty years before, through villages I couldn't even pronounce, much less hope to find people in who might remember Slanger. (Or, if somehow remembering her, be able to explain her to a guy whose foreign language skills were so pathetic he dropped out of basic Spanish in college—after the second day.)

But the deeper I got into the story, the more I felt it necessary to stand on the spot at Utah Beach where Slanger had come ashore, to imagine what these villages—Fauville, Beuzeville au Plain, Orglandes, Bethancourt—looked like. To see the field in Elsenborn, Belgium, where Slanger had died. And to walk through the cemetery where she was originally buried.

Sally looked at me. "You need to go to France. Just you. We can't afford both of us going."

"Hey, we can't afford one of us going," I said. Then, thinking of my mother's mantra from my childhood—"when-the-movie-sells"—I was about to say how $5,000 on a trip to France would be swallowed whole by a six-figure advance, when I decided otherwise.

"I really want you to come," I said. "I need you to come. It'll be great. You're a good language person. You picked up Creole before going to Haiti. I didn't. I can't do languages."

"I don't know if I can get off work."

"Work. Schmerk."

Then came the words I was longing to hear. "I'll think about it," she said.

ON JULY 2, 2001 while working on a column at *The Register-Guard*, I made a phone call that had nothing to do with Frances Slanger but ultimately would take the search to a new level. I had written a column on a woman who had helped get her Vietnam-vet father his long overdue Purple Heart award. When I'd asked her how she knew where to begin, she said she'd gotten detailed advice from a co-worker at the health insurance company where she worked. His name was Pat Gariepy.

I was about to send the column to my editor but, even though I'd doublechecked the spelling of his name in the phone book, I called him to confirm I had it correct. I did, but, for some reason, instead of saying thanks and hanging up, I asked how he had known where to begin the Purple Heart search. He explained that he was something of an amateur military historian. Had done a little work for the British government, in fact, regarding the Battle of Galapygos in World War I. Had been in the army himself. And, having quit that health insurance job, was now something of a house husband—he and his wife had no children—who spent a lot of time on the Internet to fuel his passion for military history.

"That's interesting," I said. "I'm writing a book about the first nurse to die after the landings at Normandy."

"Sounds interesting," Gariepy said. "Tell me more."

I gave him the Cliff's Notes version of the story thus far.

"Need any help?" he asked. Just like that.

I honestly hadn't been fishing for that question. It took me by surprise. But did he really want to help or was he just looking for a consulting gig that paid actual money, something that was in short supply on this informational search-and-rescue mission?

"This is a pretty low-budget operation," I said, mentally thinking, *It's just me and Uncle Visa.*

"I'm not looking to be paid," he said. "But I might be able to help."

In the weeks, months and—yes—years to come, that would prove to be an understatement. Gariepy infused the Slanger research campaign with insight and energy. He knew rocks to look under that I didn't even know existed. I'd e-mail him a question about the red crosses on the helmets of medical personnel, and he'd write back:

> The reason the red crosses weren't painted on the helmets was specifically because the army thought the Germans would target medics. That's because the division in the area, the 352nd Infantry Division, had just come from Russia, where the Russians DID shoot medics. Hence, the German medics arrived in the area before the invasion carrying pistols, which was against the Geneva Convention, and had to be told to remove them because the Americans didn't target them.

I'd e-mail him to ask how much the steel helmets weighed that Slanger and the others would have been wearing while wading ashore. "Three pounds," he'd say, then show up in *The Register-Guard* lobby half an hour later with an actual helmet. "I collect a lot of this stuff," he said, as if almost apologizing. He had the earnestness of *Superman's* Jimmy Olsen, and nearly always had answers for my questions—and plenty of questions himself. Like: "Have you filed an FIA for her casualty records?"

"Uh, no." I was vaguely familiar with the Freedom of Information Act but clueless about casualty records.

"They'll tell you exactly what happened that night. And include everything she had in her possession. Stuff like that."

The two of us started meeting at the Giant Grinder once a week, going over the book like *Dragnet's* Joe Friday and Frank Smith going over a case.

"We need to get death certification and naturalization certificates for Frances's parents," he said. "The naturalization papers might well include their Polish names so we can tell if they were, in fact, the 'Regina, Chaja, and Friedel' from those ships' records you found at Ellis Island. It was common for Jewish people to change their names once they got to America—or have someone change the name for them at Ellis Island. And, hey, we need to find out why that hospital was shelled. That just didn't happen in the European theater. The Germans respected those giant red crosses on the field hospital tents. Something went wrong."

"I've found this woman in Houston on the net who thinks she can help us with some Jewish genealogy stuff," I said, "but, you're right, we have to confirm those names. Say, how's your Yiddish? I need someone to translate Yiddish."

"Not good," Gariepy said, "but I speak some German. Learned it in the army. Was stationed there. So what else have you found?"

"I found another woman who's written a book specifically about Jewish nurses," I said. "She's returning my e-mails. Very helpful. Says Jewish women in the thirties were discouraged from becoming nurses by their parents."

"And there were quotas for Jewish doctors in medical school."

"Didn't realize that," I said. "Of the Forty-fifth's docs, only one wasn't Jewish—Bonzer, the guy here in Eugene. So you could sew up your country's wounded, but only so many of you were allowed to go to med school at one time."

"They had it better than blacks," Gariepy said. "In the South, during the war, German POWs would sometimes get served at a lunch counter while blacks had to go around back."

SUMMER'S HOMESTRETCH began. The Red Sox, having led the American League's East Division, lost to the Chicago White Sox 13-8 on July 22 and would never regain the division lead. Oh, well, maybe next year, 2002, they would finally win a World Series. Meanwhile, back home, we slogged down the info trail.

Sally ultimately agreed to go to France with me. Milton Zola, out of nowhere, sent a detailed map of his South End neighborhood from the 1930s that helped me see more clearly where Slanger lived her life. And, in what was the biggest news on the info-gathering front, the Slanger family's naturalization papers arrived, confirming that "Regina Slanger, 41, Chaja Slanger, 11, and Freidel Slanger, 7" were, in fact, Eva, Sally, and Frances Slanger. They had arrived at Ellis Island on the *Nieuw Amsterdam* on September 7, 1920. David Slanger, I learned, had arrived in 1913, leaving behind his eldest daughter, Chaja, and wife, Regina, who was pregnant with Freidel. In other words, Frances wouldn't have met her father until she was seven years old.

"So, like lots of Jewish fathers, he came to America from Poland to get work, in his case as a fruit peddler," I said to Pat one day over my minestrone soup.

"With the idea," he said, "that once he had enough money, the family could join him. That was 1913. A year later, World War I breaks out, immigration grinds to a halt and, bingo, the family is split apart until after the war."

We were moving forward, Pat's involvement the catalyst. Still, there were days like this:

Aug. 22. I make three phone calls this morning, all with high hopes of connecting with someone who has info on Slanger. The first is to Betty Vose, who may be the woman who was a 10-year-old girl at Cape Cod with Slanger in 1931 [based on caption information by a photo in the Sidman family album]. The woman on the phone message [who would, if she were the right one, be about eighty years old] sounds thirty. I leave a message. The number of the Belgium Consulate in Boston is no longer in service. And the recorded message for a guy who I'm thinking might be Dr. Martin Hirsch, a Philadelphia physician whose father may have been Hank Hirsch, a doctor in the Forty-fifth, says: "Yo, wassup? I'm not in right now." Something tells me this isn't a match.

In the information search, two bits of childhood advice from my mother proved prophetic. One, offered when I couldn't find, say, a second sock, was: "What would you do if you were the last person on earth and had to find that sock?" The inference, of course, was that you'd simply find a way to find it. That became my search mantra: Look harder. Find a way. Assume your life depended on finding it. The other advice was: "You always find something you're not looking for when you're looking for something else."

I was following a Web trail regarding Edna St. Vincent Millay's poem, "The Murder of Lidice," about a 1942 massacre of Jews in Lidice, Czechoslovakia. Slanger, having seen it published in *Life* magazine, had thought it important enough to clip and paste in her scrapbook. It was a raw-edged poem that includes a chilling portion about a soldier confronting a Jewish woman who'd hidden her newborn baby son under a bed, only to have the Germans bang " ... his head, / While the mother clawed at their clothes and screamed, /And screamed, and screamed till they shot her dead." I clicked on a link and found myself on a site about a place in France called Oradour-sur-Glane. Something about Germans massacring an entire village on—by now, the date jumped out at me like a headline—June 10, 1944, the same day Slanger and the nurses had arrived at Utah Beach. At 2 P.M.

I reached for "Notebook 1: 45th Field Hospital (Team)" and flipped to a report on the 128th Evacuation Unit, which, had been on the same *William N. Pendleton* ship as the Forty-fifth's nurses and, thus, after being ferried ashore in different LSTs, would have hit the beach at the same time. "The ship," said the report, "arrived in the bay off Utah Beach at 0730 hours (7:30 A.M.) 10 June 1944. Debarkation started at 1400 hours."

That was 2 P.M. If there was no geographic link between Oradour-sur-Glane and Utah Beach—Normandy was about 250 northwest—the time link was uncanny. At the same hour German machine gunners began mowing down 642 innocent people, Frances Slanger and other Forty-fifth Field Hospital nurses were clamoring down rope ladders, into landing crafts and coming ashore. If ever there were a chilling contrast between those who would kill and those who would heal, this was it.

BEFORE LEAVING for France, it was time to test a chapter on Sally. We were at our family's cabin on the Oregon coast, near a small town called Yachats (YAW-hots), where Sally had listened to me read fifteen pages to her. It was like pulling the sheet from a piece of art after nine months of work—and the audience being underwhelmed. I knew the manuscript was flawed. So did Sally, according to my journal's account:

> At first Sally gives her usual "very good." "No, it's not," I say. Slowly, in a painful 15-minute discussion, she agrees. But by the time we're finished, I realize it's been an extremely valuable 15-minute session. She's right. I need to "keep the camera at eye level." I need it to feel more like good fiction than deep academic. I need to take more chances, look at the world through Frances's eyes, not my own "eyes in the sky." So Sunday morning, I awake at 5:50 A.M. and, feeling the pit of failure in my stomach, realize I have two choices. Quit or make it better. I put on my glasses, throw on my sweats and here I am, just me and the seagulls awake at this hour. Both searching for the day's sustenance.

Sally and I had never been the "off-to-Europe" types; our idea of a vacation extravaganza was, say, going to Yachats and getting a shake to go with our burger baskets at the nearby Big Wheel Drive-In. So, in the weeks before leaving for Europe, we tried to learn even a few French phrases. For me, it was like flossing the night before a dental appointment: obviously too little, too late. A week before our September 8 departure, we invited a couple over who went to France about once a year. Carl Davaz, *The Register-Guard's* deputy managing editor, and his wife Kim, who wrote a culinary column for the paper, offered us all sorts of helpful information.

"And what, again, is your itinerary?" Carl asked.

"Arrive in Paris and rent a car," I said. "Drive south to Oradour-sur-Glane, this village the Germans wiped out on the same day Slanger and the Forty-fifth came ashore. Drive to Normandy. Two days there. Omaha Beach. Utah Beach. The cemetery you saw in the opening and closing scenes of *Saving Private Ryan*. Up the coast to leTréport. A long day from the English Channel to Elsenborn, where Slanger died. Her cemetery near Liege, Belgium. Back to Paris. And home."

"And you have reservations along the way?"

"No, only for the first night and the last. We figured the fewer places we had to find, the less potential for getting lost," I said.

He laughed slightly. "So you're coming into de Gaulle, renting a car, then driving around France, right?"

"Right."

"The airport is outside of Paris, to the north," he said. "Whatever you do, don't drive into Paris. Crazy traffic. Bad idea. Really bad idea."

"Roger."

"And you're doing some interviews along the way?"

"I tried to set some stuff up but couldn't. Mainly we just need to see these places."

Of all that was said on this evening, two things would stick with me most. The first was Carl's suggestion—odd, I thought at the time—to take a compass. "If you're driving and get lost, unlike here in the states, you might not have a clue where you are," he said. "With a compass, you can at least look at a map, surmise where you are, and figure out which direction you need to go to get back on track."

The second was a set of emergency questions I'd had Kim write out in French. If I got in a language bind, I figured, I could hand people this note about who I was and what I was seeking.

In the early hours of D-Day 1944, the paratroopers who'd jumped into the darkness of Normandy were weighted down with all sorts of equipment, including survival kits. Our "survival kit" was lighter and less cumbersome: a compass and a few questions written in French. Along with maps, these were what we had to help us manage this leap into the darkness, where we didn't know anybody, the language, or the land.

Only later would we find that what we were up against wasn't the unknown, but the all-too-familiar. That for all our lack of language skills and familiarity with road systems and cultural nuances, what would challenge us most in France would be an enemy rooted deep in the history of humankind. An enemy embodying the same evil that had once left broken hearts—and bodies—in a village called Oradour-sur-Glane, on the beaches of Normandy, and in a field hospital in Elsenborn, Belgium.

Chapter 8

September 9-18, 2001
France and Belgium

An adventure is only an inconvenience rightly considered.
An inconvenience is an adventure wrongly considered.

— G.K. Chesterton

Pope dies, Sox still alive

—Teaser on Boston's WBCN after Pope John Paul I died in 1978

THE ONLY THING that saved us the first day in France was a sense of humor. After flying from Eugene to Seattle to Chicago to Paris, we managed to get the car rented despite the language barrier and having not slept for nearly a full day. Things went downhill from there.

Heading south from Charles de Gaulle International Airport—"Hey, this is a breeze," I told Sally in the same way the captain of the *Titanic* might have said "smooth sailing ahead!" after leaving England—we quickly got into a disagreement about a freeway exit.

"Is this it?" I said as the pilot. "Do we exit here?"

"No. Yes. No. Yes," she said as the navigator, wrestling with a map in her lap. "I don't know!" Neither did I.

We exited. We shouldn't have. A sign with an arrow pointing down said: "Paris."

Bad idea. Really bad idea. Carl Davaz's words chided me without mercy. I exhaled in disgust, my sense of humor having not yet kicked in. "We're heading for Paris," I said. My stomach churned with fear. I had to find a way back to the main north-south freeway, N-20, I thought. I took another exit, which veered us away from Paris but toward nothing we recognized. We went from freeways to stop-and-go streets. Drizzle started sprinkling the windshield.

"Their stoplights are hard to see," I said.

"I know," Sally said. "You just ran a red."

I rolled my eyes. Turned right. Left. Went straight. I felt like someone stuck in quicksand: the harder I tried to extract myself from my lostness, the deeper I got lost. The drizzle turned to rain. Visibility turned from miles to meters. I didn't have a clue where I was or where I needed to be. I didn't know north from south, east from west.

"I need to stop and look at the map," I said, swinging into the parking lot of an apartment building on a slight hill.

"Did you see that sign back there?" Sally said. "I think we're in Versailles."

Hey, if you're going to be lost, you might as well be lost in a hot bed of world history. I looked at the map, tilting my head one way, then the other, like the undecided CEO at the start of *Planes, Trains & Automobiles*. I looked out the front window, then out the side.

"Hey, what about the compass?" Sally said.

I perked up. Of course! Davaz's last-minute suggestion saved the day. We knew we were west of the north-south main drag we needed to be on. With the help of the compass, we were able to tell exactly which direction east was, thus able to head that way. Somehow, we got back on track.

After three hours of driving, we stopped for gas and snacks. It took me nearly five minutes—and a station attendant—to figure out how to open the gas-tank cover (with the remote button on the key chain, it turned out, something I'd never experienced on a vehicle). Plus, I tried to pay for two pops and a bag of pretzels with the French equivalent of a $100 bill. Oh, well.

Finally, late in the afternoon, we arrived in the village of Oradour-sur-Glane. We found our hotel in the middle of the compact village. It was called the Hotel de la Glane, which, I believe, is French for "everything is really small, like the trash can, which looks like a twelve-ounce soda pop." We had been up for twenty-eight hours, flown for fifteen, and driven for six. We flopped on the bed and promptly fell asleep. It was about 5 P.M.

When we awoke, my watch said 7:40 A.M. It was semi-dark outside; the sun had just come up. Or had it just gone down? We didn't know which. I can never trust the A.M./P.M. indicator on my watch because it's seldom set right. Sally's watch had hands, which made it useless in situations like ours. The room had no clock.

Nobody wants to impress his new foreign hosts by calling the front desk and saying, "Hi, we're the dumb Americans in 205 who just checked in. Is it night or day?" We could call home, but you don't want to waste a Lifeline on a night-or-day question when you could be asking something significant, like: "Why are there no pickups in France, and hasn't anyone told these folks about the smoking/cancer link?"

It was cloudy. No sun to offer a clue. No cell phone coverage to phone home and ask our kids for the time there, then add nine hours. I looked out the window and thought of that scene in *A Christmas Carol* where Scrooge asks the boy outside his room what day it is, and the lad says, "Why, it's Christmas Day, sir." Though our hotel and village looked a tad Dickens-esque, there was no lad outside and, besides, I couldn't figure out how the windows opened. So I decided to go outside and smell the cafes for breakfast or dinner scents. But the door was stuck shut, and we couldn't get it open.

At this point, we both did the only thing we could: began laughing hysterically. I imagined hearing Monsieur George Bailey, aka Jimmy Stewart, saying, "Look here, Ernie, straighten me out. I've got some bad liquor or something." (The latter was totally impossible because, with my deep knowledge of French, had I tried to get some bad liquor I would have ordered, instead, a passport, an ATM machine, or tickets to the Louvre sautéed in a lemon-butter sauce.)

Sally solved the stuck-door dilemma. I ventured downstairs, a man on a mission. Our host was setting a table. But for breakfast or dinner? I desperately wanted to ask but none of my French-at-a-glance books had prepared me for such a question. They taught me to ask, "Which bus do I take?" but not, "Is it day or night?"

I walked down the street, which, like most French streets, was a two-lane route just wide enough for a kid on a scooter. "Bon jour," said a man I passed. Ah-ha, I said to myself with the zeal of Inspector Clouseau himself: That means "good morning" or "good afternoon." We had, indeed, slept an entire night! But, then, where's the French's linguistic dividing line between afternoon and evening (bon soir)? And what if he was just an ignorant tourist who didn't know the language, a guy like me who earlier had greeted a service-station attendant with a hearty, "Au revoir!" ("Goodbye!")

I headed back to the room. "I've got it," Sally said. "Check the time on your laptop." Bingo! Within minutes, I had discovered that we had slept for exactly two hours and 40 minutes. It was evening, not morning. Suddenly, our confidence in our ability to survive in this foreign culture was buoyed. We knew night from day. What could stop us now?

We laughed more, in hindsight like people subconsciously taking deep gulps of air before diving under water. As if that oxygen would have to sustain us for a dive far deeper into the depths than we'd anticipated. Because as we fell asleep, we were ignorant of the tumultuous winds of the world that were mustering themselves back home. Sometime in the night, midnight arrived. At least in this part of France—six hours ahead of the U.S.'s Eastern Daylight Time—a new day had arrived: September 11, 2001.

MORE THAN anything, what I remember about Oradour-sur-Glane is the charred and rusted tricycles that no child ever rode again. The sewing machines that never sewed a dress again. The watches that never told time again, seared by flames, their hands frozen near 2 P.M. on June 10, 1944. On that day, time stopped for lots of people in this village: 642, to be exact, not to mention those friends and relatives for whom it might as well have stopped.

Here we were, nearly sixty years later, a couple dozen tourists speaking an array of languages and yet, I assume, feeling the same pits in our stomachs as we toured what once was Oradour-sur-Glane and now was a shrine. (After the massacre, a new village, where we'd stayed the previous night, had been built to replace it.)

"Man's inhumanity to man," muttered a Frenchman next to me in broken English.

The village nestled on a gentle knoll, 150 miles southwest of Paris. In 1944, the Germans had occupied France for four years, but, with more pressing concerns, had all but ignored the community. Then one day, everything changed. A soldier's boot kicked open the front door at the infants' school, freezing the children in fear. *"Raus!"* a soldier yelled, telling the children to get out. *"Raus!"* Vicious shouts peppered the village. Children started crying.

Trucks and half-tracks rolled by, packed with 130 soldiers who fanned out, yelling at the townspeople. *"Tout le monde sur la place!"* Everyone was to go to the marketplace. Shots rang out. Within an hour, hundreds of men, women, and children stood in the marketplace. A handful of German soldiers hastily mounted MG-42 machine guns on tripods. Women and children were forced into a church, men into barns and garages.

As, far away, Frances Slanger and the other nurses scrambled into landing crafts near Utah Beach, nearly everyone in Oradour-sur-Glane was killed in the next half hour. Nearly every building was set on fire. Of the dead, 190 were school children.

Near dark, the convoy of German soldiers—drinking, singing, and laughing—loaded up and headed for other business. The Allied army, they'd learned, had landed 250 miles to the northwest, in a place called Normandy. Some Oradour-sur-Glane residents who'd been out of town that day would return in shock and horror.

Neither Sally nor I spoke a word to each other for the first few minutes on our self-guided tour. Like the others, we just looked at the rubble, tried to imagine what it had been like, then felt all the worse for having done both.

"Why?" Sally asked. "Why the attack on innocent people?"

"Nobody knows for sure," I said. "Some believe Oradour was mistaken for another village that was a hot bed for the French Resistance. Others that it was targeted as revenge for the Resistance's killing of a German officer."

Twenty-one soldiers were tried by French courts; though found guilty and some sentenced to die, all escaped death.

As we left the shrine, we walked beneath a rusted archway whose single word explained why we needed to see the village where time, in essence, had stopped: *Remember*.

THE NUMBNESS wore off the farther we drove away from Oradour-sur-Glane; that is the privilege, and pity, for those with only a temporary connection to horror. We are the Monopoly player who, when landing on Jail, is always "just visiting." We move on with the next roll of the dice while the victims—and friends and relatives of the victims—remain forever imprisoned.

Heading northwest, to the Normandy coast, we drove down narrow, twisting roads, through villages with houses and rock walls that hugged those roads. Cows dotted the fields, leaving Sally-the-born-on-a-farm girl in bovine heaven. Every few hours, we'd go through some major city—Tours, Le Mans, Caen.

"Caen—I think the British and Germans had a huge tank battle here," I said. The sense of World War II history was profound, even if the fighting had been over for nearly sixty years.

We arrived at Normandy's beaches just before dark. We had hoped to stay at a place at Omaha Beach that Sally had found in the guidebook. But, we discovered, it was full. Not what we needed after eight hours of driving, but we wound our way south down the coastline about fifteen minutes, to Grandcamp-Maisy, where *60 Minutes* commentator Andy Rooney had spent some time soon after the invasion as a war correspondent. It was a few miles north of Utah Beach and a few miles south of Omaha. We soon came across a hotel/restaurant—Le Duguesclin—right above the sea wall.

Did they have a vacancy? "Follow me," said a woman. She took us to a neat room: two levels, two rooms, with a window notched in the slanted roof and opening to the English Channel. It was as if the ocean were lapping at our feet. We took it on the spot, which, of course, didn't mean we had a clue how much it cost. Everything, we would find, was less "official" here, people seemingly more trusting than in the country we'd left. We would be at this hotel two nights and would eat four meals without having paid a cent, nor having been required to register. They just knew us as the "Room 7" couple.

"Would you like dinner?" the woman asked.

"Oui," I said, smugly proud of my command of the language.

"Ten minutes," she said with the lilt of a school headmistress.

We stowed our gear, splashed some water on our faces, and came downstairs to the dining room. Judging from the quiet dialects around us, we may have been the only Americans at the dozen or so tables. It was shortly before 9 P.M., my mind already subtracting nine hours from French time to remind myself the time at home in Oregon: Almost noon. In Corvallis, Ryan, our elder son, would probably be doing some sort of graphics design work at his and Susan's apartment; she would probably be in class at Oregon State, where she was a senior. Jason, our younger son, was in his second week at Linfield College. And, hopefully, the four cats—Sally doted on them—weren't hacking up fur balls on the furniture.

We finally relaxed, knowing we not only had a spot to stay, but also a fish dinner to arrive, and adventures to be experienced in the week to come.

"To France," I said, lifting a glass of white wine to Sally's.

"To France," she said. We clinked glasses.

The fish was superb. The atmosphere pleasant, if a bit formal. The two of us were more relaxed than we'd been since leaving for the airport the previous day. As we ate, I noticed that the couple closest to us—a tad older than us—would occasionally glance our way, almost as if either listening in or making reference to us. Sure enough, in a few moments, the man dabbed his mouth with his cloth napkin, turned, and, with a concerned look on his face, said, "Excuse me, but you're Americans, aren't you?"

"We are," I said, wondering whether his accent was Scottish or Irish.

The man leaned closer. "We're sorry about what happened today in your country," he said.

Puzzled, Sally and I made quick eye contact with each other, then back to him. We'd occasionally come across what sounded like news reports on the car radio, but, of course, not speaking French, hadn't understood them.

"We haven't heard any news," I said, suddenly concerned. "What happened?"

BOB WELCH

He swallowed. "There was an attack on your country. Terrorists. Three planes were hijacked. Two crashed into the World Trade Center, one into your—what do you call it? The—"

"Pentagon," said the woman with him. "We're so sorry. Really we are."

The news was so overwhelming that, at first, I'm not sure it registered. My journal from that night said:

> Midway through the story, when the Pentagon was mentioned, I had the fleeting thought that I was being taken for a ride by an Irishman who'd had one too many ales; it was all too incredible, something you'd see advertised in front of the Gateway Movie Cineplex.

Buildings. Planes. Crashes. Fires. This meant dozens, perhaps hundreds, of people were dead. That I can't remember a thing about the rest of the dinner—beyond the couple saying they were from Dublin—suggests how the revelation stunned us. It was as if we'd been flying and suddenly fallen from the sky. Everything stopped, our mental "black box" recording only that which had been said before the point of impact.

We quickly finished our meals—you may pay when you check-out, our hostess said—and headed upstairs to our room. We couldn't understand the TV commentary, but the images were as clear as they were horrific: the man had been telling the truth. We watched, over and over, the planes explode in fireballs when hitting the two towers that only last spring I had seen from Ellis Island. We saw the gaping hole in the Pentagon. And something about a plane having crashed in a Pennsylvania field. We tried to imagine what the witnesses were saying, their eyes and gestures speaking the universal language of shock and horror, but their French-dubbed words meaning nothing.

"Unbelievable," Sally said.

"We need to call the kids," I said.

But on this night, there was no getting through to the United States, though we tried for nearly an hour. The lines were jammed. I put down the phone, feeling unconnected in more ways than one, and watched more of the newscast. I slowly shook my head. We were like those people from Oradour-sur-Glane who'd left for the day—the "lucky" ones—only to return and find their home attacked. Disbelief. Anger. How can this be?

I walked to a skylight window in the slanted roof and opened it. Outside, the light surf of Normandy was folding ashore. Behind me, the French reporters chattered on about the terrorist attack, the juxtaposition of history almost too present, too real, too large to comprehend.

The targets change. The villains change. The methods change. But man's inhumanity to man—as the Frenchman had said at Oradour-sur-Glane—continues. History repeats. Hitler in the 1930s and 1940s. The Japanese attack on Pearl Harbor in 1941. Terrorists in 2001.

I looked south to where Utah Beach lay somewhere in the darkness. At the moment, Frances Slanger's coming ashore—her helping save lives of soldiers whose victory would end Hitler's slaughter of the innocent, her letter, her life—seemed almost inconsequential to the more powerful forces at work in the world. What did her long-ago ripple on the water matter amid such tsunamis of hate, one of which had stormed ashore in America only eight hours before?

It would only be later, removed from such cynical undertows, that I realized it was precisely because of the Hitlers and the terrorists that stories such as Slangers must be told. To give us the one thing the bullies can't take from us. Hope.

THE AMERICAN FLAG flew half-staff at the American Cemetery at Colleville above Omaha Beach on this Wednesday morning. This was the cemetery where nearly 10,000 American soldiers were buried, many of them dying on D-Day on the beaches below. This was the cemetery used for the two scenes that bracketed the riveting movie, *Saving Private Ryan*. "Think not only upon their passing," said a phrase etched in a marble wall, "remember the glory of their spirit."

The chimes played "My Country 'Tis of Thee." Of all I would see and do on my first day in Normandy, including walks on Omaha and Utah beaches, nothing would touch me more deeply than this moment: hearing those chimes, seeing that half-staff flag, and scanning these headstones of soldiers who'd died for our country. The emotions were only deepened by the tragedy back home.

It's hard to appreciate the size of this graveyard from ground level but the white crosses and stars of David go on and on, etched white against the green grass. Omaha Beach, below, looked peaceful and pleasant: a quarter-mile swath of brown beach below a blue sky in which hung cotton ball clouds. A horse and cart zipped along the surf line. Two sand-sailors slalomed the beach. Frankly, it was hard to imagine the hell on earth of June 6, 1944.

At the Omaha Beach Museum—this was no organized tour, just the two of us following my "must-see" itinerary—Sally struck up a conversation with a British schoolmaster whose private-school kids, extremely well behaved, were touring. Someone in the group had a cousin from Portland, one hundred miles north of our home in Eugene. After we moved along, we couldn't help but hear what the schoolmaster said to his students. "We need to be extra respectful of these people," he said. "They are Americans, and their country has just suffered a terrible loss."

We walked the beach, read the monuments, noted the juxtaposition of then and now, innocents and horror: a miniature golf course on the edge of a beach where once had lain hundreds of bodies, partially buried in the sand.

Because I had expected to be moved by Omaha Beach, because others had told me of how moving the experience had been for them, I felt slightly guilty that the beach hadn't stirred more inside me. But moments of deep emotion, I'd come to realize, were often like sneaker waves, catching you when you least expect them.

After my father died in 1996, I was told to brace for tough times at Christmas, his birthday, the anniversary of his death. But, no, for me it was the smell of Old Spice, the *Trout in the High Country* flier in his belongings, and his fishing creel. Moments before I was to offer a Father's Day message at church—my first Father's Day without him—I saw the creel that Sally had placed at the foot of the podium, teeming with wildflowers she'd carefully arranged. I broke down on the spot. And it would be no different in France, I would learn: the emotional avalanches—as we'd learned the night before—would come at unexpected times. Just not now.

Midway between Omaha and Utah, we visited Point du Hoc,

where U.S. Army Rangers on D-Day had climbed the cliffs using rope ladders, more than 500 beginning the assault and fewer than 100 still fighting two days later. We saw the barest remains of the once-vaunted Atlantic Wall, a concrete barrier that the Germans had spent years building to fortify the coast and which Allied troops had conquered on what's referred to as "the longest day." We walked through German pillboxes, where men had killed and been killed. I remembered the story Joseph Shoham had told me, about Frances Slanger, faced with taking care of a badly wounded POW—a German, like the guys stuffing her relatives into furnaces. "She looked at him, then began dabbing his forehead with a cool rag," Shoham had told me.

We moved on. By then it was mid-afternoon—early morning back home—so, upon reaching Ste.-Mére-Eglise, the first Allied-liberated village in France, I tried again to reach our kids by pay phone. As I stood in a phone booth, trying to get a call through, I could see the "dummy" paratrooper hanging from a rooftop spier to commemorate a paratrooper whose parachute on that D-Day morning had snagged on that same rooftop. Finally, after numerous failures, I got through. My daughter-in-law Susan was on the other end of the line.

"We saw the news last night," I said, then asked one of those questions you ask as a father whether it's warranted or not. "You guys are all OK, right?"

"Yes," she said. "We're fine. It's just so terrible."

"How many dead?"

"Thousands."

"Thousands?"

"Yes. They've closed the airports."

"Around New York?"

"No, everywhere. All over the country. For security reasons. All flights have been grounded, everywhere."

For a brief moment, I thought about our return trip in six days.

"And who do they think is responsible?" I asked

"Terrorists. Nothing specific."

With each question, I realized that the magnitude of the attacks was far larger, and the outfall—like a nuclear mushroom—far wider than Sally and I had imagined.

"It's the only thing on the TV, radio, the newspapers," Susan said.

We talked for a bit more, I said we loved them, and said goodbye.

AFTER AN HOUR in Ste.-Mére-Eglise—two platoons from the Forty-fifth had been through here, though Slanger's Second Platoon wasn't one of them—we drove west, back to the coast, to Utah Beach, where the Forty-fifth had landed. Again, like Omaha Beach, it looked benign. Peaceful. Undeveloped. Not unlike many spots on the Oregon coast, the low dunes beyond the sand reminding me of an area just north of Florence, as, heading that direction, you begin a climb up Highway 101.

The English Channel was calm, a single wave folding onto the sand. The wind was light. I could see Point du Hoc and Grandcamp-Maisy to the north, and, inland, to the east, a few Belgian gates—steel obstacles that the Germans had used to rip the bottoms of Allied army landing crafts—poking up from the beach grass in the dunes. Not far from the remains of a German concrete pillbox, where machine gunners once tried to mow down those who had come to liberate France, I heard laughter. It came, I soon realized, from what looked to be a mother—maybe thirty—and her little girl. They were flying a kite.

"I think it's a little bit more this way," I said to Sally, trying to find the "Uncle Red" swath at which the Forty-fifth had come ashore. I'd done my homework, looking at military maps of the D-Day invasion to determine exactly where "Uncle Red" was. Upon arrival, I had double checked my findings with a historian at the Utah Beach Museum, who took us out on a deck and pointed to the precise spot.

Satisfied that I had the coordinates down, I nodded to Sally to get the video camera. She shot back a "yes, master" look. For one of the few times on the trip, tension clouded the air. Part of it was jet lag, plain weariness. Part of it may have been a mother being separated from her grown children back home—and, no, it didn't matter that the terrorist attack was on the other side of the country. And part of it was my having waited so long for this moment and, thus, wanting everything to be just right. Authors, frankly, aren't the easiest people to live with.

"This," I said, when the camera's red light shone, "is where the Forty-fifth Hospital came ashore on June 10, 1944 ... ."

With the taping over, Sally fished out the plastic, zip-lock sandwich bags and handed them to me. I knelt down and, using my fingers as a shovel, scooped three or four handfuls of sand into the bag. Once home, I would mail a plastic pill bottle of it to each of the four nurses, and to John Bonzer, Joseph Shoham, and Fred Michalove. Just a small reminder that though their footprints were long gone, they hadn't been forgotten.

THE DAYS THAT followed were mainly spent driving, loosely following the Normandy-to-Elsenborn path of the Second Platoon. Here and there, we picked up snippets of information about the terrorist attacks—an international newspaper here, a BBC broadcast there. Everywhere: photos at news stands of the aftermath. But because of the language barrier—we would go four days without interacting with anyone in English—we continued to find ourselves in an emotional place that few Americans were. On one hand, we were protected inside an informational cocoon, buffered, as it were, from the hour-to-hour grind of reliving the media-sustained horror people back home faced. On the other, we were feeling a certain amount of guilt and helplessness for that very reason. Disconnected. Not pulling our weight. AWOL.

Near Le Havre, Sally read an international newspaper aloud as we drove. On the cover was a photo from New York: men and women in business suits, covered in dust, clothes torn, handkerchiefs held to faces wrenched in pain. And I thought: *No, no, no, there's been some sort of terrible mistake. This is America. You've got the wrong family photo album here. This thing does not happen to us.*

But as we drove along, through places that I'd read about in my World War II research—Dieppe, for example—I was reminded that such terror, such interruption of the usual routine, had been status quo for much of Europe during World War II. Only instead of exploding in a handful of fiery crashes, this terror haunted civilians each day for years, in the form of German soldiers who had taken over their country.

On Friday, three days after the attack on America, Sally and I made our most difficult trip, from le Tréport, on the English Channel, to Robertsville, Belgium, just outside Elsenborn, only three miles from the German border. We had driven all day, circling dozens of roundabouts. Along the way, we would see constant reminders of the Allied army advance, roadside markers—*Liberation!*— and more occasional reminders of the current tragedy in the states: American flags, here and there, draped from windows, wrapped in black bands in memory of those who had died in the attacks.

We drove through the village of Bethencourt, where the Second Platoon had set up tents to work on soldiers, and Charleville-Mézieres, where they had done the same thing five days later, and Bastogne, four days later. The Forty-fifth had spent two stints in Bastogne: one in early September, with Slanger, the three units treating a unit-record 2,822 casualties in only eight days; the other in late December, without Slanger, during the cold and snow of the Battle of the Bulge. Between the two, Slanger had been killed. The next morning, Sally and I would see where.

We climbed east into the hills of Luxembourg—our third country of the day—and then north. Darkness descended. We drove back into Belgium—Luxembourg being smaller than the Oregon county I lived in, Lane—and through St. Vith.

"Hope and Crosby played for the soldiers here," I pointed out. In Malmèdy, I brought up a more sobering fact: "About a hundred of our soldiers, POWs, were mowed down in the snow by the Germans here." Finally, we slalomed up a ridge and to a plateau on which sat the back porch of Elsenborn, a small town called Robertsville.

After three turn-downs, we found a bed and breakfast, a 270-year-old former livery. It was just us and a couple from The Netherlands, dining in a dark, quaint room with broad wood beams, antique hutches, and a floor that sloped more than some golf greens. We loved it, not only because we had never stayed in a place that had been built in 1745—a century before the Oregon Trail started hopping—but because we'd been on the road for twelve hours and it was nice to have a place to simply rest.

The woman who operated the inn, a tad younger than us, spoke little English, but enough so we understood she was curious about what had brought us here. We did our best to explain about Frances Slanger and Elsenborn. She listened intently. "I must go," she said, after serving us what turned out to be ostrich—and quite good. "I must call the mayor of Bütgenbach."

RAIN FELL lightly the next morning as Sally and I drove through Bütgenbach, just south of Elsenborn and only a couple miles from the Belgium-German border. Our host thought the mayor might be able to help make a connection to World War II-era people who could help us, but he wasn't in his office.

We drove toward Elsenborn, home to about 900 people, stopping to take video footage of the fields east of town where, according to those in the Forty-fifth, the Second Platoon had been hunkered down on the night of the attack. Like spots in Normandy, this, too, reminded me of Oregon, specifically the northern Willamette Valley, between Corvallis and McMinnville on Highway 99.

"So this is it?" Sally asked.

"Near as I can tell, this is it," I said. "Shoham said it was just east of N647, the Bütgenbach-Elsenborn Road, just outside of town. It's not like there's going to be a monument here. I doubt anyone remembers the Forty-fifth, much less Slanger. It was a big war."

We drove into town, our only choice being the journalistic equivalent of a cold call: find people and start talking to them, even though you don't speak their language, which could be French, Flemish, German—who knew? With the rain, we hadn't seen a single person outside.

"This doesn't look good," I said.

As we approached the main east-west road, I realized something. "Hey, here's the road that was changed to 'Adolf Hitler Road' when the Germans took over in 1940."

"Look, over there," Sally said. "Some people, in front of that church."

Sure enough, despite the rain, a handful of guys were putting up a banner that said something I, of course, couldn't understand, though I was pretty sure it wasn't: *Welcome, Welches! Slanger Info Here!* I had no choice. *What would you do if you were the last per-*

son on earth and had to find that sock?

I parked across the street from Bartholomeus Catholic Church, grabbed my notebook and pen, and tried to approach the men without putting them on the defensive. They looked to be in their fifties and sixties, probably not even born, or only babies, in 1944.

"Hello," I said, having no idea what I was going to say. "Uh ... World War II ... nurse died here." I pointed down. "In Elsenborn. October. Nineteen forty-four."

Four blank stares.

"I'm writing a book," I said, acting as if I were writing something.

Four more blank stares. I exhaled. The good news: for some strange reason, they hadn't returned to their banner hanging. Instead, their dispositions seemed to say: *We'll help if we can. Keep trying.*

Then I thought of it. I pulled out my wallet, not to pay them huge sums of money to speak English, but to get my survival kit: the note in French that Kim Davaz had written for me if I ever got in a jam like this. I handed it to one of them.

Brows furrowed. Heads shook sideway. Did they not know French or did they not know of anyone who had been alive here in 1944?

"We speak German," said one man in broken English.

I nodded my head as if to wave the white flag of surrender to my own ignorance.

"Merci anyway," I said, nodding, then turned to leave, thinking I shouldn't have said "merci" because they don't speak French. That's when I heard it.

"Erich," someone said. "Erich Dahmen."

I turned back. "Who? What?" I said.

One of the men pointed across the street. "Erich owns ze hotel."

"OK," I said, waiting for more, my eyes hopeful.

"Little boy"—he held his hand to the side, palms flat to the ground—"when German army comes. Now maybe sixty-five years of age."

"A man here, Erich, lived in Elsenborn during the takeover?" I said, seeking clarification.

"Ja," he said, again pointing to a hotel 150 feet from us.

"Merci, er, thanks," I said, then shook all their hands.

Five minutes later, Sally and I were sitting in the kitchen of a closed-for-the-season hotel while Mr. Dahmen, actually sixty-eight, made us coffee. (I hated coffee, but given we were on the brink of getting actual information, gladly took it, lest our host be offended.)

He joined us at a thick, wooden table that Sally-the-antique-lover was admiring greatly. We weren't surprised to learn he'd never heard of Frances Slanger but pleasantly surprised that he remembered Elsenborn in the forties. And the war.

"May ten, nineteen-forty, ze war comes to Elsenborn," he said as I started taking notes, my tape recorder's "on" light lit. "In walk ze German troops. Either you become a soldier for ze Germans or join ze underground. By end of forty-one, forty-two, men as young as fifteen, sixteen are going in ze army."

"And fighting for Germany?"

"You are either for Hitler or ze Jews, there is no choice. He wanted us trained so we could go to England when he took over, when he occupied it. We lost 100 young men to ze war, soldiers dying for Germany. Fifteen was ze draft age. I was eleven. We thought we would win ze war; now that idea seems crazy."

At the time, I mentally lurched when he said "we." Then, he offered context. "My sons—whenever they hear ze voice of Hitler on TV they say, 'How can you have followed such a crazy man?' But if you're young, you know nothing else. With Germany, there was no—what you say in America, if I gave your wife something to take care, I, I?—"

"Trust?" I said.

"Yes, trust," he said, nodding his head. "No trust."

During the war, he said, Elsenborn was caught in the middle: a dozen citizens killed, its young men forced to fight and die for Germany, and virtually the entire town forced by the allies to move to nearby Malmedy "because the American soldiers heard ze accents and assumed ze people were Germans and that they were in Germany. Ze mother tongue was German but we also spoke French, Dutch, Flemish."

As Erich shared, I realized that this war, though he was only seven when it began, had followed him his whole life.

"One family in Elsenborn had three sons, all forced into ze German army. One died in ze Battle of Stalingrad, ze two others elsewhere. Here, I will show you a photograph." He walked into another room. I quickly poured my coffee down the sink. Moments later, he showed us a photo of a man with three sons, a photograph that, since that day, reminds me that, though we might like to believe otherwise, war is complex and rarely as simple as "good guys" and "bad guys."

"Three sons. Dead. Ze father could not handle it. He had a heart attack and died." A Belgian-German version of *Saving Private Ryan*, I thought to myself, and a reminder of how easily we forget that soldiers on "the other side" die, too, and have families who grieve their losses. As the father of two draft-age boys, I was too preoccupied to be thinking of what question to ask next.

"To lose family," he continued, "is tough. In New York"—a reference to the terrorist attack—"it is ze same. Life is done. You cannot have more children."

Sally and I stayed for another hour, as Erich gave me more useful details about Elsenborn in 1944: the weather, the foliage, the culture. I later returned—Sally stayed at the inn to nap—for a second visit in which he offered even more: photographs and detailed maps of Elsenborn that were invaluable for my being able to describe this area. "Here," he said, holding the map. "It is yours."

I thanked him deeply and left. I drove back to the Elsenborn-Bütgenbach Road, where, according to what I'd been told, Slanger had died: a field and beyond that, rolling hills, more fields, and Germany. Looking at it, I tried to imagine that stormy night, Frances Slanger, perhaps the only one awake, composing her letter to *Stars and Stripes* at "0200" from her field hospital tent, "the wind howling, the tent waving precariously, the rain beating down, the guns firing, and me with a flashlight, writing."

I tried to imagine the following night, that letter already in the back of a truck, en route to Paris, the canvas hospital tents in the darkness, the sudden sound of artillery shells, "like a railroad train" Shoham remembered. Then, the panic of people scurrying for cover, the screams, the cries of "I'm hit, God, I'm hit" that Bonzer and Shoham remembered, the discovery of Slanger's stomach shredded by shrapnel, the panicked attempt to save her, the last words—"Oh ... my ... poor ... mother"—and Dr. Isadore Schwartz saying, "shalom."

Nearly sixty years later, I said a prayer of thanks for Frances Slanger at that spot. Nothing of length, depth, or creativity. Just a thank-you for giving her life for the rest of us. I bent over and picked up three small stones to remember this place. One for each of Slanger's nephews. A reversal of the Jewish custom to leave a rock, I realized. But a gesture that I hoped would say the same thing: *we were here*.

OUR FINAL STOP before returning to Paris was the American Cemetery and Memorial at Henri-Chapelle. It was here, on this slight hill near Liege, about twenty miles northwest of Elsenborn, that Frances Slanger's body was first buried. Here that, as a rabbi prayed in front of her Star of David marker, snow first blanketed the western front since the Allied army invasion. And here, on Memorial Day 1945, that U.S. Ambassador to Belgium Charles Sawyer stepped to a podium and, with an audience that included such dignitaries as General Dwight D. Eisenhower, honored Frances Slanger.

> Her friends said that she knew she was dying but uttered no word of complaint. She lies here in Henri-Chapelle with the rest of you who will not go home.
>
> The GIs to whom your letter was written cannot talk to you, Frances Slanger. They who could talk are not here; they are scattered all over the world—millions of them—and so for them and for all Americans I say this to you in answer to your letter:
>
> We thank you for the things you have said about the GIs; they are better said by you than by any other. If there is in heaven and in our hearts a special shrine for those who have given the most and the best, it is held sacred for the American nurse ... her courage, her strength, her endurance, and her unfailing hope are the essence of the things which have given us this victory and which we believe will never die.

Given the option, Frances's parents chose, in 1947, to have their daughter's body exhumed and reburied in West Roxbury in a traditional Jewish ceremony. But even though I knew Frances's body wasn't here, I needed to be here. To get the framing for what it might have looked like in 1944, freshly established, the bodies coming in by the truckloads from the Battle of the Hürtgen Forest, the Battle for Aachen, and, a couple months after Slanger had died, the Battle of the Bulge. Then, it was all dirt, mud, and ramshackle white crosses with a sprinkling of Stars of David; now, it was lush grass, immaculately trimmed. In either case, a sober reminder of war's bottom line.

It was raining. I was tired and emotionally drained, having spent a week trying to connect with a woman gone for six decades while being disconnected from a homeland that had been attacked. At Oradour-sur-Glane, I'd seen the charred tricycles. Above Omaha Beach and here, the endless headstones. On TV, the CNN images of the World Trade Centers turned into fireballs. In Erich's photo album, the Elsenborn man and his three sons. Now, more death: a cemetery with 7,989 markers, which didn't include the 450 soldiers never found, still lost out there somewhere in the hills of Belgium or Germany. Here I was, sifting through all this pain—for what? A book with no agent, no home, no guarantee would ever be published.

But something happened at Henri-Chapelle that seemed to say "here's why you've come." He was a man of World War II vintage, holding a bouquet of daisies. He spoke German. The cemetery guide could not understand on what grave he wished to leave the remembrance. Finally, she understood. Sally and I understood, too.

Not any single grave. Not for any single soldier. He wanted them placed at the foot of the half-staff American flag. "For New York," he said. "For Washington."

It reminded me of a letter in response to Slanger's, written by a young soldier in Belgium named "Spec" McClure, who wrote about "a dead girl whom I never knew but whom I, doubtless, along with countless others, felt I knew":

> She wrote as a GI Jane to a GI Joe deeply involved in a bloody business called war, asking not for understanding, expecting no mercy, but giving to her limits in both.

And we knew there wasn't a false word in the letter. ... We knew it for our world, and we grinned in appreciation, knowing that we read the letter of a girl already dead, and her words fixed beyond alteration. They were sealed with her blood ... .

During this war, as both civilian and soldier, I've seen ideals trampled in the mud by those who most profess to uphold them. I have seen this too often to have much faith left. And I have seen, as all who make an honest effort must, a thousand forms of betrayal and stupidity. And in weariness I have told myself a thousand times nothing remained to believe in—that the ancient enemies of mankind, greed and ignorance, were too great for our mortal strength to conquer. But now I know that this is not altogether right.

For somewhere in the sordid, selfish, shameful business that makes up most of our petty lives there is a nobility that will not perish ... .

That's why I'd come to France, I realized. And to this cemetery. Not to wallow in the darkness of a world where nothing's left to believe in, where the "the ancient enemies of mankind, greed and ignorance," must prevail. Not to wallow in the hopelessness of all that, but to remember a "nobility that will not perish." A nobility found in a nurse who gave her life after blowing on the embers of soldiers' lives. In a man at a cemetery, perhaps a former German soldier, who brought flowers to honor America. And in all the other candles in the darkness whose stories we must tell.

Chapter 9

*Writing a book is an adventure: it begins as an amusement, then it
becomes a mistress, then a master, and finally a tyrant.*
— Sir Winston Churchill

W HEN OUR PLANE touched down in Chicago, virtually
everyone aboard burst into spontaneous applause. Tuesday,
September 18, the day we flew home, was the first day de Gaulle
International Airport had allowed flights out since the terrorist attacks.

We'd flown to France on a plane with metal silverware and had
flown back using plastic. Sally had crocheted on the way over but
hadn't been allowed to on the way back. Instead of walking from
the terminal through a jet-way to the plane in Paris, we had walked
out onto the tarmac, where a bus took us to our already-near-the-
runway plane.

"You are returning to a country that's different than the country
you left," a flight attendant told us.

In Chicago, able to purchase a copy of *Newsweek* magazine, I
understood, for the first time, the depth and breadth of the terrorist
attack and why O'Hare International Airport was nearly vacant.
Though not to the extent that the flight attendant had suggested,

things were different in America. Nine of my first ten newspaper columns after returning had something to do with the terrorist attack. There was talk of war.

As the Willamette Valley leaves went into their annual turn-and-fall routine, I slowly got back into my book routine. By now, I was, like a short-order cook at mid-morning, fixing both breakfast and lunch. Research and writing.

We'd struck out on finding any Slangers in America or "Schlangers" in Israel; nobody had responded to the letters my son Ryan had sent out. I confirmed that the last nurse I thought might still be alive, "Tex," was dead, news that wasn't easy to pass along to her friend Sallylou Bonzer. Fourteen, I'd confirmed, had died, including Margaret Fielden, who had risen to be head nurse at Atlanta Hospital and had died in January 2002, even as we were searching for her. Only four of the eighteen nurses were still alive. And I was increasingly becoming frantic about finding someone to translate Yiddish. It's not as if you can find someone like that in the Eugene, Oregon, Yellow Pages.

But I forged ahead with the writing, returning to my 5 A.M. routine as days got shorter and temperatures cooler. Along the John Day River, my friend Jane Kirkpatrick got up at 4 A.M. to write, so whenever I felt like just hitting the "snooze" button—virtually every day—I thought: *Jane's already been up for an hour*. And I'd get up, rewarding myself not for simply being awake but for progress: hot chocolate (with whip cream) at 6 A.M. and cereal (Grape Nuts Trail Mix) at 7:30 A.M.

Writing was easiest on rainy mornings; there was something cozy about tapping those computer keys as a lone candle burned and raindrops tattered the rhododendrons outside the window. And hardest on summer evenings, when our old, un-air-conditioned house was at its heat-baked worst. For now, in the early weeks of autumn and nine months into the project, I was looking forward to finishing the book before a second round of summer's heat.

To help create and sustain the muse, I relied on soundtracks from three movies that played almost constantly as I wrote the book: *Saving Private Ryan, Schindler's List,* and *Pearl Harbor*. Weirdly, I never tired of any of the three. John Williams' score for *Saving Private Ryan* made me feel that pit-in-the-stomach realism of war. Itzhak Perlman's sweet violin on Williams' *Schindler's List* score drew me deeper into the Jewish scenes I was writing. And Hans Zimmer's *Pearl Harbor*—minus the cheesy Faith Hill song—seemed as if written for the Forty-fifth's nurses, its bittersweet melodies reflecting women whose time in Europe was twined with agony and adventure.

The office that I used to share with Sally reflected my deepening obsession with the book. Nine months into the project, she finally waved the white flag and established her own sovereign nation upstairs in Ryan's bedroom, now that he'd gotten married. Given more room, I hung up a one-by-four-foot photo of the entire Forty-fifth Field Hospital Unit at Fort Bragg so I could see the people I was writing about; a list of names of nurses, doctors, and soldiers, so I could spell them correctly; a list of the Second Platoon's every stop from Normandy to Czechoslovakia; and calendars for key years such as 1943 and 1944, so I could know what day of the week certain events had taken place.

Beyond that, I was surrounded by maps, photos, books, and the thirty-one notebooks for which I had built a special double-level, pine book shelf. A few dozen World War II-related books stood ready on my built-in shelves. And, if necessary, I would make quick dashes outside to the library annex, aka my carport shed, a storage/workshop room so cluttered that a book I was looking for might be buried beneath a Christmas wreath, a variable-speed drill, and 1999's tax records.

For each of the twelve chapters I was writing, I mounted photos on foam boards to remind me, say, what immigrants at Ellis Island looked like in 1920. I had a cell phone to my left, with speed dial so I could bounce detail questions off folks such as Pat Gariepy, Sallylou Bonzer, Irwin Sidman, and Ron Palmer. (Palmer, like Gariepy, was a local man and World War II buff who had become an informational lifeline). On my right I kept a magnifying glass for atlas perusals, not far from a foot-long metal ruler used for measuring the distance between places on such maps.

Above me on two shelves: key reference books that I often referred to, the most oft-used being *The Chicago Manual of Style*, the book publishing industry's standard for proper usage. Should the "Forty-fifth" in "Forty-fifth Field Hospital" be indicated in words or numerals? Should "colonel" be spelled out or abbreviated? Proper usage could be amazingly complex. Every rule seemed to have exceptions: "Titles of television and radio programs are set in roman type and quoted unless they are continuing series, in which case they are italicized." Like it or not, *Chicago* was the ultimate arbitrator.

What made style particularly challenging was working a day job as a columnist that required me to follow *The Associated Press Style Guide,* a different set of rules; for example, *AP* style requires names of states be abbreviated if listed after a city (Springfield, Mass.) whereas *Chicago* wants them spelled out (Springfield, Massachusetts). Sometimes, arriving at *The Register-Guard* in the morning after working on the book, I'd almost need to mentally tell myself: *OK, you're a columnist now.* And mentally install my AP style preferences.

Back home that evening, I'd take off the columnist hat and put on the author's hat—Boston Red Sox, of course—and return to a story that had grown so large that I'd created more than a dozen files just to guide me. Among them, a:

• "Time Line Spreadsheet." A ten-page, color-coded document that listed everything of passing significance that happened to Slanger, from her father's birth on May 20, 1881, to her death on October 21, 1944.

• "The Cast." A list of name, rank, serial number, age, hometowns, and "live-or-dead?" status of twenty-seven Forty-fifth Field Hospital doctors, nurses, and enlisted men I was tracking.

• "Story Structure." My theme? "Good can overcome evil when ordinary people, drawing on the God-given power of the heart, make extraordinary sacrifices for something beyond themselves."

• "Slanger's Choices." A nine-column spreadsheet that showed what obstacles Frances encountered, how she felt about them, what she did about them, and whether she fell victim to them or overcame them.

• "Outline." An eleven-page scaffolding of the entire book, including what each chapter would include, emphasize, and foreshadow.

• "To do." An ongoing list, being added to nearly daily, of action steps necessary to complete the book, everything from "get

Lidice poem permission" to "find someone who knows Yiddish" to "run first-night-in-Normandy dialogue by Dottie Richter to see if it's how she remembers it." Not to be confused with:

• "To Find Out," which was more informational in nature and included such questions as: "Were the Slangers orthodox Jews? Anyone alive who knew Tiny Schwartz well? Was Ike actually at that Belgian cemetery on Memorial Day 1945 when Slanger was honored?"

Now nearly a year into the project, I wanted a rough draft done by February 1, 2002—thirteen months after my start date—and the book finished and sold by June 1. That way, I figured, the publisher could roll it out in May 2003, the same month the new World War II Memorial in Washington, D.C., was to be dedicated. The media would certainly be in a World War II mode, particularly with big names such as Tom Brokaw (*The Greatest Generation*) and Tom Hanks (*Saving Private Ryan*) backing the memorial. I would ride this final World War II wave as far up on the publicity beach as it would take me.

IN MID-NOVEMBER, with three-fourths of the book at least roughed out, I began the writer's equivalent of putting up drywall: the dirty, exhausting, often-monotonous job of feathering in information from books and interviews and reports that I hadn't used in the first go-round.

What I'd learned over nearly thirty years in journalism is that you first write something from the "story on out"—from what you know—and then go back and write it from the "information back in," what you overlooked during the first write-through. In describing the nurses' first night in Normandy, for example, I first wrote the scene with information I'd known, mainly from the interviews with the nurses. But by the time I was ready for the second go-round, I'd been to the National Archives and seen the Forty-second Field Hospital's statistical report, the "seventeen-truckloads-of-wounded-soldiers" stuff suggesting the nurses had actually underplayed the pain and horror. So, I feathered in that.

In a month's time, I went back through every page in the thirty-one notebooks, every page in my file-cabinet files, and the dozens of computer files to make sure any pertinent details, descriptions, quotes, or statistics had been inserted.

The challenge of writing a book is that, like making a quilt, the larger it gets, the more unwieldy it is to work with. What began as something I could read in thirty minutes was now something that would take nearly a full day. If I were to make only one "fix" every other page, that would still mean some 150 fixes. At, say, two minutes each, that would be five hours of work for simply that task. As the book grew, then, working on it morphed from the equivalent of giving a small dog a bath to wrestling, and pinning, a tyrannosaurus rex.

As a nonfiction author, you're like a lake with an outlet stream (the writing) and an inlet stream (the information). Each night before bed, I would read books and articles that would help me better understand my story. And, occasionally, watch movies that would give me a better feel for war (*Enemy at the Gate, Saving Private Ryan*), for army nurses (*Charlotte Gray, The English Patient*), and for the Jewish experience (*Schindler's List, Life is Beautiful*).

The harsh irony? The more you learn, the more you have to learn more. When I discovered through school records that Slanger had once worked at the Massachusetts Knitting Mills, for example, I needed to learn where that was located, what it looked like, and how she would have gotten to and from it. When I found a list of twenty students who attended Boston City Hospital's School of Nursing, I needed to try to contact those students. (I was zero-for-twenty.) And so whether the subject was war, nursing, Boston, or knitting mills, each new fact might require taking a bunny trail— or five—from the main route.

In Slanger's "buddy book," one of her fellow nurses referred to someone as a "gold britches." What did that mean? Slanger trained at Fort Bragg in North Carolina. What did the camp look like? Often, instead of getting closer to finishing the book, I'd be somewhere off in the bushes, trying to find out what a loblolly pine—lots of them at Fort Bragg—looked like. Or e-mailing my brother-in-law the doctor to find out what "circumpolar pallor" means. Or searching the Web to find out what time the sun came up in Normandy on June 10, 1944. Or showing a photo of Penny the dog to our veterinarian to confirm it was, as Shoham had told me, a wire-haired terrier.

At year's end, as I took stock of where I was and where I needed to be, I realized two things. First, after my screen started flickering on my Macintosh G3 laptop, I needed to replace the computer—and did so, with a Macintosh iBook. The day the computer store transferred the information from my old computer to my new one was like sitting in a hospital waiting room while a loved one had a heart transplant; yes, I'd backed up the manuscript itself on a disk, but not many of the Slanger-related files. Fortunately, the operation was a success.

Second, I needed to make a late-winter trip to Boston and the National Archives in Washington, D.C. I couldn't ignore the truth: I had too many holes in this drywall that needed patching. And, no, try as I might, I couldn't justify waiting until April, when baseball would have started and my Red Sox would once again be trying to reverse the curse.

IT CAME IN THE night. The how-could-I-be-so-stupid question I should have asked Rivka Freudenstein, the woman from Jerusalem, long ago. I'd been reading Dorothy Kearns Goodwin's *No Ordinary Times*, about the Roosevelt administration during the 1930s and 1940s. In particular, I was interested in how reluctant Franklin was, despite prodding from Eleanor, to come to the defense of the Jews. Instead of bombing the train rails to the death camps, as some had suggested, Roosevelt contended that the best way to save the Jews was to win the war. Amid reading this, I remembered Rivka, the Jewish woman who'd sent the "lost" book back to the man in Cottage Grove.

"Where you going?" a half-asleep Sally asked as I slipped out of bed.

"Gotta send an e-mail."

"Now? At 1 A.M.?"

"Sorry."

Writing a book means always having to say you're sorry. It's an experience that's far easier on the one having to apologize than the one being apologized to. But as I got deeper and deeper into this—like a spelunker repelling into the darkness of who-knew-what—Sally maintained a steadfast support for me, even when I told her I needed to go to Boston and Washington, D.C., in March.

It helped that I was building the five-day trip onto a men's retreat I was leading for a Methodist church in Tampa, Florida. I'd get a round-trip ticket to the East Coast paid for and I figured what I made at the retreat would pay for my other flights, food, and lodging to do more research.

I e-mailed Rivka and asked her if, by chance, she knew Yiddish, explaining that I desperately needed someone to do some translating for the book. The next morning, December 8, I tossed some clothes in a shoulder bag, piled a dozen books and twice that many notebooks into an old suitcase, then left for a long weekend to write at the coast. By Christmas, I wanted to send a semi-polished copy of the manuscript to a half-dozen friends who'd agreed to offer editing evaluations. And I needed to pay more attention to my wife, an irony since to do that—to get this project done—I was leaving her for four days.

That was hard. The road work was easy. I would sometimes arrive at the cabin on a Thursday night and return Sunday night, having worked for forty hours, the equivalent of two weeks of piecemeal time at home. And be so immersed in the story that I wouldn't want to leave it.

In part, that's because there were no distractions. No Internet to use for information gathering, which forced me to do nothing but write. No TV to distract me, though I found exceptions for University of Oregon football and basketball games on the radio, a challenging alternative given that the mid-coast radio reception came and went like wispy beach fog. No phone calls because the cabin had no land lines, and cell coverage was a cross-your-fingers proposition at best. In short, for nearly four days, I didn't need to be responsible for anything but plugging thousands of words into a laptop computer. Beyond stoking the fire—the lone source of heat in a seventy-year-old cabin with no insulation—all I needed to do was eat a little, which you learn to do, like ultra-marathoners, while not stopping; sleep a little; and go to the bathroom.

All of this "easy writing," of course, assumed that the cabin, roughly the size (and temperature) of a three-car garage, would remain functional, which, this particular weekend, it did not. On Thursday night, a thirty-knot wind from the south was rocking the cabin more than usual and the leak above the refrigerator, which sat on the stoop in the garage because it wouldn't fit in the kitchen, seemed leakier than usual. I always got a bit worried when the water would drip out of the light socket above the fridge. But, with a flashlight in hand and ladder under foot, I checked the roof amid sideways rain that stung my face. It was still there.

Sometime in the night, though, the south end of the garage's composition roof peeled back like a sardine can. The garage, including the wood I needed to keep the fire going, was soaked. And so there I was Friday morning, the fourth guy in line at a hardware store in nearby Waldport, looking for a plastic tarp.

"Your roof, too?" I asked the guy in front of me.

"Boat shed."

I didn't imagine any of these guys had books due to sub-editors in two weeks; they looked too intelligent for that.

"Heard the really strong winds aren't coming until tonight," said the guy behind me.

In winds now gusting to forty knots, I tried to pin down the blue tarp using nails, two-by-fours, and driftwood. It was like trying to affix newspaper pages to a floor vent with the heat on. But when I finished the project, the rain wasn't pouring into the garage anymore. I called it good, being careful when opening the refrigerator not to touch the dripping light socket overhead. I stacked soggy wood beside the fireplace to dry it out.

Then, I resumed the position of a writer, my back to the pine-paneled south wall. I was wearing double socks, double sweatpants, a turtleneck and two sweatshirts, a blanket on my lap. The Michellen tire guy had more mobility. I could blow and see my breath. But I was able to keep writing.

By evening, I realized the guy behind me in line was prophetic; the wind was so strong—gusts beyond fifty knots—I literally could feel the wall pulsating against my back. The electricity, the writer's lifeblood in the computer age, stayed on, though I could see what looked like sparklers from atop a nearby power pole. Meanwhile, I kept feeding the fireplace, but the wet stuff was only smoldering. The cabin thermometer had risen to 62 degrees. But no way, I realized, could I get through the weekend with only the wood that was left.

The next morning I drove my pickup to a nearby grocery store, scanned the classified ads of the local weekly, and found a guy offering "dry fir, split," which, in Oregon, means "not quite as wet as most other guys' stuff." Desperate, I headed inland, along the Yachats River, and, checking the address, turned into the driveway of a place that triggered the sound track from *Deliverance*. I've never loaded wood so fast. But, I was soon back at the cabin with most of a two-day weekend left in which to write. I buckled down and wrote tons.

"How'd it go?" Sally said when I came home Sunday night.

"Good. Got lots done. Lost the roof. Lost heat. Lost feeling in my lower extremities. But good."

Before going to bed, I checked my e-mails. One was from Rivka Freudenstein in Jerusalem, a woman I'd never met but whose e-mail message I could scarcely believe as I looked at it:

"Thanks for asking. It so happens that I'm a trained linguist, expert in Hebrew and Yiddish. I'd be glad to help you with your translations of Yiddish."

Chapter 10

March 2002
Washington, D.C.

A book is like a man—clever and dull, brave and cowardly,
beautiful and ugly. For every flowering thought there will be a page
like a wet and mangy mongrel.

—John Steinbeck

YOU LEARNED early on who the troupers were on this journey, and Joseph Shoham was among them. Since I'd interviewed him in Latham, New York, Shoham had moved to Reston, Virginia, to be near a son, Michael. Having wrapped up my
presentation at a three-day men's retreat in Tampa, Florida, I was
to go over some facts and to ask some follow-up questions with
Shoham at 8 o'clock on a Sunday night, soon after touching down
at Dulles International Airport.

That in itself, I realized, was pushing the etiquette limits, particularly since Joseph and his wife Ethel were nearly ninety years
old. But it would get worse: a flight delay in Tampa would push
my departure back two hours, I learned, and my Monday schedule
was full. Though I considered Shoham the book's best eyewitness
source, I couldn't push the interview to another day. I called from
Florida before the delayed flight left. Would he still be willing to
meet with if I didn't arrive until, uh, 9:30 P.M.?

"No problem, Bob," he said. "Ethel and I aren't going anywhere."

By the time the delayed flight got delayed more and, upon landing, I rented a car, I didn't arrive at his apartment complex until 10:30 P.M. But Shoham greeted me with a hug and Ethel pampered me with food and drink—"you must be famished"—until she headed off for bed an hour later.

Until well after midnight, Joseph and I went over the book. He helped me correct fact errors, add detail, make sure the dialogue was as close to the truth as he could remember. And, of course, found ways to brag about Ethel, whom he'd eloped with in 1939. As we talked, I noticed, on the table, a card he'd given her—for their sixty-third Valentine's Day. Shoham was more than a source, he was an inspiration, even if the card made me miss Sally.

After a night in an inexpensive Arlington, Virginia, hotel, I took the subway to the Pentagon Monday morning, not for anything book-related, but to see the rebuilding progress after the terrorist attack for a possible *Register-Guard* column. I hadn't been there five minutes when a guard started peppering me with questions about what I was writing down, then, hardly listening to my answers, confiscated my notebook. Suddenly, my entire trip was in peril. I didn't care about the notes I'd jotted for my column, but all of my appointments—and phone numbers and addresses for those appointments—were in that notebook. If I didn't get it back, a four-day trip was going to be almost impossible to pull off. When the notebook was returned five minutes later with no apology, I wasted no time leaving.

I headed to the National Archives in College Park, Maryland, where I found, if not a mother lode of information, lots of good details from Forty-fifth and Forty-second hospital reports. I took the subway to the Jewish War Veteran's museum where, for a second time, I was unable to locate the *Stars and Stripes* newspapers I needed for the summer of 1944. Then, I flew from Baltimore to Boston where I planned to plumb the depths of the Boston University archives for Boston City Hospital School of Nursing records. I'd learned it had such records; if so, wasn't it possible that some might make specific reference to Slanger?

I was right. By mid-morning, I'd come across "Boston City Hospital/n98/Box 52," which, for the first time, took me inside the walls of the mid-1930s nursing school. As the morning unfolded, and I found other boxes, the interesting tidbits bubbled up as if from a bottomless well: letters about supervisors in trouble, controversies over a handful of black applicants, and the records of Frances "Fannie" Slanger.

Nothing in my research to this point confirmed Frances Slanger's giving spirit—and absolute passion to be a nurse—like these records. In her application for the school, Slanger had written:

> I have always loved to comfort those who were sick. I realize fully that I must give my time up to work and study and I am prepared to go into it heart and soul ... . Even when I was a very little girl I used to say I was going to be a nurse. My people used to laugh at me, but now they are quite willing that I should be. To put my real reason into a few words: I want to serve (those) who are less fortunate than I.

Goodness, Slanger seemed fairly "less fortunate" herself, given her life thus far. But Slanger had a tendency to see others' needs and not her own. In a letter, she offered to volunteer on Saturdays until school started. Wrote one of her teachers from Practical Arts High School in response to a questionnaire:

> What is her moral character? "I know of no defect. She is bright-minded, conscientious and honorable." What do you consider her faults? "I know of no outstanding fault unless it is in her persistence to get a higher education in spite of the opposition of her parents. I think Frances Slanger will be a joy to you as a student nurse. I know her only from the teacher's viewpoint, but all her teachers I'm sure will agree with me that she is an earnest, sincere, ambitious, and conscientious student. If she does as well as a student nurse as she did as an academic student you need have nothing to fear. I highly recommend her and hope you will give her a chance."

During the thirties, many hospitals had quotas on the number of Jewish male students they would accept. I found nothing in these records suggesting Slanger had been discriminated against nor that she believed she had been. But I did find, of nearly three dozen supervisors' reports, a handful of teachers who considered her unfit to be a nurse. From one: "Miss Slanger is somewhat blundering and her judgement [sic] is often poor." Digging deeper, I found what amounted to a Slanger box score: of twenty-nine reports, how she rated in each of fifteen categories. Jackpot. I could see, in a glance, that Slanger was esteemed by her supervisors. Not perfect. She scored low in "speed," "sense of humor," and "adaptability." But high in categories such as "courteous," "sympathetic," "takes criticisms," and "dignified." "Frances shows good executive ability and shows intelligence and culture," wrote one supervisor. "She appears very much interested in her work and anxious to learn."

Shortly before the archives closed, I packed up and left. I was stoked. I walked east down Commonwealth Avenue to the Barnes & Noble across the street from the Buckminister and rewarded myself by buying three books about the Boston Red Sox.

I HAD DINNER that evening with Edward Schwartz, son of Isadore Schwartz, the doctor in whose arms Slanger died. It was a fruitful two hours, helping me understand his father much better. I spent an entire day and part of another going through the nursing records, and a full day in the Boston Public Library going over old city directories, maps, and newspapers for specific information that I knew was missing—from the weather on the day she said goodbye to Irwin in 1943 to where her father had lived in 1913.

I glanced at my watch, barely caught a subway that took me as far west as the "T" line went, and took a cab the rest of the way to West Newton for a scheduled interview with Hazelle Ferguson. She was a graduate of Boston City Hospital Class of 1937, a year ahead of Slanger, and, though only knowing Frances slightly, could help me understand what nursing school had been like.

Nobody answered the doorbell. No neighbors were home. I called on my cell phone. Nobody answered. After half an hour, worried that I didn't have enough cash for a cab fare, I walked an hour to the subway stop, then returned to the Hotel Buckminster and checked out. An entire afternoon wasted. But, later, I learned it wasn't Ferguson's fault; she'd been taken ill and was at a hospital.

Irwin and Joan Sidman were taking me out for dinner that evening, then dropping me off at the airport, where I had decided to spend the night to save $114 in hotel and cab fare. It sounded strange, but I had a 6:15 A.M. flight the next morning, meaning, with the beefed-up post-9/11 security checks, I needed to be there by 4:15 A.M., meaning a half-hour, $25 cab ride at 3:45 A.M., meaning I would need to get up at 3 A.M. Was four hours of fitful sleep worth $114 plus tax? I didn't think so, though later the next day I would have serious second thoughts.

About 10 P.M., the Sidmans, while suggesting I was out of my mind, nevertheless dropped me off at passenger check-in and drove away. There I was: just me, my bags and, as I walked into the airport, what appeared to be the entire U.S. First Army. I'd already forgotten that Pentagon lesson. These weren't the times to be hanging around Pentagons or, at least in the middle of the night, airports. (And this one had been the starting point for one of the doomed United Airlines flights.) Tough-looking soldiers patrolled the airport interior like gun-toting locusts.

I had imagined enough late-night passengers so I could blend in as I slept in a chair. But I appeared to be the lone civilian in the airport. In these days of heightened security, I realized that a guy showing up eight hours early for a flight might cause some suspicion, so I opted for a backup plan: I lugged my bags across a skywalk to a Hilton Hotel.

I spent two hours in the lounge, watching basketball. Then, at midnight, I found a comfortable chair on a second-floor mezzanine. I plugged in my laptop and wrote a *Register-Guard* column, occasionally congratulating myself on what a cozy setup I'd managed. But at 2:30 A.M., a tall man in a blazer and security badge suddenly appeared in my cozy setup. He startled me.

"Do you have a room here, sir?" he asked

"Uh, no, I don't."

"Then I suggest you get one—now—or leave. We've had surveillance cameras on you for two hours."

Let's see: Kicked out of the Pentagon parking lot. Kicked out of a hotel. Like TV's "Fugitive," I slunk away with my bags, stopping halfway across the glass-enclosed skywalk. I sat on a steel beam, staring across Boston Harbor at the lights of downtown, thinking of all the people asleep in their nice, soft hotel beds. Other than a few minutes here and there, I never slept that night. Now all I had to endure was a return trip to Tampa to fulfill my roundtrip requirement, then a cross-country flight to Oregon. It would be Boston-to-Atlanta-to-Tampa Bay-to-Denver-to San Francisco-to-Eugene.

At 4 A.M., in an eerie quiet that I'd gotten used to, I dragged myself to airport check-in and was greeted by the surreal sight and giddy sound of hundreds of teenagers bound for Nassau and spring vacation. Just what I needed after twenty-two hours without sleep and a five-stop, cross-country trip ahead of me: a terminal crawling with hyped-to-the-max seventeen-year-olds. It was like having a pounding migraine and walking into Circuit City. But I survived. I made Atlanta. I made Tampa. And I made Den—

"We're being diverted," said the twenty-something kid next to me, who was listening on headphones to plane-to-tower communication. "Colorado Springs."

Suddenly, I expected John Candy to appear from *Planes, Trains & Automobiles*. The Colorado Springs landing was one of those "If-I-survive-this-God-I-promise-to … " sort of landings. A woman behind me started humming hymns. A little kid puked all over his Buzz Lightyear doll. (*"To infinity and—yuck."*)

Once on the ground, the captain assured us we would be quickly refueled. We were quickly refueled in the same way an old growth forest quickly matures. Eventually we got to snowy Denver, where most passengers, desperate to catch West Coast connections, were like bronc riders waiting for the rodeo chute to open. But the plane inexplicably stopped 200 feet from the gate and remained there for ten minutes. A pilot announced that one of our two engines had failed and, with the slippery conditions, we'd need a tractor to pull us in.

At this point, I leaned toward the guy one seat away from me, a man from Arcadia, California, whom I'd earlier learned worked for a medical company that made physical-restraint products.

"Can I see your catalog?" I asked. "I might need to place an order. Like, *now*."

We got to the airport. I'd missed my flight to San Francisco and, thus, to Eugene. I had been away from Sally far too long. I threw myself at the mercy of a United agent like the *Home Alone* mom, so desperate that I mentioned the airport/Hilton/no sleep thing. She punched enough keys to write a short novel, then said, "Ah. Portland. Departs at 7:45 P.M., forty-five minutes from now."

Portland is a two-hour drive from Eugene, but I didn't care. "Thank you," I said. "Thank you!"

The flight was delayed three times and, naturally, I was one of the handful of people pulled aside for the quasi-strip search. But, finally, at 1:30 A.M., having been awake, other than an occasional cat nap, for nearly two full days; having spent the night on a sky-walk; having flown five legs; having had relatives pick me up and drive me from Portland to Albany (one hour) and Sally drive me from Albany to Eugene (a second hour), yeah, I was home. Even if my luggage was still somewhere else.

AN AUTHOR'S BOOK is never truly finished. It's just that at some point, you must send whatever you've written to an agent or publisher. In the spring of 2002, that's what I needed to do. I had, for the last few months, asked a handful of friends and family members to edit *Somebody's Daughter* and to give me their honest thoughts. They had.

The consensus was: good book, needs lots of work. Show more, tell less. Quit editorializing, just tell the story. And add more Slanger. "I'm worried that you'll find all this terribly disheartening," wrote one sub-editor, "and I wish you wouldn't because I don't think it should be. You story is still there and I feel confident you can make it work … if you can just be hard enough on yourself to stick to the story and not let your love for the whole subject make you sloppy."

She was right, of course—first, that the book needed massive remodeling and, second, that I'd find her response terribly disheartening. Not her fault, but the timing couldn't have been worse. I'd just invested more than a year, all four weeks of my allotted vacation time, and enough money to seemingly buy my own publishing company. I'd been away from Sally so often that I needed to show I.D. to prove I was her husband. I was tired. And still had thirty-nine items on my "To Do" and sixteen on my "To Find" lists. And no agent.

In that context, the critiques, though fair and helpful, stung.

Hungry for approval and tired from more than a year of work, I read right past the encouraging words and my sister-in-law's occasional happy faces to the harder stuff. But, ultimately, I realized that the very thing that hurts so badly is the very thing that would make the book better. My humility, my willingness to listen, my openness to change weren't comfortable, but they were necessary. And, hey, I'd asked for it. Would I have preferred they lie through their teeth and pump me full of false praise?

Editing is like that C.S. Lewis quote about God and people: "We're like blocks of stone, out of which the sculptor carves the forms of men. The blows of his chisel, which hurt us so much, are what make us perfect." So, while not agreeing with every suggested change, I spent about a month re-writing and polishing.

Meanwhile, along with Pat Gariepy, I was still doing some last-minute research. I finally found a way to see all the *Stars and Stripes* newspapers published in 1944—on microfilm, through UO's Interlibrary Loan system, the rolls coming from somewhere in the Midwest. Based on his name on a 1942 postcard to Slanger, I talked to a man, Nathan Freidman, who used to sip sodas with Frances at a lunch counter near Boston City Hospital. And I put together a proposal package for agents—forty-two pages' worth.

Book writing, I'd come to realize, was like trying to ride a bicycle while assembling it at the same time. Even though the book wasn't done, I needed to find an agent. Most publishers won't even look at a proposal that hasn't come through an agent. An agent is a publisher's weed-wacker, cutting down all the unsightly grass that just clutters up the publishers' in-basket garden. And most agents won't even look at a book proposal without first seeing a one- or two-page query letter.

In a weekend at the Yachats cabin, I had identified twenty-two agents in the 394-page *Guide to Literary Agents* whose interests seemed to touch on at least a couple of the nonfiction/military/history/women categories. My sister, Linda Crew, was a young-adult novelist and, long before, had offered to have her agent take a look. In my naivety, I'd always thought: *oh, Linda's agent will represent me*.

Within a week, the assistant to my sister's agent e-mailed and asked for the proposal. A few weeks later, the agent politely declined to represent me but offered some good insight. A few days later I got a phone call from an interested agent who'd been the favorite on the list. Jim Hornfischer was the rare non-New York agent, living in Austin, Texas. He was writing a World War II book himself, about sailors, and, more importantly, had represented James Bradley, whose World War II book, *Flags of Our Fathers*, was superb and selling fast. Hornfischer was enthusiastic about the Slanger story. We talked books, Texas football, Oregon football, the works. I sent the proposal. I was confident he was going to say yes. So confident that that weekend at the cabin, with friends, Sally and I popped a bottle of champagne to celebrate.

Prematurely, as it turned out. Weeks later, Hornfischer sent a nice "close-but-no-cigar" letter. I was numb, having thought this was our breakthrough. I wrote back to Hornfischer in a last-ditch effort to change his mind. "Unfortunately," I wrote in an e-mail to Ron Palmer, who was helping me with my World War II research, "Jim Hornfischer denied my appeal. But there are other agents in the sea. I have only begun to fight!"

But it was hard sustaining such resiliency. My April 18, 2002, journal entry:

> I'm as down as I've ever been on the project. I know God works in mysterious ways but this is getting too mysterious for me. I find my confidence drained with each rejection. It's like: Can I even write? Is there even a single chapter that's any good? It's just hard plugging on when the only positive feedback I've gotten are from a few friends who read it and from the family. [My sister] Linda says: step back. Take some time off. But I don't want this project hanging over my head forever. I want to get it done, sold and return to my regularly scheduled life.

As I waited for more replies from agents, I redid some of the book and read a "problem-child" chapter to Sally. April 22:

> She winces. It is, she says, too distant, too encyclopedic, too non-Frances. And I know she's right. I want to quit. This is déjà vu. A few months ago, I'd read her the same chapter and she'd winced even more. I thought I had it fixed. I was wrong. I admit: I'm tired of getting back on the horse and riding.

There's only one thing worse than being an author who gets criticism from a spouse, no matter how gently she presents it: that's being the spouse who delivers such criticism. The spouse who must put up with the sulking, wounded writer who loves to say, "Be, honest, really. It's for my own good. I can take it." And then melts into a pouting two-year-old when the assessment is anything short of glowing. "You should have married an insurance agent," was among my go-to lines when I was trying to clean up after one of my pity parties.

At times the mounting financial pressure, the lack of time together, and the waning hope for publication threatened to erode our marital bond like waves against the banks in Yachats. But just as the beach rebuilds itself after a storm, so did we find ways to rebuild after whatever blow we'd taken, our ultimate hope being our belief that God had us on this journey for a reason.

Scouring the agents directory a second time, I sent out a dozen more queries. A week later, one of the dozen responded with an e-mail. "This sounds like a winner," wrote Ellen Geiger of New York. "Do you have a proposal yet?"

I sent one, via FedEx, the next day. A week later, I returned from a noon-time run at work and there was a message from her. "You've got something here, Bob," she said. "You have a very appealing style."

I wanted to shout, but I had learned my lesson with Hornfischer. This fish might be in the net, but it wasn't in the boat. Two days later, the bottom fell out of the net. Geiger had had lunch with a Simon & Schuster editor who told her biography, unless it's a well-known subject, had a tough time selling. Maybe I would be best to consider a university press, she suggested. Meanwhile, she said she would mull it over and get back to me.

Biography not selling? Had she heard of *Seabiscuit*, which, at the moment, was sweeping the nation? And it was about a horse! But two weeks later, Geiger e-mailed.

> Dear Bob, After much soul searching, I've decided I'm going to pass on representing the Slanger project. I'm just not convinced I can make the kind of big sale you're expecting. What's more, a

big book on women in WWII just sold, and I'm sure the Slanger book would be compared to this larger, more comprehensive work. Maybe in a few months the climate will have improved. I'm sorry, but in this ultracompetitive climate, you need someone who can represent the work with 100% enthusiasm! I wish you the best of luck with it.

I sent letters to three other agents, people who had represented authors who'd written World War II books I'd liked. I sent check-up e-mails to three others. Worked forty-four hours—polishing, polishing—at the beach cabin. Called the Forty-fifth nurses to wish them happy anniversary. (Fifty-eight years since they'd stepped foot on Utah Beach.) And sent a proposal to *60 Minutes* commentator Andy Rooney, who, I'd learned in his book, *My War,* had been a reporter for *Stars and Stripes* during the war. I included a photo of Grandcamp-Maisy, where Sally and I had stayed in Normandy, because he'd mentioned staying there shortly after the invasion. Maybe it would tug on his heartstrings, assuming he had some beneath that curmudgeonly exterior; then again, maybe he'd open his next Sunday night commentary with: "Do you ever get tired of groveling writers who think we care even the least bit about their inconsequential little *books*?"

Meanwhile, rejections trickled in like search-and-rescue workers coming back to base camp with no sightings. Most were short and unsweet: "Dear Author, Thank you for contacting (us) about possible representation. I'm sorry to say, however, that your work is nothing which we feel we can successfully represent ... ." Others: "It didn't generate enough enthusiasm ... alas, not for us (written across my letter and returned) ... what you have here is a magazine article ... ."

A few offered details. "This needs to be either a historical novel or nonfiction," wrote an agent. "Choose one. I'd chose historical novel. Focus it on her and the war. I don't care about her past. All I care about is her once she's joined the army. I also think the title should be *Hi-Ya Babe*. This is the perfect title." The agent proposed sending the book to a writer he knew who might be able to jolt my manuscript to life with her ICU "novel" paddles. No thanks. "You need to create more emotion," he wrote. "You need to get beyond being a newspaper guy."

More rejections arrived. One night, I took a yellowed newspaper clipping that I'd cut out long ago and taped it to my computer. It pointed out that Pearl Buck had been rejected 12 times for *The Good Earth* and James Joyce 22 times for *Dubliners*. There's comfort in numbers, it's been said. Not much. But some.

Chapter 11

June-October 2002
Eugene, Oregon

Call dug the grave with a little hand shovel. In his condition it took most of a day; at one point he grew so weak that he sat down in the grave to rest, sweat pouring off him—if there had been anyone else to shovel he would have been inclined to be buried there himself. But he pulled himself up and finished the work and lowered Augustus in.
"There," he said. "That will teach me to be more careful about what I promise."
—Larry McMurtry, *Lonesome Dove*

God sometimes does His work with drizzle instead of lightning.
—Anonymous

SO, WHAT are your options, Welch? It was late June 2002 — the Red Sox had lost their division lead and would once again miss the playoffs—when the question kept nagging at me like a squawking crow looking for a handout. If this were a presidential race, the early returns were in and, at this rate, I wasn't going to win even Rhode Island. Maybe the answer wasn't sending more letters. Maybe the answer was making my manuscript better.

But then my pride protested. I began mentally defending myself. I disagreed sharply with the agent suggesting Slanger's past was irrelevant; to me, that was precisely what made her story so compelling. Prior to stepping off that landing craft, people were continually telling her: *You can't make a difference in the world. You're a nobody. You're not worthy.* She was detained at Ellis Island (and placed in a cage as most detainees were, awaiting second opinions). Scolded by teachers for bad grammar. Told by her parents that nursing wasn't for a Jewish girl. Told by supervisors that she'd never be a good nurse. And told by the Army Nurse Corps that she would have to serve stateside because of bad eyesight. Slanger's story was little without her past; I wouldn't have written the book if she had been a farm girl from Des Moines who'd breezed through life. To picture seven-year-old Frances Slanger in a cage at Ellis Island, a little girl who, at that moment, had no country (in limbo between two), no family (separated from her mother and sister), and hardly had any human standing (she was in a cage) was to picture someone powerless to make a difference in the world. And yet look what she had done: instilled hope in thousands of hopeless soldiers.

She had grown up amid the squalor of World War I, Lødz a virtual battleground for the Germans and Russians. With the exception of one person, Slanger's entire extended family in Poland had been killed by the Germans in World War II. Her scrapbook—I called it a "chapbook" in *American Nightingale*—had pages of newspaper and magazine articles regarding Hitler and the Jews. And she had put her life on the line to aid soldiers who were putting their lives on the line to oust Hitler and to end the murder of the Jews. Given as much, to ignore her past was to ignore much of her motivation for being on the front lines with those soldiers.

The problem was, venting like this—to Sally, Pat Gariepy, or running pals who'd been listening to my Slanger play-by-play now for nearly two years—may have cleansed my emotional sinuses but didn't get us closer to having the book published. So, I reviewed the feedback. If there was a consensus between my subeditors and the agents it was this: I needed to give the book more emotion, make it read more like a novel than a history tome, and, above all—the agents were adamant about this—forget trying to tell Slanger's story in cradle-to-grave fashion.

"You can do that with John Lennon or Madonna," one agent said. "The reader's willing to follow. But with an unknown person, no. You must give them some context. Keep it in the present and go back in time to fill in her past."

My practical side said yes, make the changes. My pride said no. As a tiebreaker, I called Jane Kirkpatrick. I told her nothing about the feedback, not wanting to prejudice her assessment in any way.

"Would you be willing to take a look and give me some advice?" I asked.

"Perfect timing," she said. "I'm in Los Angeles at a book conference and have tons of down time. Can you overnight-it?"

I did. A few days later, she e-mailed me that she liked the book a lot. But loosen up your writing, she said; give it more emotion. Quit thinking you're Stephen Ambrose and be Bob Welch. Above all, forget telling the entire story in cradle-to-grave fashion. "Stay in the present," she said. "Then take trips back in time to fill in her past."

I was like a wild horse that had finally been broken. Jane's agreeing with the others confirmed it. I need to make some major changes. Two days later, Sally and I had a week's vacation—a working vacation obviously—and I would take the block of time to restructure the book. But where was my model for this? What target was I trying to hit? What other books or movies have been done in this trips-back-in-time style?

What came to mind, after some thought, was *The English Patient*. I'd seen the movie about a badly burned World War II pilot being taken care of by a nurse. It wasn't so much about now; it was about then. Who was this man? Where had he come from? How had he gotten here? Novelist Michael Ondaatje established his base camp as Italy 1944, but then took trips back in time from there. I watched the DVD, then bought the book and skimmed it, all in the three days before our vacation.

In Yachats, the weather cooperated fully: Oregon's "coast crud," a not-uncommon summer condition when the valley heats up, created a winterish strip of fog down the shoreline, meaning we weren't anxious to be outside. Everywhere else in the country, people were baking in summer heat. In Yachats it was fifty-six degrees with a steady ten-knot wind. I got a fire going. Sally crafted to her heart's delight. And I started my remodeling project. After making a backup, I started copying and pasting like a madman. All day. Day after day.

Instead of opening with Slanger flailing in the Utah Beach water, I began with her writing the letter in Elsenborn. I included the entire letter. Without me having to say a word about who she was, the letter showed who she was. Showed her grit. Her compassion. Her admiration for these wounded soldiers. And when I revealed that she had died after sending that letter to *Stars and Stripes*, the reader would naturally think: *Who was this woman and how had she died?* The reader, I hoped, would care.

In the Chapter One re-write, I placed the nurses on the *Pendleton*, poised to load into the landing crafts, then shifted to Poland from 1913 to 1920 to understand Slanger's early years. Later, the nurses load into the LCVP landing craft. Using boats as the common theme, I shifted back in time to Freidel (Frances), her mother, and sister making their way to America aboard the *Nieuw Amsterdam* in 1920. And continued that pattern for more than half the book before settling into the present: 1944.

The key, I began to realize, was to not go back so often that it would be jarring to the reader. Quite the opposite, I wanted to raise questions in the present that only the past would answer; that way, the reader would want to return to the growing-up Slanger. Joseph Shoham, in the early days in Normandy, asks Slanger how she became a nurse. Boom, we're back in Boston in the 1930s to answer that question. The effect, I began to realize, was even more powerful than I'd anticipated. Reading the book now was like working a puzzle inward from two separate corners, the past and present complementing one another to gradually reveal the full picture of who Slanger was.

Late in the week, I stopped what I was doing and started to read the new version to myself. I like this, I thought. But I'd liked other versions, too, and they were, in retrospect, terrible. So, I read it to Sally, five chapters worth. She liked it. A lot. The changes, we agreed, had taken the book from "information heap" and "really long Slanger timeline" to "focused story." It had suspense. It had ebbs and flows of action. It had a whole new sense of emotion that people had said was missing.

After returning home and completing the revision, however, I felt uneasy. I'd just made a major move from one house to another. Had all the furniture made the trip after this rearranging? When you work on a thirteen-inch computer screen—and, no, most authors don't write on laptops, but I love the flexibility of being able to work wherever I am—it's hard to get a sense for the broader scope of your book. Out of a 300-page, 85,000-word book, you can see only a few paragraphs at a time.

I needed perspective. I needed to somehow get inside my book. I needed—the light went off—Carl Davaz, *The Register-Guard's* assistant managing editor who had helped us with our France trip.

"You want to do *what?*" he said when I told him my idea.

"On some weekend when the newsroom's photo studio isn't being used, I'd like to tape all 300 pages of my manuscript to three walls," I said.

He laughed, then, head still shaking, OK'd my bizarre plan. After printing out the book, I color-coded, with bright highlighters, sixteen categories I wanted to visually chart, from emotionally intense sections to foreshadowing to flashbacks. I wanted to see how often, in description, I got beyond the "default" sense of sight to the easily-overlooked senses of smell, hear, feel, and touch. How long I sometimes went without a mention of Slanger. How often I went without dialogue.

After spending much of a day doing the color-coding, I taped the manuscript to three walls of the studio, roughly the size and appearance of a racquetball court. Five rows of pages. Two hours of time. I stepped back. (OK, hobbled back, my leg in a brace after I'd torn knee ligaments playing a game of touch football that my son Jason thought was tackle.) Yes! The strategy had allowed me the new perspective I was seeking. I was literally inside my book.

With the color coding, I could see long stretches without Slanger material. I took out my laptop and transferred my visual observations onto a specially created spreadsheet. My middle chapters, I realized, were virtual droughts of action, Chapters Seven through Nine nearly devoid of anything emotional, Chapter Two through Four empty of anything lighthearted. The point wasn't to build a book that was equal parts this and that, but the all-day exercise had succeeded grandly in showing me changes I needed to make.

Once home, I polished and polished and checked facts, over and over, a daunting task. Despite my well-organized cataloging of information, it still took time to search for, say, a newspaper clipping that confirmed how many caskets, including Slanger's, were aboard the *Connelly* when it returned to New York Harbor on October 26, 1947 (6,248). Or to find the page in a book on the Holocaust that confirmed how many Jews were sent to the gas chambers the day Slanger died (513). One Saturday, Pat Gariepy and I spent six hours going through every fact in the book to ascertain each was correct. If every page has a dozen facts, a 300-page book will will require an author to be certain of more than 3,000 names, numbers, descriptions, quotes, etc.

That's why fact-checking is the literary equivalent of doing plumbing in a crawl space. Critical, laborious, but no fun. Sometimes, of course, you can confirm the accuracy of something in the thirty seconds it takes you to run a Google search. Other times, you must trace back to notes you took a year ago, make a phone call, or find the photo of a ship in a visual encyclopedia—*What's What*—to confirm where an "after mast" is located.

There's always this subtle temptation to rationalize—to think the reader won't know the difference between "coveralls" and "overalls" and won't care where, exactly, nurse Christine Cox died, so why bother double-checking. But readers do care. After three decades in journalism, I try to remember that it's not good enough if ninety-nine percent of your readers won't catch a slight error; one percent will and that's one percent too many.

By August 1, the third, and final, draft was finished. I'd been sustained by a number of forces, among them my faith that, despite my occasional whining, God was at work in all this; my friends; and my subject. The deeper I got into this story, the more Frances's inspiration became part of my strength. If she could overcome what she did—growing up amid World War I, moving to a new country, refusing to believe people who said she'd never make a difference in the world—then who was I to complain about a few rejection letters?

Twenty-six rejection letters to be exact but, then, who was counting? One morning I awoke and walked into the office for another 5 A.M. work session and was reminded of another force that kept me going. There, by my laptop, was a miniature Rosie Riveter lunch pail, along with Rosie's proverbial statement: "We Can Do It." It was encouragement from Sally, the one who, for nearly two years now, had been looking at the back of my head while I clicked computer keys. The one who'd trusted the huge financial risk I was taking. The one who would have had every right to pull away from me. Tired and touched, I looked at that lunch pail, buried my face in my hands, and cried.

MY SISTER Linda suggested a new strategy for getting an agent: instead of writing to them, go meet them face-to-face. The Willamette Writers Conference would be held in Portland in early August. You pay $15 for a ten-minute chunk of one-on-one time. "You'll have a better chance meeting someone in person," she said. "Bob, you're great with people."

I wasn't sure about this, but, then, if my hopes of getting the book published once floated gloriously in the sky, they now were looking more like the flaming Hindenburg on descent. I was desperate. I set up three appointments with agents, none of whom I knew anything about except all were interested in non-fiction. My first appointment was at 10 A.M. Saturday. I would leave at sun-up for the two-hour drive north.

On the night before, I was at home, printing out the manuscript. I'd read that most agents, even if interested in your work, don't want a full manuscript to lug home on a plane, but I've always been an over-preparer. What if an agent were actually interested and she was the rare bird who *did* want the manuscript—but I didn't have it? I couldn't take that chance. Not me, the guy who, as a kid subbing on a paper route, had laid out 104 rubber bands on the floor the night before to save time the next day.

I watched the printer spit out the sheets, one after another. My book. My baby. My millstone, clutching tighter around my neck, driving me into debt, driving me crazy.

Chk-chk-chk-chk-chk-chk. Pfffffft.
Chk-chk-chk-chk-chk-chk. Pfffffft.
Chk-chk-chk-chk—

What the—? I looked at my printer, which was blinking "OUT OF INK."

I looked at the clock. Ten o'clock. Well, of course. I had the appointment of my life in twelve hours in a city two hours away and my printer runs out of ink, conveniently after the stores have closed. And, of course, there would be no time in the morning. Why now? Why me? Why this?

What would you do if you were the last person on earth and had to find that sock?

Kinko's, the 24-hour copy shop. Of course! I copied the book onto a disk, said goodbye to Sally—a familiar word to her by now—and headed downtown. Sure enough, a clerk said she could have it for me by about 2 A.M. Wonderful. I needed to be on the road by 6 A.M. to meet the requisite Welch "hour-early" rule. "Go for it," I said and started to thumb through all those magazines that I'd never otherwise read.

Shortly before two—I was barely still awake—she brought me the printed manuscript. It looked all wrong. The words had gaping spaces between them. No thanks.

"What about Wal-Mart?" said the only other customer desperate enough to be in a copy shop at 2 A.M. "They're open twenty-four hours and they have printer cartridges."

I'm not a Wal-Mart regular and hadn't stopped to consider that it never closes its doors. "Thanks, man." I drove five miles to Wal-Mart, bought the cartridge, raced home, and replaced the spent one. But the printer now wasn't working at all. It had juice, but my computer wasn't reading it. Serious panic. It was 3 A.M. This was not happening. Yes, this *was* happening. This was happening because in the fifteen years that I'd owned printers, nothing like this had ever happened before, and so, naturally, it would happen now. Please, God, please.

What was wrong? Why wouldn't it work? Who do you call at 3 A.M. to help? Suddenly, I realized I had plugged my mouse cord, not my printer cord, into the side port of my Mac. Oh. All better.

The final sheet rolled off at 5:30 A.M. I kissed Sally goodbye. "You never came to bed, did you?" she said. "Nope. Sorry." (There was that word again.) "Off to Portland. Wish me luck." I showered, shaved, dressed, and left, rehearsing my spiel as I headed up Interstate-5 in my pickup.

So critical were these author-agent interactions that Willamette Writers offered day-long workshops just to help people know how to make the ten-minute pitch. I'd have to rely on instincts. In some ways, my frantic transition from Eugene to Portland helped; I was too tired to be nervous. In my mind—and on a cheat-sheet outline—I winnowed my pitch to four sections: an overview of the book, Slanger's intriguing past, my credentials as a writer, and the timely marketing opportunities. Now that the new World War II

Memorial dedication had been pushed back to May 2004, the book could come out in, say, January and ride that publicity wave along with the June 2004 sixty-year anniversary of D-Day.

I arrived just before my 10 A.M. appointment with an agent named Robert Shepard from San Francisco. I jumped into my verbal routine with the enthusiasm of a well-caffeinated carnival barker. After a minute, Shepard raised a hand.

"Whoa, whoa, OK, I'm convinced you have a story. Now, let me ask you some questions." He was clearly enthused. In fact, when my ten-minute session was up, Shepard told the room monitor, "Mr. Welch is going to be staying for another session. I have an opening." He took two sample chapters and the proposal.

After a night at the hotel, I met with another agent from San Fransisco. Ted Weinstein seemed genuinely interested, but not, it seemed, on a level with Shepard. Weinstein didn't want to take a proposal and sample chapters with him, but asked if I'd send them. A third agent, Lisa Dicker of New York, was encouraging but seemed less enthused than the other two.

I called Sally. "It went great," I said. "I really think this Shepard guy might go for it. He was so impressed he gave me his second time slot so we could keep talking."

That night, in my journal, I wrote: "Came home Sunday fired up. Was worth the entire conference fee!"

But then came the waiting. One day. Three days. Ten days. Finally, came an e-mail from Shepard: "You've made a complete, compelling, and enjoyable proposal that makes a strong case for this book," he said. "The sample chapters go all of this one better: you write with real feeling, and bring home to the reader both the impact of Frances's beautifully written letter and her death ... ."

I knew by this point he wasn't going for it. I was the retired general in *White Christmas* reading the letter that said, between the lines, that the army wasn't interested in him returning to active duty. And I was right. It was an encouraging rejection—I appreciated Shepard's sensitivity—but, in the end, he said, "I just don't feel as passionate as I'd need to be to be sure, and that's part of the alchemy of selling every book."

Before I could even decide which bridge to jump off, the phone rang. It was Weinstein. He began by telling me how much he loved the story itself. But Shepard, too, had started off with encouragement and look where that had gotten me.

"I think I can sell this," he said. "The writing is great."

"You do? Really?"

"It's a great story about a human being in war time. I think there are movie opportunities, too. It's going to make you and your agent a lot of money. I think you're looking at an advance somewhere in the $25,000 to $100,00 range."

I mentally froze, so unaccustomed to acceptance. Someone believed in me—someone who could make this book a reality. Better yet, someone believed in Frances Slanger. In us.

I SPOKE WITH three other authors who'd been represented by Ted; all lauded the work he'd done for them. He sent a contract. I signed it. "I think we can have a deal by Thanksgiving," he said. "I'm looking at an imprint from a major publishing house."

He wanted the proposal polished to strengthen our case. Meanwhile, he started talking up the book. In mid-October, an editor from Little, Brown & Co. called and spent forty-five minutes asking me questions; Atria Books, a Simon & Schuster imprint, was also interested.

It was as if, after almost two years, our ship was finally out of the harbor and sailing. Seemingly out of nowhere, two people stepped forward with good, eleventh-hour information for the book, one a soldier who'd sailed on the *Frances Y. Slanger* and remembered how everyone, upon boarding, was given a handout about the woman for whom it was named.

After I sent him a shot-in-the-dark letter, James Bradley, author of the best-selling *Flags of Our Fathers*, a guy who knew nothing of me, agreed to look at the manuscript and consider an endorsement. Judith Bellafaire, chief historian at the Women in Military Service for America, would be sending an enthusiastic "blurb." So, too, would Evelyn Benson, author of *As We See Ourselves: Jewish Women in Nursing*.

On October 22, 2002, I was speaking to a Sweet Home High School English class in a small town in the foothills of the Oregon Cascades when my cell phone rang. Normally, I wouldn't think of leaving my phone on, but Ted had told me a deal was imminent.

As I started my talk on writing, I told the students they might be watching "history" here today. "Not like it's the armistice ending World War II or anything," I said, "but still ... ."

When the phone rang, I put it to my ear. The students eagerly watched.

"We do?" I said, after Ted told me he'd gotten us a deal. "Yeah!"

The class cheered. We had an offer. Atria Books, the Simon & Schuster imprint, was offering a $20,000 advance, a quarter of it to be paid at each of four points: at signing, at deliverance, at hardcover publication, and at softcover publication. Did I want the deal? It was lower than the low-end that Ted had anticipated, but at this point I wasn't about to dicker. We'd just take less money up front and more at the back.

"Yes, yes," I said. "Take it. Yes!"

I was just happy to know my book was going to get printed. And happy to sign with an imprint that had the financial oomph and prestige of Simon & Schuster behind it.

"And," as I told Sally that night, in what sounded like my father speaking, "he thinks it has movie potential."

We hugged. I thanked her for sticking with me. And she said what she often says: "I have no choice. I'm the mother of your children."

That night, Sally and I took Pat Gariepy and his wife Karlann out for dinner to celebrate. It had been nearly two years since I'd reluctantly returned that phone call from Nathan Fendrich. And seemingly that long ago since I'd toured Roxbury with Milton (*"Get in the caw"*) Zola, opened the Ark of the Covenant at Boston University, heard the Irishman at Normandy say "You're Americans, aren't you?" and stood in the Belgian field where Frances Slanger had died.

In many ways, it felt like the end of a long, long journey. But would soon prove to be the beginning of another.

Chapter 12

January 2003-May 2004
Eugene, Oregon

M: An editor can't expect to be loved, only respected. And that's not easy. My rejection letters started out as four pages of single-spaced hand-wringing and advice. Now they're down to a kindly, vague paragraph.
J: Does that help authors feel better?
M: Of course not, nothing helps. This is real life, "history." History is what hurts, somebody said.
J: An author, I'll bet.

—Ernest Callenbach, *Publisher's Lunch*

THE FIRST TIME I gave a speech about the book—to a Rotary Club in Eugene—I concluded with the revelation that "the military named the finest hospital ship in the fleet in honor of Frances Slanger." At that, a man near the back of the room stood up and began clapping. Others joined in. I was surprised. And encouraged.

Other encouragement started trickling in. In mid-February, my agent Ted called to say Barry Levinson, producer of such movies as *Diner, Analyze That*, and *Possession* called him "about twelve minutes" after seeing the book proposal. How soon could he get a copy of the manuscript?

On the "blurbs," or endorsement, front, we were making good progress. Bradley, the *Flags of our Fathers* author, surprised us with a solid endorsement: "Bob Welch has done the country a service … I recommend you enrich your life and read this touching story." Pulitzer Prize-winning columnist Paul Greenberg—I got to him because a *Register-Guard* colleague, Paul Neville, knew him—sounded interested in perhaps endorsing it as well. But a few months later, Levinson decided against a movie deal. Ted wrote on May 22, 2003:

> No news from Hollywood. Both Barry Levinson's and Elton John's production companies were all hot and bothered and then decided not to pursue. I'm headed to LA next week for BookExpo and have meetings with a few more Hollywood folk. Will continue on this path and keep you posted. If nothing comes before publication, the presence of the physical book will certainly help generate new interest.

Twice I had sent books and DVDs to *60 Minutes* commentator Andy Rooney with no response. But knowing Rooney was going to be receiving a lifetime achievement award at the same National Society of Newspaper Columnists conference in Tucson, Arizona, that I'd be at in June, I planned to ask him in person. He obviously wasn't the warmest guy around, but I was hopeful I could land an endorsement from him, based on his emotional connection to the war.

At a wind-whipped social hour before the evening banquet, about a hundred of us mingled on a roof-top patio, sipping drinks and making small talk. Suddenly, there was Rooney, holding court with a dozen or so people.

From a distance, I clutched my copy of *My War,* his book. I'd hoped the book might at least grease his ego so a pitch might slide more smoothly. I joined the ring around Rooney and realized just getting to him was going to be hard enough, much less getting a chance to chat. But one by one and two by two, the group thinned, and soon it was just one man telling a Charles Kuralt story to Rooney. And me.

I tried to pretend I was the third part of this conversation, nodding and looking interested. Once, Rooney, dressed in a dark suit and holding a drink at chest level, nodded at me, which I took as a subtle sign that he'd somehow welcomed me around his campfire. But I knew I didn't belong. This was, after all, one of the most recognizable faces on the planet, a man who can tell stories about sharing a tent with Ernie Pyle. Author. Columnist. Commentator.

And all-around equal-opportunity offender. A guy who's honked off presidents, gays, blacks, Republicans, Democrats, the French, and a truck driver in New York whom he yelled at for littering.

Suddenly, it was just Andy Rooney and me. We shook hands. His eyebrows, I noticed, looked even larger in person than on TV, like those cotton ball eyebrows kids used to glue on their construction-paper Santa Clauses. He was a small man, around five feet tall. His cheeks weren't as rosy without makeup. He walked with a serious stoop. (Heck, he was eighty-four; he had a right to.)

I'd considered leading with a quick "ice-breaker" about some hard-hitting issue he'd opined on—something like, "You're right, Andy, naps *are* underrated"—but instead I began stammering about my book. About this nurse who wrote a touching letter to the same *Stars and Stripes* newspaper for which he had written in 1944—and then was killed in a field hospital tent the next night.

I showed him a copy of the nurse's letter as it appeared in the newspaper. He looked at it. His brow furrowed. "Yes, yes, yes," he said, nodding. "I remember this."

My heart quickened. I'd survived the preliminary heat; now for the finals. "So would you consider reading the galleys and perhaps—"

"No, no, no," he said, about as subtly as a belly flop. "I never do endorsements. I get a handful of offers a week, and I turn them all down. No time for that." He looked at the name on my badge—"wanna spell it right"—and wrote in the book: "To Bob Welch. Tucson. Andy Rooney."

After dinner, I found myself next to him in the dessert line. "Don't suppose you've reconsid—"

"No," he assured in that no-means-no style.

Frankly, I appreciated Rooney's bluntness. At least he didn't offer false hope, which, too often, I came to believe in from others. In terms of helping me out on the book, people, I came to find, funneled into three categories: those, like Rooney, who said they wouldn't help and didn't; those who said they would and didn't; and those who said they would and did. The latter, of course, were the rare finds. But the difference they made was the difference between me writing a book and me not writing a book.

I LIKED MY editor, Brenda Copeland, from the start. Liked her straight-shooting, metaphor-tooting style. Once, I mentioned how a number of groups I'd spoken to about the book had mentioned that Slanger's story would be perfect for *Oprah!* "I wouldn't get my hopes up about Oprah," she wrote back. "I know *Somebody's Daughter* is very good, but I hear 'Oprah would love my book' as much as I hear 'Do I look fat in this?' "

I liked how blunt she was. Liked the way she lived in a totally different world than mine, me calling her from laid-back Eugene, Oregon, where you can see blue jeans at the opera, and she calling me from upscale New York, from high up in The Avenue of Americas Building or walking home from work, cell phone to her ear: "Whoops, almost got hit by a taxi, but as I said we should be able to get the edits to you—whoa, now I'm going by a marimba band—I should be able to get the edits to—sorry, nearly ran into a Santa Claus … ." And liked that she genuinely liked the book. "It's really a pleasure to work on," she said to me in an e-mail. "I wish we could clone you."

Not that I was exactly Atria's priority author. At the same time Brenda was editing my book, she was editing *Playboy* pinup Pamela Anderson's novel *Star*. Anderson was everything Frances was not: rich, famous, beautiful, and shallower than the thin retreat of a *Baywatch* wave. But I had an idea which one of us was going to get the bigger slice of the promotional pie, and it wasn't me.

Brenda was organized, encouraging, and passionate about the book business. "This is a good book," she wrote me with her eleven pages of suggested fixes. "We're going to make it better." No, we didn't always agree on everything. Most of our spirited debates, though, had to do with the exterior of the book—and its release date—and not the contents. She won a few battles. I won a few. And, with one glaring exception, the decisions reached were the best decisions.

Atria didn't like the name *Somebody's Daughter: The World War II Hero Time Forgot*. They—meaning she and some "committee" that decided such things—thought it leaned toward the Harlequin romance side. I could understand that. They wanted something bolder, more gallant. They liked the word "American" but didn't like the word "nurse." What could they match "American" with?

"Did the soldiers have any sort of nickname for these nurses?" Brenda asked.

I thought it over. "Some of the GI's letters, in response to her letter, referred to the nurses as 'modern-day Nightingales,'" I told her, "after the well-known British nurse, Florence Nightingale." Thus was *American Nightingale* born. I grew to like it far better than *Somebody's Daughter.*

The subtitle was more problematic. Atria wanted: *The Story of Frances Slanger, Forgotten Heroine of D-Day.* I liked everything but the "D-Day" reference. It wasn't accurate, I told Brenda. She dug in; "D-Day" was a powerful phrase that would catch readers' attention, she said. I agreed.

"But Slanger was back in Southampton, England, on D-Day, June 6," I said. "For all I know, she was playing gin rummy on D-Day."

Atria's folks weren't budging. But, then, once the book came out, Atria's folks weren't going to be giving a talk at some Hilton ballroom and have to answer the question from the audience, "Why does the subtitle say she was the heroine of 'D-Day' when she didn't arrive until four days later?" No, *I* was going to be giving that talk. And *I* would have to answer that question. I said as much to Brenda, who, finally, understood. Atria backed off and went with "Normandy."

I loved the cover from the first time I saw it: the bold, sans-serif words in white across a gray-sky background—*American Nightingale*—and soldiers wading ashore at Utah Beach. But the initial mock-up had had an inset of Slanger in her dress uniform. No, that wasn't right, I thought when seeing it. I suggested using a photo of Slanger cropped from a group picture: she in her fatigues, hands in pockets, with the hands of a nurse behind her on her shoulders as if to say: *the one who wrote the letter, the one who died, the one who had the ship named in her honor.* These were women who jumped out of a landing craft in fatigues and were greeted by seventeen truckloads of wounded soldiers. Women who wiped the blood off handsaws that had just taken a soldier's leg off. Please, no dress uniforms. Brenda was convinced. Atria went with the photo I recommended.

The only other issue of contention was when the book would come out. In December 2002, I learned the book wasn't coming out until June 2004. June? That was way too late. By now, the World War II Memorial dedication had been pushed back from May 2003 to May 2004, which was wonderful timing for us. The sixty-year anniversary of D-Day was June 6, 2004. Some 100,000 World War II vets were expected in Washington, D.C., for the memorial dedication alone. But the book needed a few months to create any sort of a buzz for the wave to build and peak with the May-June commemorative events.

Brenda did some checking. Actually, it should be on the shelves May 11, she e-mailed me. I was stunned. That was still too late, almost a year and a half away. From my vantage point, it could easily be published a few months earlier. Why not, say, January? I asked. If published in May, there would be no chance to build up word of mouth about the book so when bookstores and the media might be featuring World War II books, we could ride the wave. Nope, she said.

"Brenda," I e-mailed, "I'm afraid that a May release will be like showing up at a New Year's Eve party at about 11:50 P.M. as a single. Yeah, we're there, but we don't have time to meet anybody. The result? Nobody to kiss at the stroke of midnight."

"To co-opt your lovely metaphor," she promptly e-mailed back, "publishing in January would be like arriving at a New Year's Eve party at about 4 in the afternoon. By the time the rest of the guests arrive you'll be drunk in the corner with salsa stains on your dress. Finding someone to kiss will be the least of your worries."

In hindsight, I wish we'd split the difference and shown up for the party at about 8 P.M. But, with comebacks like that, I had to admire Brenda Copeland. I'd never had so much fun disagreeing with anyone in my life.

ON OCTOBER 16, 2003, the Boston Red Sox were leading the New York Yankees 5-2 in Game Seven of the American League Championships Series and fives outs away from going to the World Series. They lost 6-5 when light-hitting Aaron Boone homered in the eleventh inning for New York. Boston Manager Grady Little was fired.

IT'S A WARNING nearly every rookie author gets at writers conferences and in publications: unless you're an upper-echelon author, don't expect your publishing house to do much to promote your book. In discussions with Brenda, I never was promised, nor did I expect, a gourmet dinner—some twenty-city tour and interviews on major TV networks. But neither did I expect what I ultimately got: self-serve.

I kept asking when Atria's promotional person would contact me so we could map out a plan, but got tired of waiting for a response. I realized if I wanted publicity, I'd need to drum it up on my own. And so I knocked on whatever door I thought might open, always keeping a written, computerized trail of what I had done and what I needed to do. I was averaging about ten knocks per day; meanwhile, my list of doors-yet-to-knock-on was almost always in the two-dozen range.

While I did this, I put together a grand plan for the kickoff of the book and sent it to Atria. In the proposal, I offered to pay $11,550 and suggested that Atria pay $9,650 for a multi-fronted publicity campaign that would included sending 5,000 postcards, my spending two weeks on the East Coast as the book launched, plus a few other regional appearances. The silence from the publisher was deafening. I soon realized I was going into this battle alone.

Raising awareness about the book would prove to be a task far more time-consuming, costly, and aggravating than I had imagined. But we did at least one thing right. With no help from Atria, we pulled off a publicity coup. It began—and you might say ended—in our kitchen. That's where, in December 2003, my twenty-four-year-old son Ryan was hanging out with his friend Adam, who was just starting in the prescription-drug sales field.

"I can't get these doctors to listen to anything I say," he said, "but if I whip out my laptop and pop in a DVD, they're *there*."

Later, it hit me: why not create a DVD to promote *American Nightingale*? I'd been a newspaper features editor; I knew how little time an editor or producer had to read, or even skim, a book. But someone, if curious, might slide a five- or ten-minute documentary into a CD/DVD tray.

I sketched out what I imagined as a quick-hit documentary of the project. We could bring in the man who started all this, Nathan Fendrich, and Pat Gariepy, and Sallylou and John Bonzer, for "in-studio" interviews.

"We need some black felt or something to make the kitchen look like a studio," I said. "Some solid background."

"I can get that," said Sally, our resident craft expert.

Ryan's company, AO Creative, did promotional films for businesses and nonprofits; he could handle the technical side of things. Jason, our twenty-one-year-old son, was a multimedia design major at University of Oregon; he could handle sound and other details.

"We've got dozens of World War II photos from the Bonzers and the video footage I took at Utah Beach and Elsenborn," I said. "And there are areas of Florence on the coast that look just like Utah Beach. We could shoot some stuff of me being interviewed in the dunes. Gariepy has World War II helmets, uniforms, the works."

"Jason has that fog machine," Ryan said.

For music, we decided to see if McKenzie Stubbert, a young man who attended our church and was a great piano player, would help. His dream was to write film scores; maybe he'd write something for us. Within days, we had McKenzie on board and finalized the plans for a low-budget documentary; only Ryan, Jason, and McKenzie would be paid. In peanuts. Because of our tight schedules, it would need to be filmed and recorded in two days: December 22 and 23.

We did voice-only stuff the first day. A friend, Rodger Terrall, had a wonderful voice—he was the announcer at University of Oregon women's home basketball games—and did the documentary's narration. Susan Honthumb, a *Register-Guard* colleague, grew up in Boston; she and her slightly Northeastern accent were the voice of Slanger reading her letter. Three male friends pretended to be soldiers reading snippets of GI's letters in response to Frances's.

The next morning, at 7 o'clock, with breakfast burritos in our laps and a stepladder and three-wheeled camera dolly in the back of our Ford Explorer, Jason, Ryan, and I headed for the coast seventy-five minutes away. It was raining. Not good.

We arrived at a beach near the north jetty of the Siuslaw River, a ten- to twenty-knot wind chilling us as soon as we got out of the car. Almost as if on cue, the rain slowed to a light drizzle, then stopped altogether. The surf pounded. We could not only see and hear the fury, but feel it. Not what we needed for what I'd envisioned as the opening shot—a lone helmet in the shallow backwash. In a foot of water that numbed the feet in moments, Ryan took a few steps up the aluminum ladder to shoot down on the helmet while I steadied the ladder and Jason made sure the helmet didn't get washed out to sea. I semi-directed, but mainly made sure Ry and Jas didn't get hit by sneaker waves. We shot about ten minutes' worth of helmet footage. We were already shivering.

"Let's try the dolly for shots of the back surge!" I yelled above the din of the wind and surf. The "Wally Dolly" was a three-wheeled, triangular-shaped cart created by Ryan's father-in-law, Wally Anderson, a guy who builds his own experimental aircraft and can whip together anything technical as if it were made by NASA engineers. The dolly's purpose was to allow a shooter to film while moving, someone else gently pulling it along as if it were a wagon.

I envisioned the mini-documentary beginning with boot prints in the sand (the nurses coming ashore) and the backwash wiping away those prints (the nurses being forgotten). At the end of the film, we'd run the wave in reverse, revealing the footprints (nurses being remembered). Ryan sat on the dolly. Jason started to pull him—or tried. The dolly sunk into the soft, wet sand. We tried it again. Same result. We hadn't had the time or foresight to do what the Americans had done before sending tanks up Omaha Beach— one night, months before the invasion, they sent a single soldier to the beach in mini-sub to take sand samples to see what kind of weight the beach might withstand.

"Let's bag it," I said.

Ryan shot the shots without the dolly. He filmed shots of Jason walking on the beach, wearing John Bonzer's actual olive-green field jacket, complete with an authentic Red Cross arm bandage that Pat Gariepy, of course, loaned us. Then it was up into the dune area where, with beach grass blowing in the wind and the video camera rolling, I talked about how *American Nightingale* was born. I offered a short overview of Frances Slanger and explained why we must not forget her and the entire World War II generation. Just as I finished, the rain returned. It was 11:15 A.M. Right on schedule.

"Let's go," I said. We slurped down clam chowder at Mo's, a popular place on the waterfront, and headed back to Eugene. Our three in-studio interviews were scheduled to be shot at 3:30 P.M., 4:30 P.M., and 5:30 P.M., with miscellaneous indoor shots after that.

En route home, Ryan filmed Jason in army gear, writing a letter to Slanger along a creek. Then they switched roles, Ryan writing a letter in a forest clearing.

"We need one more soldier," I said as we rolled into Eugene. "Adam?"

"He's working," said Ryan.

"Mart," Jason said, slipping out his cell phone. "I'll call him."

In twenty minutes, we had Jason's friend, Justin Mart, in army garb, writing a letter in a field, Interstate-5 just out of the frame. We zipped home and started fine-tuning the set and lighting for the "studio" shots in our kitchen. The Bonzers were probably already en route to our house for our first interview. We were still wet from the beach footage.

"This light's just not right," said Ryan, adjusting the sophisticated lamp I'd borrowed from a *Register-Guard* photographer. We did test after test, adjusting the light, bouncing it off the ceiling, but the results were the same each time: terrible. The space was small, the light intense, like shining a flashlight into a thimble. My face felt like it was on fire.

We didn't need this. I looked at my watch. Three-fifteen. The Bonzers would arrive any minute. Here we'd concocted this grand plan and yet were stymied by something that, at first glance, seemed small but was actually huge. Above all, the documentary had to look and feel professional, even if it were being done by a bunch of rookies.

Later, our challenge would remind me of an obstacle the Allied army faced in Normandy: their tanks couldn't bust through hedgerows fortified by roots and centuries of time. What saved them was improvisation. Some GIs welded pipes, steel "teeth" and metal bumpers to the fronts of the Sherman tanks, enabling them to bull their way through the dirt-and-root mounds. Stephen Ambrose, in his book *Citizen Soldiers*, suggests little things like that ultimately won the war for us.

Improvise. Improvise. It was a gene that had somehow gotten passed down from my father, the guy who could fix anything if given five minutes and a roll of duct tape. Only this time, the gene seemed to have skipped a generation because I didn't have an answer to this dilemma.

"You have one of those shop lights on the little stands?" Ryan asked.

"Sure, but won't that be yellowish light?"

"It's worth a try."

I glanced at the kitchen clock. "A shop light, Ry?"

"Dad, we gotta do something."

When the red "record" light went on for the interview with Sallylou Bonzer, the light on her face might as well have been provided by some *Good Morning America* lights crew. It was perfect. So were the interviews with her and John, who did wonderful jobs as I asked questions, Ryan filmed, and Jason worked sound. Beyond the Bonzers' grandson, Aaron, who was acting as their chauffeur, we couldn't have fit another person in the kitchen, though our four cats slipped in and out with no problem.

When I asked Dr. Bonzer about the night Slanger died, his eyes grew watery. "Oh, yes, I remember that night well. A major, a private were killed. And Frances." He paused, his rosy cheeks glistening. "It was terrible," he said, his voice cracking. "Terrible."

As the Bonzers finished their interview, Nathan Fendrich arrived. "Here's the man who's responsible for all this," I said to the Bonzers. "Nathan, this is Dr. John Bonzer and Sallylou Bonzer. John, Sallylou, this is the guy who first told me about Slanger's letter."

I will never forget the response from Fendrich, a man who'd lost extended family in the Holocaust. He saluted the Bonzers. "It is," he said, "my privilege to meet people whom I consider to be true heroes."

The Bonzers hardly knew how to respond. Aaron, their grandson, looked on with pride. The Bonzer's own children barely knew their parents' World War II backgrounds. And a buddy of John's once said he'd played golf with him virtually every weekend for decades and hadn't even known Bonzer had served in the war.

We interviewed Nathan, then Pat Gariepy. That evening, in our "wet" unfinished basement—half dirt, half concrete—we fired up Jason's fog machine and filmed another soldier-as-letter-writer scene, then did the same on our back porch, Jason, the kid who'd never smoked in his life, puffing on a non-filter Camel for authenticity. Finally, we filmed my daughter-in-law Susan's right arm, in a jacket, as if she were Slanger writing the letter from her field hospital tent.

Ryan, after Christmas, hunkered down and, along with the still photos I'd sent him, started editing the footage into what would be a twelve-minute film. When, a week later, Ryan had the film roughed out—it looked wonderful—he got a copy to McKenzie, who, unbeknownst to us, showed it on our church's projection screen and, using his brother as a sound engineer, played the song he'd written to fit the images. He repeated this over and over, until he got the timing just right, the ebbs and flows of the music one with the images.

"But what if it's just not at all what you wanted," Sally said on the night I was to go hear McKenzie's song.

"I just have this feeling it's going to be good," I said.

When I first heard his song "American Nightingale," I wasn't surprised. I should have been, but I wasn't. It *was* good. Soft, hauntingly sweet piano music that, within thirty seconds, had taken me from McKenzie's clutter-everywhere bachelor pad to the beaches of Normandy.

By February 1, we began sending out the first of some 300 copies of the *American Nightingale* DVD to the media and anyone else who might be interested in the story of a heroic World War II nurse.

THE MONTHS leading up to the book launch were chaotic. I had never run a national publicity campaign and every day was on-the-job training. But I was fueled by a sense of urgency.

Within a few weeks of learning whom Atria had assigned to be my book publicist—Brenda spoke highly of this veteran, buoying my hopes—I learned she had decided to quit the book-publishing business and move to Seattle. Her replacement was a rookie.

I was frustrated. But Ted, my agent, was as steady as I was impetuous. He calmed me down as if to say: *The pilot has blacked out and this young co-pilot is the only one with a prayer to land the plane. Work with her, Bob.* I would. I had no choice. Meanwhile, though, I would also try to figure out how to trigger the landing gear and operate the flaps myself—just in case. Months before, I had bought two books—*1001 Ways to Market Your Books* and *Guerilla Marketing for Writers*—to guide me through the marketing shoals.

"When planning your marketing budget, follow the rule of seven," I read in *1001 Ways*. "This rule states that if you want your prospects to take action and buy your books, you must connect with them at least seven times within an 18-month period." I scoffed. Impossible. Unnecessary to go to such lengths.

I began planning what would be an eighteen-day trip to Boston and Washington, D.C., in late May when the book would be released. Not that, in the beginning, I had any actual appearances scheduled, other than a Red Sox-Orioles game on Memorial Day at Fenway Park. But these events, I figured, would come.

With Ryan's help, I created postcards, their catch-phrase customized for six groups: Jewish publications and bookstores ("A Jewish Heroine"), hospitals and nursing organizations ("A Nurse of Honor"), libraries ("Hero for the Ages"), Boston audiences ("Pride of Boston"), military audiences ("Combat Nurse"), and Oregon audiences ("Oregon Author"). We had a combined first printing of 5,000. The postage alone would cost us $1,150.

I put together thirty-five data base lists, including ones for newspapers, magazines, radio stations, TV networks, organizations, libraries, museums, bookstores, and individuals who'd purchased books from me in the past. I started contacting any group, near or far, to whom I might speak. I e-mailed newspaper editorial page editors about writing op-ed pieces regarding Slanger for their 2004 Memorial Day editions. Jason built a Web page and taught me Adobe Photoshop software so I could work with photos. Ryan taught me Adobe inDesign so I could create my own press packets.

Each morning, at 5 A.M., I'd be on the phone or computer, trying to line up something: a speech, an interview, a guest editorial. And what I quickly learned was this: That book was wrong. It didn't take seven contacts to produce results. It took way more.

The double-edge sword for authors, I began realizing, was our imaginations: just as we can picture a story being written—just as we can imagine creating something from nothing, so can we visualize the same in regards to publicity. At some point, I read that Don Hewitt, the creator and soon-to-be-retiring executive producer of *60 Minutes* had, like his friend Andy Rooney, been a war correspondent, for *Stars and Stripes*. I immediately pictured his eyes misting up as he watched the DVD. I pictured him getting on the phone and telling some editor to get a crew ready to ship out to Eugene, Oregon. Perhaps he'd use the Slanger piece in the final show he would produce: a tribute to his own, heroic generation. But though I did wind up talking to a fairly high-up editor, I never even got close to talking to Hewitt. I doubt he ever saw the DVD.

Promoting the book without serious help from the publisher was, as the one book title suggests, guerrilla warfare. After hearing about an organization called the American Association for the History of Nursing, I thought: *perfect fit*. Perhaps I could speak at its annual conference. Instead, I learned you had to be a member to speak and that only entitled you to write an abstract, with hopes that, if yours were accepted, you could make a presentation. *Whatever it takes*. I paid the $100, joined, wrote the abstract—and, months later, was turned down. It did nothing for my ego to learn that while the story of a heroic World War II nurse had been rejected, among those abstracts accepted was one called "Rethinking the Tuskegee Syphilis Study."

There went one hundred bucks, essentially lit on fire. But every money decision had to be made quickly and required a risk. Once, at Kinko's, I spent more than $350 on color copies for a press packet I was putting together; the numbers on the digital counter clicked upward like a ninety-mph taxi ride. The alternative was to trust that Atria was going to take care of me. And nothing I'd heard from them suggested that was going to happen.

IF THE SPRING of 2004 was chaotic, it was also comforting because every now and then, I'd get good news. For starters, the Boston University Barnes & Noble bookstore, the one at which I'd said, "Someday I'm going to have a book signing right here," OK'd my request for just that in early June. Atria's associate director of copy editing wrote, "Just to let you know, the copy editor thinks your book is wonderful, and this comes from someone who can be hard to please."

Weeks later, the feeling became mutual; the editing job, done by someone with a nursing background, was superb. Boston's largest bookstore, the downtown Borders, offered a signing, one of only three events Atria would land me. Boston University's Gotlieb Archival Research Center invited me to speak at its annual meeting in April, which, as I recalled, was during baseball season; I couldn't wait to see the Red Sox play again in the magic of Fenway Park. Maybe 2004 would be the year Boston finally reversed the eighty-six year curse and win the World Series.

Among the most encouraging responses to the DVD came from a guy named Dick Foth, a friend who'd keynoted a Christian writers conference I'd attended near Santa Cruz, California, and now lived in Washington, D.C. "It's wonderful," he said. "I have a friend, Dr. Timothy Johnson, who is the ABC medical editor. Would you like me to forward a copy to him?" I forwarded one to Johnson myself, two days later, dropping Foth's name.

We were rolling. Meanwhile, I tried to keep people on "Team Slanger" apprised of our progress. One day in early March, I was saying goodbye to Joseph Shoham on the phone when he said what he always said when our conversation was ending. "Say hello to that old tent mate of mine, Johnny Bonzer, out there in *Ara-gawn*, Bob."

Shoham, a Jewish man from the East Coast, had been close friends with Dr. John Bonzer, a Catholic man from the West Coast, in the war. But they hadn't seen each other since soon after the war in Europe ended in 1945. I hung up the phone and, for a rare moment, stopped. Did nothing. Nothing but think about Bonzer and Shoham and what it must have been like, operating on soldiers from Normandy to Czechoslovakia, the two of them knit together with a bond of blood, pain, and purpose.

Then, an idea came: *What if … .*

"You want to have a reunion for the Forty-fifth in D.C?" Sally asked that night when I mentioned it to her.

"Nothing big. Maybe some punch and cookies at the community center of Shoham's apartment complex. I'll be back there for nearly three weeks. All the nurses and captains we've been able to track down—maybe a dozen—are all from the Northeast. All we'd need to do is get the Bonzers back there."

The look in Sally's eyes said: *And just who would pay for this?* We'd gotten the first of three advance checks, which in terms of bringing our Visa debt to its knees, was like trying to fell a grizzly bear with a BB gun.

"Great idea, really, but we still have to pay for your trip and—"

"It would only be maybe two or three hundred dollars," I said, sounding like a guy who routinely put on reunions for a dozen people, three time zones away, with a couple months' notice. "Maybe five," I said, thinking seven-fifty, max.

Sally nodded "OK" in that I'm-going-to-lose-this-one-so-why-bother way. Taking that as undivided support, I sent postcards to three dozen people, plus the adult children of the folks who would be our special guests: the four nurses (Bonzer, Richter, Montague, and Belanger); Dr. Bonzer, Shoham, and two enlisted men we'd come across, Charles Willin and William King; and Slanger's three nephews. The idea was to plumb the interest and see if enough people would come to even make such an event practical.

Within two weeks, the postcards started cramming my post-office box. Fifty-two people said they'd be there. I mentally gulped and came back to Sally with the, uh, good news.

"Fifty-two?" she said.

"Yeah. Nearly all the honored guests. A ton of adult children. And a dozen people from here in Eugene who helped us. Ron Palmer and his wife Linda were already going to be back East seeing their daughter, who's in the Air Force. They wanna come. So does Nathan Fendrich, of course. And Gariepy wants to bring along some World War II memorabilia to authenticate the experience for the guests."

There was a pause, Sally undoubtedly thinking the same thing I was but that I could probably more easily slough off: *what are we getting ourselves into?*

"Hey," I said, "maybe Atria would pay for it. Sort of sponsor it. It'd be chump change for them. Maybe even some publicity for the book."

But a check with Brenda triggered a "sorry" response. By now, humor was the only way to get through Atria's unwillingness to do little more than pay for overnight-express expenses when I was sending stuff to them. "I've got an idea," I said to Sally in one of my more cynical moods. "For my publicity trip back East, I'm gonna have myself Fed-Exed back east. That way Atria will pay for my trip."

Meanwhile, I kept mulling the reunion idea. For some reason, I really wanted to make this happen. And for some reason, after praying about it, I really believed the money part of it would take care of itself. That night, when the subject came up, I looked at Sally, this woman who'd already followed me way too deeply into this black hole and had every right to just tell me to stop.

"What do you think?" I asked.

She leaned forward on the couch to speak. I subconsciously bit my lip. She put her face in her hands, then removed them.

"What?" I said, having no idea where she was on this matter.

"With fifty-two people," she finally said—I braced for the worst—"we're going to need more than some community center. We're going to need a hotel ballroom."

I'd been thinking the same thing. "And you're OK with that?"

She nodded yes.

"I think it needs to be a bit more than a reunion," I said. "I think we call it a tribute. Show the DVD. Introduce each person. I'll bet we could get some people from the Army Nurse Corps to make some presentations."

"Maybe have a little cluster of American flags for centerpieces," Sally said.

"Put up some photos on the walls," I said. "Giant posters of them all."

Within a week, we'd booked a banquet room at the Quality Hotel Courthouse Plaza, a decent place I'd stayed at in Arlington, Virginia, while doing research. Sally jumped in to help plan the dinner menu, the table arrangements, and who would sit where.

We chose the cheapest entrees on the $26.95-per-guest "Jefferson Plated Dinner": grilled chicken and prawns with sweet basil sauce and mango relish, roasted garlic mashed potatoes, and steamed garden vegetables—complete with, yikes, automatic nineteen percent gratuity. Soon, I was signing a three-page catering contract obligating us to costs that approached nearly $3,000.

"Uh, who's paying for this again?" Sally asked.

"Don't worry, it'll all work out," I said, my voice sounding just like my father's when he'd tell us that the black clouds on the Cascade horizon would produce only a "little squall" shortly before a three-hour downpour turned our campsite into a federal disaster area.

Meanwhile, I found a D.C. bus company that, the morning after the banquet, would have an air-conditioned carriage to take us all on a tour of the new World War II Memorial and the Women in Military Service for America memorial. We would see the two memorials on June 10, 2004, sixty years, to the day, that the Forty-fifth's nurses piled out of their landing craft at Normandy.

When friends heard about our plans, they'd almost always ask the same thing: *Who's paying for this?* And, for some reason, I kept saying: "That'll take care of itself."

Clearly, Atria wasn't going to help. Its idea of promotion—at least in my case—was sending books and press releases to a few hundred "influencers" whose names and addresses I sent to them. The publisher got me signings at the Boston Borders and the Smithsonian, would ultimately pay for a few nights' lodging in Boston for one publicity event, and, of course, paid for my overnight-freight expenses. Nearly everything else came out of my wallet. I'd gotten all six book endorsements on my own. And our team wrote, produced, filmed, edited, packaged, sent, and paid for the hundreds of DVDs.

But, weirdly, I always felt this amazing respect from Atria's Brenda Copeland—and respected her, sensing that she would have done more if she could have. In March, after meeting her at a writers' workshop on Whidbey Island in Washington state and telling the *American Nightingale* story to a class, she e-mailed me: "You're Ward Cleaver in combat boots."

Any bitterness on my part about Atria's lack of promotional

help was buffered by a reality that I couldn't dismiss. When nobody else believed in this book enough to publish it, Atria did. Just like when no other agents believed in this book, Ted Weinstein did. For both acts of faith, I couldn't help but be forever grateful.

THE LETTER had a Manchester, New Hampshire, return address. It was from Betty Belanger, one of the four nurses. I opened it one afternoon in early April, about a month before the book was due out and two months before the tribute to the nurses in D.C. would be held.

> Dear Bob,
> Charlie and I can hardly wait for June, to see our old pals again after sixty years. Thanks so much for bringing this all together. It'll be such fun! Here's a little something to help defray expenses.
> Love, Betty

The "something" was a check for $200. I was awed. The next morning, en route to work, I was going to deposit it at my credit union when a stab of guilt poked me. You can't take money from someone who's going to be an honored guest. That's just not right. That night, after tearing up the check, I wrote her a note on my new *American Nightingale* stationery.

> Dear Betty,
> Thanks so much for your letter. And your gift, too. It moved me. But you've already given. You and the others in the 45th gave at Normandy and thirty other stops between there and Czechoslovakia, patching up wounded soldiers. For just this once, let us give to you. See you in June!
> Sincerely, Bob Welch

Three days later, I was speaking to a Learning in Retirement group in left-leaning Eugene, where any mention of war was generally greeted with great cynicism, even more so at a time when America was fighting in Afghanistan and Iraq. I spoke about Slanger. Showed the DVD. And, when finished, was taking questions from the audience, which had seemed moved by the presentation.

"I have a question," said a woman in the middle of the audience of about a hundred people. "How can we give to your banquet fund?"

The question caught me by surprise. "Uh, we don't really have a banquet fund," I said.

She reached into her purse and held up a check book. "Well," she said, "you do now." And wrote out a check for $300.

Another woman stood up. "My husband fought in the Battle of the Bulge," she said. "I'd like to give to that fund, too, in his honor."

"I despise war," said another, "but these nurses need to be honored. I'd like to make a donation, too."

That evening, I walked in the door, numbed by the generosity. "You're not going to believe this," I said to Sally, then popped open the DVD case packed with checks and bills, none smaller than a ten. Her eyes widened.

"What'd you do?" she asked. "Rob a bank?"

I told her the story. "I never asked for a cent of this," I said. "Honest."

Sally went for the calculator. The total came to $1,450.

Chapter 13

April 15-May 25, 2004
Eugene, Oregon

Fame is a vapor, popularity an accident; the only earthly certainty is oblivion.

—Mark Twain

WHEN THE BOOK galleys arrived for me to correct, I was too tired to be elated—or, for that matter, to be anguished that my name was misspelled "Bob Welsh" on the top of every lefthand page. I had been sowing promotional seeds for three months and didn't have a single out-of-town sprout to show for it—interviews, talks, nothing. "This," I wrote in my journal, "is far harder than I imagined." I kept making phone calls. Sending e-mails. Mailing promotional packages.

Setting up speaking events was easy in the Eugene area where I'd been at the newspaper fifteen years—and seemingly impossible on the East Coast despite the fact that May-June World War II fervor was going to be in full swing. Beyond a speaking gig at Boston University's nursing archives in late April, few events were getting scheduled. And time was running out.

Looking at what was left in my promotional "budget," I hired a publicist to fan some flames for me. But even if that somehow buoyed my hopes, I kept getting the feeling that the Welch-Atria relationship was one of those he-likes-her-more-than-she-likes-him deals.

It didn't help matters that I couldn't nail a single Red Sox ticket for late May when I'd be in Boston as part of the "eighteen-day promotional tour," which sounded far more high-brow than it was. I'd even hit up Alex Rankin, the Boston University nursing archives assistant director who I'd gotten to know. His response was enlightening about the Red Sox, if not encouraging about a ticket:

> The Red Sox, as you know, are an amazing team. Some people around here would even go as far as saying that they are beyond the World Series at this point. The team is noble and leaves everything on the field. But the fans, the story is in the fans.
>
> Eighty-six years is a long time to stew on the fated turmoil of a loved one. Most fans say they hate this whole Bambino business but underneath the veneer, cannot help but wonder about the pattern. They can quickly flash back to Buckner and other post-season flops. The fans don't forget these things. They hold them, and to borrow from David Halberstam, chew on them like salted nuts.
>
> Red Sox fans are elephants of the game and fanatical in their devotion. In perhaps only Philadelphia or New York will you find fans willing to spend a night in jail just to tell a player exactly how bad they think he is playing, and then turn around and not hesitate to take a bullet for the player the next day. After a home run.
>
> There is no logic, no calculation to the cheering frenzy (the horribly unliterary chant "Yankees Suck" can be heard at any Boston sporting event at any time.) During home games, there are always the high profile aristocrats seated on their thrones along the baselines and the thousands of season ticket holders who have been coming to the same seat every year for decades, or the lowly fan such as myself who scrapes together the timing and luck to pick up two tickets and sneak away for a few hours to the park. The rest of the horde are fans that are for the most part living in rural-ish communities throughout New England. These fans drive with their families or friends from 1 to 12 hrs away, clutching the most expensive bleacher tickets in the country.
>
> They spend at least $25 for parking and a couple hundred on a hotel room in hopes the game isn't rained out. For many fans, a trip to the ballpark is their family vacation for the year, or their bachelor party, or their graduation present. All this amounts to heavy drinking, boisterous antics (a guaranteed minimum of 2 fights per 9

innings if the Yankee are in town), and wonderful camaraderie. Of course, no fans compare with the kind, courteous, and drunkenly friendly St. Louis fans. But Boston has an intensity I didn't feel in San Diego when the dreaded Dodgers were in town.

Fenway is a special place. A wonderland of history. In no other park can a single become a home run due to garage doors in left and center. Nowhere else does an outfield have to contend with a massive wall and a ladder where a ball can bounce from rung, to rung, to rung, to … . You get the idea. Fenway is New England's sandlot and the Sox our Sweat-hogs.

Rankin's insight only intrigued me more about this ball team I had fallen for. The season was still young. Could this be the year?

Meanwhile, back in Oregon, Sally and I took a rare break to watch *About Schmidt,* a film starring Jack Nicholson. It was about a sixty-something man who retires from the insurance business. His wife dies and he contemplates how he's living a meaningless life. So meaningless that the idea of returning to his go-through-the-motions job somehow has renewed appeal to him. But his employer won't hire him back. So he wastes his days in the routine of insignificance, the exception being a letter he occasionally writes to a young man in a Third World country to whom he's begun corresponding because he once donated money to an organization helping such people. At the movie's end, a letter arrives from the young man, thanking Schmidt for the huge difference he's made in his "foster son's" life. Schmidt had no idea what a difference he was apparently making in this single life.

It touched me deeply. I'd been thinking of my elder son, Ryan, who, only twenty-five, was nevertheless working with teenagers through Young Life, a Christian nonprofit that builds relationships with kids with the idea that God is not some white-bearded fuddy-duddy but a loving Creator who, more than rules and regulations, seeks relationship with us. Who sheds His grace on us. I fired an e-mail to him about the film:

It was an odd movie but one that makes you think. Near the end, Warren (the guy) says: 'When I die, the world will be no different than when I was alive. I've made no difference.' Then, of course, he realizes that he's made a difference in the life of this Third World 'foster' child.

You don't get many strokes in your Young Life stuff. But you're making differences in kids' lives, even if you might never know how. Even if no kid ever sends you a picture of the two of you. Never forget that. Never. Love, Dad.

Of course, as with many things in life, it was far easier for me to exhort my son about such things than to believe them for my own life.

MY CELL PHONE rang about 2 P.M. March 31. I was in my 1995 Nissan pickup, heading north on Eugene's Delta Freeway.

"Bob Welch?" said a man.

"Yes."

"This is Dr. Timothy Johnson, ABC's medical editor."

"Uh, hello." I turned on my blinker and eased to the side of the road. My heart pounded as if a retread tire had just blown and I was limping to safety. I instinctively tried to calm myself, to pretend that this was a business-as-usual sort of call, in hopes that my mouth might actually work should I attempt to reply. As if I'd just gotten off the phone with, say, CBS's Tom Brokaw and had NBC's Ann Curry on hold.

"We've seen your DVD on Frances Slanger," Johnson said, "and think this might make a good segment for *Good Morning America*."

His words were like iced water to a marathoner's lips late in the race. Johnson was serious. In my letter to him, I'd mentioned the June 9-10 tribute in Washington, D.C.

"We're considering reuniting the nurses live on the show in New York," he said.

The idea petrified me. Yes, it sounded good, but, having been in contact with some of the nurses and their families, I knew how difficult just getting them all to Washington, D.C., was proving to be. Some had already made their reservations. Throwing in a trip to New York for live TV was, in my mind, a logistical nightmare. Too fraught with things that could go wrong.

"Uh, sure, we could do that, but it's a bit risky," I said. "These women are almost ninety. You know, I'll be in Boston in April for a speaking engagement; could we tape something at that time instead?"

Johnson, it turned out, lived in Boston. He liked the idea and, after we talked further, agreed that the "live" approach might be difficult to pull off.

He e-mailed me a couple days later. "The next person you will hear from is Thea Trachtenberg, a producer extraordinaire at *Good Morning America*. She has seen the DVD, and I have filled her in on our conversation. I have a feeling this will happen. Blessings."

Two days later, she e-mailed. "I think it could be a great segment," she wrote. "I am out of the office tomorrow for Passover, but let me know when is good for you after that. Also, I'd love to get an advance copy of your book. The DVD Tim showed me made me all weepy. I can only imagine what the book will do to me." I stared at the e-mail, specifically the stuff underneath her name: "Producer, *Good Morning America*, 147 Columbus Avenue, 5th Floor, New York, NY 10023."

I fired off an e-mail to Brenda with the good news and later asked if Atria were going to increase the first-print numbers because of the *Good Morning America* publicity. As usual, in her polite but direct way, she encouraged me to keep my feet on the ground. The first-printing, as originally set, would be 9,000 books, she reaffirmed. I mentally shook my head, thinking that a tsunami was about to hit and my own publisher wasn't going to be prepared.

I needed to vent, so I e-mailed my writer friend Karen Zacharias, who was at work on a book, *After the Flag Has Been Folded*, about growing up after her father had been killed in Vietnam:

> Is it just me or is 9,000 the numerical language for "We have no confidence in your book whatsoever, Bob?" I know authors have unrealistic expectations. But, hey, I'm not asking for a first-print run of 100,000. Do the math, though: If one out of every 1,000 *Good Morning America* viewers buys the book, that's 5,000 books right there. (5 million watch it).

Wednesday I found out that renting a bus and driver to take the nurses & co. to two memorials on June 10 was going to cost

$480. Thursday I spoke to a group of Eugene business owners—business people, mind you!—and a woman pressed a check for $500 in my hand after I spoke. The people at the grassroots level get it. But Atria is still out to lunch. My publicist has landed me exactly—count them—two events, one in Boston and one in D.C. I haven't seen a single review of the book, which is due out in a few weeks. Yes, I think it's fair to say I'm getting panicky. Talk me off the ledge, please. I need to keep remembering: God is in control. Repeat, now, Bob: God is in control, God is in control.

Karen wrote back:

Bob: That's a really good mantra to repeat. You have to cling to that. Remember this book was never about Atria to begin with. It's about Frances Slanger. And God will put this book in the hands of the people who need it. If he can feed the thousands with five loaves … . I heard on NPR today that 1 million people are expected to be at the World War II event on Memorial Day. The world needs Slanger's story.

Your hope is based upon a Shepherd who owns all the pasture. Not on a publishing house that produces 9,000 books. I wish all of this weren't happening for you. But I believe that there must be a reason. Perhaps a contact you will make because you are doing all the footwork yourself, rather than relying on Atria for it.

Keep this in mind. When John Grisham started out he sold *A Time to Kill* from the trunk of his car. He couldn't get a publishing house interested in it. Still, he believed in his ability to tell the story and in the story itself. And his instincts proved right.

Hang in there, buddy. Think of how blessed your life was by the generosity of that woman who pressed $500 into your hand. Maybe she needed to feel ownership in Frances's story. You've given her the opportunity to do that. Listen, moments like these are what make life, for all its chaos, so wonderful. KZ.

She was, of course, right; I was suffering from tunnel vision, wallowing again in self-pity, forgetting the bigger picture. Fortunately, there wasn't much time for wallowing. Thea Trachtenberg e-mailed. The plan was to interview me and Irwin Sidman, the eldest Slanger nephew, in Boston. Perhaps go see Slanger's headstone in the cemetery. Run the segment in early June, maybe in conjunction with the sixtieth anniversary of the June 6, 1944, D-Day landings.

Perfect. Until she suggested we do the interviews in a "suite" at whatever hotel I was staying at in Boston. *No, no, no, I wanted to say. You don't understand. I stay at a hotel that has no suites. A hotel that, instead, has a sign on the wall saying what I'll be charged for stealing something. A hotel that offers a continental breakfast at a sushi bar. If you film at my hotel, there, behind Timothy Johnson's head, will be a sign that says, "Mechanical Room No. 3" behind which may lurk the ghost of Babe Ruth. You don't want your crew setting up at the Buckminster.*

I e-mailed Thea and was as genuine—and mildly diplomatic—as I could be. She understood completely. Days later, she e-mailed that we'd do the interviews at her hotel, the Fairmont Copley Plaza on St. James Avenue. "As of right now," she wrote, "it will be in the Presidential Suite." Meaning, of course, that I might be the show's first guest to be interviewed in a $750-a-night room—after taking a red-eye flight from the West Coast to save a hundred bucks on travel.

But on April 21, after my three hours of sleep, there I was, having gotten out of the cab in the heart of Boston's exclusive Back Bay district, standing in front of a hotel whose entrance was guarded by a couple of those giant golden lions: all stone and columns and regal burgundy awnings and bellhops looking at me with more respect than I deserved. I walked inside. Marble pillars in pink and black swirls flanked a chandelier that had more individual lights on it than the entire Hotel Buckminster had working bulbs. The gold-plated ceiling was about fifteen feet high. Every chair, plant, and table was placed in perfect symmetry with one like it across a blue and tan rug done in feather-like patterns.

I stood in front of the suite where the interview would be. I breathed deep, the way Red Sox first baseman Bill Buckner might have as he stood on the cusp of World Series fame, just before that easy grounder, then knocked on the door.

"Hi," said Thea Trachtenberg, the *Good Morning America* producer.

"So, you're more than just someone on the other end of an e-mail, huh?" I said, shaking her hand.

"Apparently so," said Trachtenberg, a thirty-five-year-old Wesleyan University graduate. "Would you like something to eat? We have fruit, croissants, orange juice."

She pointed to a display of food that could have fed the entire newsroom back in Eugene. All I could think of was the $18.50 I'd just spent for fruit, croissants, and orange juice, not including tip.

In walked Dr. Timothy Johnson. Like Trachtenberg, he was far more genuine, warm, and personable than I'd expected. Gentle. Humble. Marcus Welby, M.D., with a lapel microphone.

I relaxed in a bedroom-turned-hospitality suite with Irwin Sidman, Slanger's nephew, who would be interviewed first. In the living room next door, four light, sound, and camera people adjusted equipment, did sound bites, positioned chairs. Trachtenberg calmly orchestrated it all. The crew spent five minutes deciding what to put on a fireplace mantel, finally settling on a wicker basket.

I watched Irwin being interviewed. He did wonderfully by simply being himself, a guy who'd never gotten over the loss of his aunt. "She was my hero," he said, blinking back tears. As I watched the interview, I thought of how far we'd come from that night in December 2000 when I'd first called him.

I was next. One of the crew members touched up my face with makeup. ("Hey, while you're at it, could you shrink my earlobes?") Johnson drew up a chair in front of me surprisingly tight—our knees were almost touching—and, with the camera rolling, started asking me question after question, most of them good, particularly one that took me far beyond the moment to the deeper part of this story: "If Frances Slanger were alive today, what one question would you ask her?"

I didn't hesitate. "I'd ask her why, given her background, she'd turned out so selfless. Why she hadn't become bitter like so many people would if they were raised in poverty and squalor amid the stench of decaying bodies of soldiers. Why, when she applied for Boston City Hospital's School of Nursing, she'd written: 'I've always wanted to serve those less fortunate than I?' Seems to me she was pretty 'less fortunate' to begin with."

Once, he stopped the interview to point out I had perspiration on my upper lip. (So much for "Never let 'em see you sweat.") A few other times, he was bothered by noise from outside construction work. But, well-prepped by Trachtenberg and having read at least portions of the book, he made the interview a smooth-flowing conversation. Sitting cross-legged on a chair, Trachtenberg watched a small TV monitor, occasionally making minor suggestions.

We then went outside where Johnson and I were filmed walking across Copley Plaza, pretending we were deep in discussion when actually we were just saying things like, "So, we just walk along like this and talk and viewers think we're saying deep things when we're actually just flapping our lips." The piece would air sometime in early June. Back in the suite, I ate a few more pieces of pineapple—each bite taking some sting off the $18.50 I'd spent downstairs—and chatted with Johnson as the equipment guys put away their stuff.

"That DVD," Johnson said, "is what really attracted us to this story. Just curious, how much did you spend on it?"

"Oh, about $14.95," I said.

"You mean, fifteen hundred dollars?"

"No, like fourteen dollars and ninety-five cents. That's what it cost to make our kitchen look like a studio with that black piece of fabric for a backdrop."

Johnson smiled and shook his head. "It worked."

"Remember that part where Nathan Fendrich is talking about the night Slanger died?" I asked.

He squinted as if trying to remember. "Anyway," I said, "you hear these *thump-thump-thumps* in the background. It sounds like artillery fire. But it was actually one of our cats scratching on the kitchen door, wanting in."

Johnson laughed. We parted. I took the "T" subway back to the Buckminster, popping up near the Kenmore Square Barnes & Noble where I'd vowed to return someday to do a book-signing and where I had an appointment for exactly that on June 3. At the hotel, I called Sally with the news that the interview had gone well, prayed a quiet prayer of thanks, and changed back into my jeans and a sweatshirt, which always feels so good after a suit and stiff shoes. Now, I thought, let the celebration begin.

I left the Buckminster and walked across the Interstate-90 overpass to Fenway Park. The Red Sox were out of town, but the souvenir shop was open. I bought my first-ever Red Sox shirt, then went to a hole-in-the-wall hot dog stand next door and got the biggest hot dog they had. The sun was out. It had been a long three-plus years. But as I walked past Fenway, life, for now, couldn't have tasted more delicious.

IT ARRIVED at our house, via Airborne Express, at 10:43 A.M. on May 8, 2004: the first hardback copy of *American Nightingale* I'd seen, three and a half years since those notes jotted on a Wendy's napkin. Being obsessive compulsive, I photographed the package before opening it, then, that evening, read the entire book. I found four minor glitches and one major snafu: a misspelling of Charles Willin's last name—Willen instead of the correct Willin. (Despite our fact-checking and at least two Atria editors combing the book, we ultimately would wind up finding eight errors after publication.) But all in all, it looked good. It felt good. It even smelled good.

Four days later, Karen West, the owner of Eugene's largest independent book store, called. A box of books had arrived. I bought the first book, saved the receipt, and drove to the Bonzer's house to present it to Sallylou and John. She had tears in her eyes.

In the weeks before my trip back east to launch the book, everything started falling into place. The books began selling on amazon.com, our "rank" plummeting—the lower the better—deliciously from 2.4 million to 77,000 almost overnight. A Web site called "Book Babes" weighed in with our first review, saying *Nightingale* had "the golden cast of *Saving Private Ryan.*" *The Oregonian* added it to its "Hot Pick" list and called it "fascinating." Jim McKone, who did reviews for *The Monitor* in McAllen, Texas wrote:

> Across 60 years I must have read around 3,000 books. This is the only one I remember that brought tears to my eyes within the first two pages, then in the middle, again at the end. It is told with quotes and humor and horror, in crisp passages like *1984* or *War and Peace*, novels of heroism and brutal details.

A French TV network, hearing about the book because of some

connection to Betty Belanger in New Hampshire, called to set up interviews with Sallylou Bonzer and I. *Good Morning America* sent a crew to Eugene to get "B roll" shots of the Bonzers at their house and me at my house, working on my laptop computer in my cluttered office. Later they filmed me standing on my porch and walking down the street.

Ten days before my trip to the East Coast, Sally and I had a book-debut dinner for the local people who'd helped me research and write the book and for their spouses. Fifteen people total. We watched the DVD, presented each person with an autographed copy, and talked about the eighteen-day promotional trip: first I'd go to Washington, D.C., for the unveiling of the new World War II Memorial, then to Boston for the Barnes & Noble book-signing and, I hoped, other events; finally, back to Washington, D.C., for the sixty-year anniversary of D-Day and the June 9-10 tribute to the nurses, an event that nearly everyone gathered at our house planned to attend.

Suddenly, the *Nightingale* experience was rising to a whole new level. For months, my friend, Dick Foth, who had all sorts of connections to D.C. big-wigs, had been trading phone calls and e-mails with me about the banquet and, specifically, about a Retired Major General Mick Kicklighter's willingness to participate. I was amazed that Kicklighter, the Assistant Secretary for Veterans' Affairs, was finding time for us on his schedule; he was, Foth said, among those in charge of rebuilding Iraq. At times, he reported directly to the president himself. Once, while waiting for gas at a 76 station, I called Foth. He told me he couldn't talk on his cell phone at the moment. "Uh, security reasons," he said.

"Oh," I said, watching the kid outside wipe the windshield of my pickup 2,500 miles away and thinking about myself as a security threat. "I understand."

I sent copies of books to everyone who I could think of who'd offered me significant help. My only disappointment was that I couldn't track down Emory Massman, the author of the hospital-ships book, to get an address. He was the guy who had pointed me to the Boston University nursing archives, the key in finding the Slanger "mother lode" of information, the infamous "two suitcases."

At my first signing event, sponsored by *The Register-Guard,* 180 books sold. The next night, our friends Ann and Jason Schar hosted an outdoor, invitation-only event at their country home. More than a hundred books sold. The weather was perfect: clear, temperature in the mid-seventies. Later, I wrote in my journal:

> Tonight was so wonderful, sort of like the fruits of a long journey: seeing friends and family gathered with me to celebrate the book. I will never forget the great people, great food, and great weather.

Later that night, the Oregon sky opened up. It started to rain.

Chapter 14

May 25-June 11, 2004
Washington, D.C., and Boston

The life of faith is not a life of mounting up with wings, but a life of walking and not fainting.
— Oswald Chambers

Nobody dast blame this man. A salesman is got to dream, boy. It comes with the territory.
—Arthur Miller, *Death of a Salesman*

Somehow the Sox fulfill the notion that we live in a fallen world. It's as though we assume they're here to provide us with more pain.
—A. Barlett Giamatti, a native New Englander and former commissioner of baseball

IT WAS THE WORLD WAR II generation's last hurrah, a gathering of some 100,000 of them in Washington, D.C., for the dedication of the World War II Memorial. None, I presumed, had heard of a just-released book called *American Nightingale*. I would do what I could to try and change that.

Frankly, after more than six months of trying to drum up interest in the book on my own, I'd hoped to land at the beachhead with a bit more backup. I had book-signings at two major bookstores in Boston, a speaking engagement at a Women in Military Service for America luncheon in Arlington, Virginia, and a D-Day signing at the Smithsonian Institute. That's it. Any other publicity on the East Coast was going to have to be the result of seat-of-the-pants imagination, roll-up-the-sleeves determination, and down-on-the-knees prayer.

The Saturday, May 29 dedication unfolded with the scope of a World War II Woodstock. Massive blocks of seating areas stretched out across the National Mall, dominated by eighty-plus-year-old World War II vets, spouses, and adult children. Because I would write about the event for *The Register-Guard*, I had, months before, secured press credentials.

With the crowd spread out for nearly half a mile, the dedication experience was, for most, like watching a giant in-flight movie, the eight jumbo screens representing the drop-down video monitors you get on some jets.

The ceremony was organized. Dignified. Solemn but hopeful. A fitting last hurrah to a generation that, as President George W. Bush told the crowd, "gave the best years of their lives to the greatest mission their country ever accepted." But just as the war itself was fought and won far from the chambers of the elite, so was the most compelling story of this four-day commemoration found far beyond the stage, the billboard-sized LCDs, and the tidy speeches of the chosen few.

It was found in baby boomer Gary Noteware of Boston, pushing the wheelchair of his eighty-four-year-old father, Dayton, who once serviced planes for the U.S. Air Force. In the cragged face of a man in a *U.S.S. Rodman* hat, tears streaming as he sang "My Country 'Tis of Thee," one hand clutching a postcard-sized American flag on a pencil-sized stick. On the back shirt of thirty-three-year-old Deborah Wyttenbach of Reston, Virginia: "Capt. William F. Jerman Jr. KIA Feb. 22, 1942. My grandfather, my hero."

The nearly two-hour ceremony was a predictable package of speeches, music, and pageantry, the crescendo being a four-jet flyover during the singing of "God Bless America." But I won't remember that as well as I'll remember the smell of pipe tobacco, which, for some of us, brought back memories of World War II fathers (navy) no longer here. I'll remember the looks in the eyes of men who, sixty years ago, saw too much—and now scanned bulletin boards of "look-me-up" notes, with the slim hopes of finding buddies they remembered from Bastogne or Corregidor or Pearl Harbor.

"What outfit were you with?" one man said to another. "Mine sweeper?"

"Your eye is good," came the reply. And the two were suddenly long-lost friends.

I'll remember a thirty-something woman grabbing the hand of

an eighty-something man during a concert, the two of them swing-dancing beneath the Washington Monument. Fifty years difference in age; identical smiles.

The nine speakers spoke well, though none reached the emotional depths that the simple playing of taps did. President Bush talked longest but came across as somewhat reserved. Actor Tom Hanks tactfully took patriotism to a beyond-the-flag level. And NBC anchor Tom Brokaw was refreshingly real. Noting his bond with the World War II generation that he honored in *The Greatest Generation*, he said, "I'm humbled by our relationship."

In the end, that's what this was all about. Courage. Sacrifice. Honor. Yes. But, above all, relationships. Between old war buddies. Between a "we-just-did-what-we-had-to" generation and its "do-your-own-thing" children. Between people from the Bronx and people from Boise. Between a country and the 16 million veterans who served in World War II, 12 million of whom had already passed on.

Indeed, this weekend's events were, in essence, the proverbial last visit to the hospital; more than a thousand veterans were dying each day. And so you noticed a sense of urgency as volunteers for the Veterans History Project fanned out, tape recorders in hands, to mine the untold stories of these men and women.

Respect permeated the place. You saw it in the hundreds of Vietnam vets who rolled into town on motorcycles, part of an L.A.-to-Washington "Rolling Thunder" bike brigade. You saw it in boomers—imagine the opening cemetery scene of *Saving Private Ryan* on a continuos loop—who were learning, some for the first time, what this meant to their mothers and fathers. You even saw it in the cynical media, which, at least in my M-1 section, joined to offer a standing ovation to honor the men and women for whom the memorial is dedicated.

Beyond always carrying a copy of my book and conspicuously holding it up, cover out, as I pretended to scan the crowd for someone, I did nothing to promote *Nightingale* that day. I was too caught up in the tribute.

Earlier, World War II veteran Dayton Noteware, sitting in his wheelchair, pondered only for a moment a question I asked about what had been most meaningful to him. "The way so many young people have come up to me, stuck out their hands and said thank you," he said. "It took me by surprise."

I'll remember that moment. And the moth-bally smell of the navy blues worn by seventy-seven-year-old Bill Clark of Pagosa Springs, Colorado. The click of a zillion photos. The daughter of an army nurse at a luncheon filming her mother as if she were some Hollywood star. The loudspeaker playing "I'll Be Seeing You" as folks headed for buses and the Metro after the ceremony. And, finally, I'll remember sitting on the subway and seeing a man in a "101st Airborne Division" cap who suddenly realized he and his wife were on the Orange Line and needed to be on the Blue Line. The man looked confused, embarrassed, stymied.

Without hesitation, a young woman put down her book and re-assured them they could transfer at the next stop. They thanked her profusely. Soon, the stop came. The doors opened. The couple left. And the train continued on, someone else quickly taking their seats. Gone. But not forgotten.

I returned to my Arlington hotel that evening on the Metro and, to stave off loneliness, grabbed a bite at a sidewalk cafe as dusk became night. At a table next to me, a handful of "Rolling Thunder" motorcycle guys downed beers and raised the noise level from evening small-talk to an occasional whoop and holler, the kind of high spirits you'd expect from guys who'd just driven up to three thousand miles across the country to honor their partners in arms.

Soon, a white-haired man in a World War II hat shuffled down the sidewalk with, I presume, his wife. Suddenly, the Thunder stopped. To a man, the Vietnam vets stood and saluted.

MY FIRST DAY of promoting the book was a disaster. My new, compact printer I'd brought along was defective so I had to shell out $60 to buy another one, then figure out how to get both home while not exceeding the airline weight limit. And a thirty-count box of *American Nightingale* books arrived with exactly seven books in it, the tattered cardboard looking as if it had been ripped apart by Godzilla.

My first event was a disaster, too. I'd imagined hundreds of army nurses lined up to buy books after I spoke at a Women in

Military Service for America luncheon at WIMSA's memorial adjacent to Arlington National Cemetery. Instead, the theater was sprinkled with a crowd of perhaps a few dozen. Only a handful of books sold.

Other highlights or lowlights, depending on your point of view: White House correspondent Helen Thomas rankling the luncheon crowd with an anti-Bush speech, and me mistaking a childhood heart throb for someone else. She was sitting two tables away at the luncheon. "And now," the emcee said, "I'd like to recognize a woman who's been so supportive to women in the military: Connie Stevens!"

My heart fluttered like baseball cards in the spokes of my old Schwinn. As she stood to the applause of hundreds, I remembered that magical moment in 1962 when I had come home from Emery's IGA Foodliner in Corvallis, clutching the first 45 record I'd ever bought. I was eight years old. And in love for the first time. The song on that MGM record was "Vacation."

Put away the books, we're out of school
The weather's warm but we'll play it cool
We're on vacation, havin' lots of fun
V-A-C-A-T-I-O-N in the summer sun.

As the clapping faded, I looked at her. She glanced at me, almost as if she knew me. Sure, I was a married man but there was no turning back: When this luncheon was over, I wanted my photo taken with my arm around Connie Stevens.

This puppy-dog love is not my nature. Famous people are no different from you and me: just wealthier, more beautiful, more powerful, and more often to be stopped in public by some doting jerk who says something stupid like, "When I was a kid ... ."

None of which would dissuade me from meeting my 1962 heartthrob. I etched a plan in my mind: Let the Southern women in their flashing red, white, and blue flag-pins get their cheesy photos, then swoop in with a more dignified approach.

After 10 minutes, she shook the giggly gadflies and strode purposefully toward the exit, with just enough of a sideways glance to suggest she knew I was coming. And would welcome me as if she, too, had been waiting for this moment. I handed my camera to a stranger with orders to shoot on sight. Showtime!

"I can't believe it's you!" I blurted out. "How 'bout a photo?" I put my arm around Connie and smiled big. She put her arm around me and smiled, too. "When I was a kid, your song, 'Vacation,' was the first 45 I ever bought!" I gushed.

There was a slight pause, the kind of worrisome pause you get when you first see the little beach ball on your Macintosh spinning and realize your computer is locked up.

"You must mean 'Sixteen Reasons,' " she said, forcing a smile between slightly clenched teeth. Her touch on me weakened. "I didn't do 'Vacation' "

Oh. My. Gosh. I had mistaken Connie Stevens for another singer from the same era, Connie *Francis*, my true heartthrob! The beach ball kept spinning.

"Uh, yeah, right, of course, 'Sixteen Reasons,' " I stammered unconvincingly.

My smile twitched on and off like a wire-shorted lamp. Hers dimmed considerably. The woman with my camera couldn't get it to work. Dead battery. In a moment, Connie was gone, out the door. And out of my life. Forever. I bent over and buried my head in my hands, not knowing whether to laugh or cry.

ON SUNDAY, back at the National Mall, I finally started getting some media traction. My tactics were simple: start talking about *American Nightingale* to anybody who might listen, but particularly to folks with TV cameras and notebooks and microphones, of which there were many. My journalistic background helped immensely; I knew how to jump-start conversations and quickly steer that conversation to, in this case, a heroic World War II nurse. It was simple because I believed so deeply in the story and it was so refreshingly different from other World War II stories: a Jewish nurse. A late-night letter. Her death. The letter getting published. Broken-hearted GIs. And a ship named in her honor.

The women-in-World-War-II angle was a fresh one; few people knew that 350,000 women had served in armed forces during the war, more than 50,000 as nurses. Sixteen died in combat. Eighty-one were held as prisoners of war. I doubt *New York Times* columnist Maureen Dowd knew as much when she wrote that this generation "can't stop gushing and celebrating themselves," their latest alleged chest-thumping being "a kitschy memorial to honor themselves."

These women deserved honoring and *American Nightingale* would provide it for them. I talked myself into a spot on a Washington, D.C., FOX network affiliate for later in the week after my return from Boston. I was hopeful about getting to be on "Voice of America," a public-broadcast radio network that seemed intrigued with the story. And a producer for CBS's *This Morning*, through a cameraman, OK'd me calling him after Memorial Day about a possible appearance on that show.

The perfect set-up, of course, would have been to just plunk down at a table with a dozen boxes of *American Nightingales*, a big sign, and start selling and autographing books. But the four-day World War II event had strict commercial guidelines and that wasn't allowed. Still, the Mall was wall-to-wall in covered tents in which World War II vets were gathering to find old buddies, listen to panel discussions, and peruse displays.

At a panel discussion on women of World War II, I discretely went from row-to-row during the event, crouching on a single knee to hand the end person a dozen or so *American Nightingale* postcards and ask that they be passed down. Without hesitation, the person did so, as if I were some official World War II Memorial representative. I remember thinking: *Like taking candy from a baby.* Later in my journal I wrote: "I feel so cheap. But I'm a desperate man."

On that one day, walking around the National Mall, I passed out more than 500 postcards. I spent nearly ten hours talking to people about the book, handing out business cards and postcards, and getting people's names if they had any sort of connection that might help me. As evening arrived, before heading for the Metro to return to my hotel, I took one last glance inside the white tent where I'd passed out hundreds of postcards to the audience at the morning panel discussion. The floor was littered with hundreds of them, at least one folded into a paper airplane.

Maybe this wasn't going to be as easy as I thought.

I TOUCHED DOWN in Boston on Memorial Day morning and took a cab to my usual hangout, the Hotel Buckminster. This was going to be a great week. I would, later this afternoon, treat myself to a Red Sox-Orioles game at Fenway; I'd finally scrounged up a $50 ticket over the phone. Boston was leading the American League's East Division. Sox fans were growing hopeful again. On Friday, I would get to watch the *Good Morning America* piece that Thea Trachtenberg had told me would run in conjunction with the sixty-year anniversary of D-Day the following Sunday, June 6.

For now, I wanted to see the stacks of *American Nightingales* in the Boston University Barnes & Noble store where, three years before, I'd vowed to someday have a book-signing. It took me ten minutes to find the book. And it was, indeed, just one: in the Military section, second floor.

What was going on? I hadn't expected a full front window display, but bookstores, the week before an event, usually find a prominent spot for a featured book.

"Excuse me," I said to a clerk. "I'm Bob Welch, author of *American Nightingale*. I have a book-signing here on Thursday night and am concerned that I saw only a single copy up in Military."

"Book-signing?" he said. "We pulled the plug on all summer book-signings a month ago. I wonder if someone didn't get the word to you."

I was momentarily speechless. "Are you sure?" I asked.

"Quite sure," he said. "I'm sorry. Someone should have told you."

"I'm sorry, too," I said, reminding myself that it wasn't this guy's fault. "Look, I'm all the way from Oregon. I've sent out more than 200 postcards to people here in Boston—extended family of this nurse I wrote about, friends of the family, nurses, media. I think the bookstore owes it to them to hold the event, even if only, like, four people show up."

He looked at me with an "are-you-serious?" expression. I returned a polite "yes-I-am" expression.

"Well, let's see," he said. "It's Monday. I suppose we could try to get books over-nighted from your publisher tomorrow."

"I think that'd be great," I said. "I'm staying across the street at the Buckminster. I'll be here Thursday night as planned."

The Red Sox got drubbed that afternoon 13-4 by the Orioles to fall out of the top spot in the AL East—as it would turn out, for the rest of the season. Oh, well, maybe next year.

The next morning, Tuesday, at 7 A.M., I turned my hotel room into *Nightingale* Central: a desk to work from surrounded by suitcases full of books, promotional DVDs, and padded mailing envelopes. (At year's end, my tax records would show I sent ninety-two FedEx or DSL packages involving *American Nightingale* in 2004.) I attached my cell-phone ear plug, pulled out my laptop, and started calling every Boston contact I had in an attempt to drum up attention for the book. The laptop was, for now, my life: every appointment, every phone number, every e-mail address was stored inside the white Macintosh iBook. Sally would joke: *It's your brain.*

By that afternoon, I felt like a Boy Scout trying to get a fire started using only two sticks. After a dozen calls, all I had was an interview with a *Boston Globe* rookie reporter, a Harvard grad who agreed to meet with Irwin and me at the Summer Shack, a well-known Boston lobster restaurant. The interview went well, even if my journalistic radar sensed this was a story going deep inside some back section. I wanted to say:

This book is the perfect storm of time and place—a heroic Boston nurse, the forgotten heroine of Normandy, being remembered on the sixty-year anniversary of the invasion. At least give it the cover of the Books section. A few days later, the bittersweet truth: we made the *Boston Globe*—on Page S-8. I had no idea a newspaper could even have that many sections. *S-8?* But it was true.

The next night, I showed up for my long-awaited signing at the Boston University Barnes & Noble. The books showed up. So did four people.

Alas, the day would get worse. Back at the hotel, I scanned my e-mail before heading out to dinner with Ed Schwartz, the son of Frances Slanger's friend, Dr. Isadore Schwartz. What I saw stunned me. CIA Director George Tenet, dogged by controversies over a string of U.S. intelligence setbacks, had resigned. That in itself wasn't earth-shattering to me, a guy who wasn't particularly political, but its ramifications were. An e-mail from Thea Trachtenberg said *Good Morning America* would be concentrating on the Tenet story the next morning. Something in the show's lineup had to give. That something would be *American Nightingale*.

WAITING FOR an early flight from Boston's Logan International Airport back to Washington, D.C., two days later, I thought: *This isn't happening. Please tell me this isn't happening.* An e-mail update from Thea had been at least hopeful; she thought the segment would air Monday, June 7, the day after the sixty-year anniversary of the invasion. But by now my mind was occupied with another crisis: my laptop computer had died.

I had been checking on-line about when Sally's flight was to arrive in Washington, D.C., later that evening and going over some plans for Thursday's tribute to the nurses when, zap, the screen had gone dark. I'd pressed every defibrillating set of keys I knew—keys that always seemed to bring it back from its "sleep" mode—but this time it wasn't waking up. The contact information for a D.C. television show Sallylou Bonzer and I were to be on later in the week: entombed. The name of the *Washington Times* reporter who had expressed some interest in covering the banquet: entombed. Dozens of other must-have bits of information for the last half of the trip, including my speech, schedule, and bus-contact names for the banquet and memorial tour: entombed.

Worse, it wasn't like at home, where I worked at a newspaper loaded with Mac experts whom I was forever calling in as "lifelines." Amid thousands of people around me in this airport, I felt totally alone. And it wasn't like I had lots of time to devote to getting this thing fixed, should I even find an Apple Store when I arrived in D.C. Finally, I thought: What if the computer is truly dead, the info irretrievable? In my go-go-go mode of recent months, I hadn't taken time to back up a thing. Stupid me.

The only even slightly good news was that, the previous night, I had sent 600 e-mails to friends, family, and folks who'd purchased books from me in the past to tell them the *Good Morning America* segment was being pushed back from June 4. "Hey," I had e-mailed back to Thea after she'd told me about the postponement, "I'm honored to be on the show whether it runs now or at 3:30 A.M. only in Cleveland. Happy weekend, kid."

"Don't be honored," she'd written back. "You tell a good story and you sell it well. You did a great job of being your own public relations person for this book. P.S. I love that you called me kid. You are officially my favorite interview subject."

If her warm response had taken some of the postponement sting away, the following morning's computer crash had my stomach broiling. I seemed so close to grabbing the proverbial brass ring on this book project. Why did it seem like I wasn't going to ever quite get it? Why did God seem to be teasing me with these trips to the mountain top, only to allow me to slide back down just as I reached the pinnacle? Why did I seem destined to be the second coming of my father, whose *Trout in the High Country* movie was now gathering dust in our carport shed alongside basketballs, tire chains, and old college textbooks?

At times during the *Nightingale* journey, I had found myself so close to the World War II people I was writing about—so close to their story of sloshing through the mud of Normandy and deep into France and Belgium—that they had become my reference points. Now, I pictured Fred Michalove, wandering off by himself, despondent, his tender-hearted emotions frayed by weeks of death. In Stephen Ambrose's book, *Band of Brothers*, such moments were called "the breaking point." Times when soldiers were so deeply wracked by war that they seemingly couldn't go on. Emotionally, that's where I was at this moment, given the Barnes & Noble fiasco, the *Good Morning America* postponement and, now, the computer crash: at the breaking point.

But, as I sat there, worrying, I slowly realized the ridiculousness of such a comparison. I thought: *You don't have a problem, Welch. Michalove had a problem. War: that's a problem. Death: that's a problem. You have a comatose computer and a delayed date on* Good Morning America. *Perspective, pal. Climb out of your pathetic pit of self-pity.*

Author Oswald Chambers said it well: "No sin is worse than the sin of self pity because it removes God from the throne of our lives, replacing Him with our own self interests. It causes us to open our mouths only to complain, and we simply become spiritual sponges—always absorbing, never giving, and never being satisfied. And there is nothing lovely or generous about our lives."

Shamed by daring compare myself to Michalove got my chin off the ground. By the time we'd touched down at National Airport at 9 A.M., I had a plan. Because it was Saturday and Apple stores were likely closed Sunday, I had to get the thing fixed that day. Do or die. On Monday, I needed to be going full throttle with publicity and preparation for the Thursday night tribute; there wouldn't be time for computer glitches. Now, the image in my mind was of Houdini. OK, so this time I not only was going to be placed in a coffin with chains around it, but the coffin was going to be dropped by crane to the bottom of an icy river. *Relax. I can do this. I can get out. I can survive.*

I had already decided that, if push came to shove, I would play the "desperate author" card. I would offer a $50 tip to whatever twenty-something MacGenius could resurrect my iBook. Arriving at my Arlington hotel, I flipped through the Yellow Pages. I not only found an Apple Store, but one with a "genius bar," the fix-it centers featuring folks who were the computer world's answer to navy SEALs. And it was in the Clarenden section of Arlington, only a few miles from my hotel. I arrived just as the store was opening, surprised to realize that I wasn't the only one needing an urgent-care facility on this Saturday morning. I checked in my computer, got in the "queue," and, realizing it would be a while before my slotted time, headed for a nearby Barnes & Noble to wait.

That afternoon I realized something profound and sobering: when it comes to book sales, the gap between my imagination and reality was the Grand Canyon in width. Back in Eugene, when thinking of a bookstore like a Barnes & Noble in Arlington, I might imagine my book prominently displayed on an end cap, being passed by thousands of would-be buyers and being purchased by dozens of people, diplomats among them.

Reality was far different. Once I found my books on this June afternoon—two copies, second floor, Military section, spine out, just like in Boston, with the "20% off" sticker conveniently placed over the endorsement from *Flags of Our Fathers* author James Bradley—I planted myself nearby to watch nobody go near them. I read, drank hot chocolate, and melted into a puddle of quiet despair.

Not only was the book in a far-off, second-floor nook, but because nonfiction is filed alphabetically, it was shelved in the lower right section. I'd encountered the same setup in every store I'd been to: my books—assuming there was more than one—perfectly positioned for, say, a right-leaning two-year-old. Why couldn't my mother have married a guy named Andrew Aardvark and named me Andrew Jr.?

In an hour's time, only a dozen or so people even moved through the section. Nobody even looked at my book. I wanted to stand up on my chair and say: *Listen up, folks! I worked on* American Nightingale *for more than three years! I'm nearly forty thousand bucks in the hole! At the moment, my computer with all the info for this rather pathetic, self-paid "book tour" is on its death bed. I drew four people for a signing at a store like this in Boston; my Corvallis High classmate Jon* (Into Thin Air) *Krakauer gets twice that interest while waiting in line at a Trader Joe's! So have a clue and buy it, please.*

Instead, being a sophisticated author, I did the only thing I could do: looked around to see if anyone might notice, then walked over to my two books. I pretended to be looking at them—*hmmm, this looks like a really good book*—then casually placed the two copies on an eye-level shelf that had a bit of extra room. Cover out. Probably right in front of some author named Andrew Aardvark.

You sit in a Barnes & Noble for an afternoon and realize that, without publicity, without people knowing about your book, you have a better chance of being named *People* magazine's "Sexiest Man of the Year" than your book has of being purchased. And yet, when doing the math, you also realize you need to sell lots of books to even earn back the $20,000 advance. My contract guaranteed me 10% of the catalog retail price on the first 5,000 sold, 12½% on the next 10,000 copies and 15% thereafter. Bottom line: initially, I would get $2.20 of every $22 hardback book sold, eventually perhaps as much as $3.30 per book—but that's only if a store sold the book for cover price, which often wouldn't be the case. Doing the math on how many books must sell to simply earn back my advance—perhaps 10,000, considering store discounts— only depressed me more as I watched the two copies not sell that afternoon. I resisted the urge to buy one of my own books for the sake of convincing myself that one had sold, which technically would be true. But desperate as authors can be, even I wouldn't stoop to that. I did, however, wonder if things would have been different had *American Nightingale* come out in March instead of late May, giving it more time to get noticed before the big World War II festivities in Washington, D.C. On this trip, I'd seen a number of special D-Day book displays but only once was *American Nightingale* included.

I headed back to computer urgent care. Forty-five minutes later, I finally got a one-on-one with the young techno-surgeon in whose hands I'd placed my iBook. He pressed a bunch of keys—a "T" and something else—and the thing started booting up. A sweet sound, indeed.

"So it's alive?" I asked.

He nodded slightly. The mother board, he said, had gone bad and would need replacing. All the data would need to be transferred onto a new board. Basically, my computer needed a brain transplant. I glanced at the clock. It was 3 P.M. The store closed at 8 P.M.

"How much time?"

"We should be able to get it done tonight."

"Wonderful," I said.

He made good on his promise. The data all made the journey from one mother board to the other and the fix was free because I had purchased a service warranty when I'd bought the computer. Of course, the back-up zip drive he recommended—and I should have already been using all along—cost $250. But I had my life back. And, after ten days of being apart, I'd soon have my wife back. Sally was arriving that evening. For a day that had started so badly, it was finishing well. As Houdini, I was wet, cold, and shivering, but walking out of the East River, the casket and chains left behind me.

After meeting Sally at National Airport—we'd been apart too long—she told me about how, on the Eugene-to-Denver leg of her flight, she'd been walking down the aisle and seen a woman reading a book. "Then I realized what book," she said. "Yours."

"*Nightingale?* She was reading *my* book?"

"Yeah."

"Cool!"

The news made my day. In all my years of writing, I'd never seen someone reading one of my books. If it couldn't be me seeing the phenomenon, this was—as the old phone commercials used to say—the next-best-thing to being there. Never mind that the chances of seeing someone on a plane reading my book were higher on a Eugene-Denver flight than on any other flight; lots of people going east from Eugene are on that flight. And Eugene was the only place *Nightingale* had gotten any significant publicity. Still, it happened. The only thing better, I figured, would be to actually see, for myself, someone reading a book I wrote. Someday, perhaps. Someday.

In Washington, D.C., the roller coaster day was winding to an end. I sighed. Life was good. Sally and I had been reunited. My laptop was alive and well. In two days, our book would be featured on *Good Morning America*. But if this journey had taught me anything, it was that roller coasters spend most of their time climbing or falling, seldom zipping along level track. My slow acceptance of that was good preparation for the next zero-G drop I would experience. Because even as Sally and I relaxed that evening, Thea Trachtenberg and others at *Good Morning America* were scrambling to redo the next morning's show, the show our segment had been rescheduled for.

Instead, it would be devoted almost entirely to former President Ronald Reagan. At 6 P.M. Eastern Daylight Time, he had died at his home in Los Angeles.

Chapter 15

June 5-10, 2004
Washington, D.C., and Arlington, Virginia

I see, but cannot reach, the height
That lies forever in the light,
And yet forever and forever,
When seeming just within my grasp,
I feel my feeble hands unclasp,
And sink discouraged into night!

    —Henry Wadsworth Longfellow, "A Village Church"

And I saw that all labor and all achievement spring from man's
envy of his neighbor. This, too, is meaningless, a chasing after the
wind.

    —Ecclesiastes 4:4

AS PREDICTABLY as Red Sox pennant flops, the e-mail arrived later that night from *Good Morning America* producer Thea Trachtenberg. I'd seen the news, read the headlines. The e-mail said exactly what I knew it would say: because of Reagan's death, the *American Nightingale* segment was indefinitely on hold. Like him or loathe him, Reagan had been one of those bigger-than-life presidents. Those in the media, *Good Morning America* among them, dropped whatever they were doing and rushed to the story like gulls flocking to a belly-up salmon.

The Washington, D.C., FOX affiliate dropped Wednesday's scheduled segment with Sallylou and me. "Voice of America" kept putting me off. I couldn't even get a *Washington Times* reporter to return my calls. And if some of my "bird-in-a-hand" possibilities had flown off for this bigger, fresher story, getting new gigs was now going to be all but impossible.

Meanwhile, amid the disappointment, I got on the Metro and

headed to the Smithsonian for a Sunday book-signing event. I considered it an honor to be signing at such a historic place on such a historic day, the sixtieth anniversary of the D-Day landings, even if I was tucked so far from the mainstream foot traffic that someone would have to be seriously lost to find me. But I talked a Smithsonian bookstore manager into moving my table to a better location.

Immediately, a man from across the room, seeing me sitting alone at the table, raced over with a sense of urgency. He looked at the stack of books. "Are you the author of this?" he asked, picking up a copy.

"I am," I said, relieved that my ship was apparently coming in.

"Wow," he said. "That's cool! So, hey, do you know if there's, like, a bathroom around here?"

It would be the most oft-asked question of the day, ranking just above, "Where's the bookstore?" and "Do you know what time it is?" I sat at that table for three hours. Thousands of people streamed by. Bus loads of school kids streamed by. The residents of entire assisted-living homes streamed by. Seven books sold.

Don't panic, I told myself. There's always *Good Morning America*. Maybe.

That night, Sally and I had dinner at a sidewalk cafe in an Arlington neighborhood that was everything Sally and I were not— young, hip, and ethnically diverse. We went to bed early. I was reading from Emily Yellin's *Our Mother's War*, a well-done book by a woman whom I'd met the previous week at the Women in Military Service for America event. Sally read *American Nightingale*, something she had vowed to do only after it was completely done. After half an hour, I put my book aside and tried going to sleep. Ten minutes later, at the brink of succeeding, I heard it: sniffling.

"Are you crying?" I asked Sally. More sniffling. "Babe, what's the matter?"

"Fr-Fr-Fr-Frances died."

"What?"

"In your book," she said. "Frances died."

I smiled and shook my head. "And you're surprised?"

"No, of course not, but it's like she's been part of us for so long and we've been so busy talking about her life ... ." She half cried and half laughed. "I didn't know I'd take it so hard. She's gone."

I held her close while she cried about the death of Frances Slanger, and we both fell asleep.

OUR SEGMENT for *Good Morning America* didn't run Tuesday and, for the first time, Thea's occasional e-mail messages weren't suggesting that it was only a matter of "when," but "if." If it couldn't be squeezed in over the next two days, it wouldn't run, period. I mentally gulped; I hadn't considered that it might get shelved for good. But Tenet's resignation and Reagan's death—what were the chances of this doubleheader?—were proving ominous. Thursday was the sixtieth anniversary of the women landing at Utah Beach; if the show lost that time peg it was like the space shuttle losing its one window of opportunity to land. There would be no other chances.

I turned to Sally. "Not looking good," I said.

"If it's meant to be, it'll be," she said. "Nothing we can do about it." It was nice to have at least one rational person among the two of us.

The only thing that saved me from becoming an emotional Mount St. Helens was a well-timed distraction: the tribute for the nurses and others from the Forty-fifth Field Hospital was only two days off. It was Tuesday. The dinner would be Wednesday night and the tour of the memorials Thursday morning. Forty-eight people were coming from six states: New Hampshire, Delaware, Massachusetts, Virginia, Connecticut, and, of course, Oregon.

Sally and I met with Dick Foth, my casual Washington, D.C., friend who'd somehow pulled strings to get some army major to at least make an appearance at the banquet and another to offer an invocation. Later, we met with the hotel's events planner to see the room we'd reserved and talk specifics about the dinner, podiums, microphones, projector screens—the works.

Back at the room, I designed and printed up programs. "Off to Kinko's," I told Sally. "Tom and Maggie arrive around six so we'll leave for the airport around three. There'll be lots of rush-hour traffic."

Tom Penix was *The Register-Guard's* graphics editor. More

than that, he was a close friend, a guy who had encouraged me on the Slanger project from the moment he heard about it. A guy with a big heart and a wacky sense of humor. Once, outside some swanky dinner before baseball's All-Star game in San Diego back in the eighties, he had pretended to be Jerry Mathers, "The Beaver" on TV's *Leave It to Beaver*. After a friend had said, "Hey, it's 'The Beaver!' he had signed dozens of autographs before the two of them bolted, nearly unable to stop laughing. He loved laughter, baseball, God, people, especially his family, and, after an L.A. upbringing, life in rural Oregon.

Not long after I'd mentioned putting on the tribute in D.C., he had asked if he could come. "To Washington?" I asked.

"Yeah. With Maggie. She loves history and we promised her a special high-school graduation present. She'd love this. I think we can get some cheap flights."

"Of course," I said. I was stunned and honored. Not only that he wanted to come, but that he and Maggie wanted to help. Maggie, I said, could help Sally in getting the room set up. If I e-mailed him photos, he told me, he'd see to it that life-sized photos of all the honorees lined the banquet room's walls. Tom and Maggie were among thirteen Eugeneans planning on coming for the two-day event.

Before leaving to pick them up, I checked my e-mail one last time. Good news, though, of course, I'd already seen good news turn bad when it came to *Good Morning America*. Thea Trachtenberg hoped the segment would air Wednesday, but made no promises. Reagan's body was being flown to Washington, D.C., Wednesday, and much depended on what live footage was available at what time during the two-hour show.

I spent about forty-five minutes sending out another 600 e-mails to those on my list, the change-after-change-after-change messages reminding me of that scene in *Airport!* where a gate clerk says: "Trans American Flight 209 non-stop from Los Angeles is now arriving at Gate seven … Gate eight … Gate … ." But what else could I do?

At Baltimore-Washington International Airport, we picked up Tom and Maggie right on schedule and headed for Camden Yards to watch an Orioles-Diamondbacks game, eat hickory-smoked beef at Boog Powell's place along "The Warehouse" in right field, and, generally, relax. It was a perfect evening: baseball amid that wonderful daylight-to-sunset-to-darkness shift. Great company. A perfect evening, indeed, until I went to the restroom and Tom decided to let his latent sense of humor out for a seventh-inning stretch. I was lined up at the urinals with about a dozen other guys when Tom, edging toward the exit, said loudly: "Hey, there's Bob Welch—in the beige shirt and shorts! He's going to be on *Good Morning America* tomorrow! Wow!" And then bolted.

So glad I invited him along.

"AND THERE'S a new book out, called *American Nightingale* ... . " In the 6 A.M. slumber of our hotel room, there was Diane Sawyer, in living color, talking about my book. It was happening. The *Good Morning America* segment was being run. A full-screen shot of the book. D-Day shots. Irwin being interviewed. Sallylou and John being interviewed. Me being interviewed. Four minutes. Good music. A wonderful segment.

When it was over, Sally and I high-fived each other. "I don't believe it," I said. "We were just on *Good Morning America*. It happened."

But, ah, the ghost of Ronald Reagan would laugh last. Three hours later, when the segment should have aired on the West Coast, I got a call from son Ryan in Eugene. We'd gotten bumped. Instead of *American Nightingale*, my mother, extended family, friends— at least the entire Pacific time zone—watched aerial footage of a vehicle taking Ronald Reagan's body to the Point Mugu Naval Air Station northwest of Los Angeles for the flight to Washington, D.C. For all I knew, the Central and Rocky Mountain time zones had missed the *Nightingale* segment, too.

"Easy grounder to Buckner. Oh, my gosh, it slips beneath his legs! The Red Sox let another World Series slip through their fingers!"

So close; so far away. I felt like the night my Kidsports team's championship game was rained out and we were deemed "co-champions." I didn't lose, but I didn't feel as if I'd won either. I shook my head sideways. But there wasn't time to contemplate, celebrate, grieve, or engage in whatever mixed emotions I was experiencing with this good news/bad news scene. I had to turn my attention to that night's banquet and to other matters. The *Washington Times* was on the line, trying to set up a pre-banquet photo of some of the nurses. Dick Foth called; Retired Major General Mick Kicklighter was going to be able to make it, but only briefly before having to leave for another meeting. If OK with me, he said, he'd invited another retired major general, Robert Drees, to offer an invocation. "Sure," I said. "Sounds good."

Sallylou Bonzer, energetic as ever, called to say she had arrived at the hotel and was meeting Betty Belanger (Quinn) in the lobby; did I want to come? To see two army nurses meet after being apart nearly sixty years? Of course.

On the way down the elevator, Sallylou told me John was tired. At eighty-five, he was already in shaky health; the cross-country flight from Oregon had been hard on him. But, she said, he was excited about seeing his old tent mate, Joseph Shoham, that night at the banquet.

As we exited the elevator, the first thing I saw was a newspaper photographer from the *Washington Times* fiddling with her camera bag. The second was Betty. I hung back. Sallylou, of course did not.

"Betty?" Sallylou said. "Betty Belanger?"

"Is that you, Sallylou?" The two hadn't seen each other since 1945. They lit up like school girls before a prom, hugging and holding double hands, stepping back to look at one another. A few people in the hotel lobby couldn't help but stop and watch the reunion with curiosity.

"We got older!" Sallylou said.

"I'll say we did," Betty said.

The two sat on a couch, still holding hands, still looking into each other's eyes and probably seeing 1944. Meanwhile, the *Times* photographer clicked away. In that moment, listening to two women try to catch up on six decades of life, I sensed this tribute event was already worth it.

I excused myself, my mind back on the utilitarian chores of getting things done—and, of course, worrying about obstacles. Among them: the increased traffic that we'd face the next day because of Reagan's body lying in state in the capitol rotunda.

"Bad timing," I told Penix as we fought some rush-hour traffic to get a projector so we could show the DVD at the banquet.

"Bobby, there's nothing we can do about it," he said.

"He's following me."

"Who?"

"Ronald Reagan. First, he knocks us off the West Coast. Now his traffic is going to clog the streets, and we're going to be stuck on a bus with forty people, most of whom are nearly ninety years-old and it's going to be hot and—"

"Have some faith, man, it's going to work out."

That's the problem with believing. We never believe enough. We say we believe, but our worry suggests the opposite. We fret when we should be remembering the words, "Be still and know I am God."

When we returned, Sally and Maggie were already getting the banquet room ready.

"I'm a little worried about John Bonzer," I told Sally, still worrying. "Sallylou said the trip was tough on him. He's pretty frail."

We taped up thirteen life-size posters of the honorees that Tom had brought, including group shots of the Forty-fifth Field Hospital Unit and a picture of the *Frances Y. Slanger* ship with explanatory captions for each. We draped red, white, and blue bunting over the podium, placed bouquets of small American flags at the center of each table, and sprinkled sand I'd taken from Utah Beach at each place setting, along with programs:

> *A tribute*
> *to the memory of Frances Slanger,*
> *represented by her three nephews:*
> *Irwin Sidman, Jerry Sidman & Francis Sidman,*
> *And to four nurses of the 45th Field Hospital:*
> *Sallylou Cummings Bonzer, Mae Montague Bowen,*
> *Dottie Richter Lewis & Betty Belanger Quinn.*
>
> *And to three others of the 45th:*
> *Dr. John Bonzer, Joseph Shoham & Charles Willin.*
>
> *Arlington, Virginia*
> *June 9-10, 2004,*

60 years from the date the 45th splashed ashore in France.

Honors presented by
Lt. Col. Christine Johnson & Maj. Jennifer Petersen,
U.S. Army Nurse Corps,
& Lt. Gen. Ret. Claude "Mick" Kicklighter,
Assistant Secretary for Veterans' Affairs

Social hour
Invocation: Maj. Gen. Ret. Robert Dees
Dinner
Film Presentation: American Nightingale—*An Overview*
Honoring of our "Heroes of the 45th"
Sharing, toasts

As we tidied up, in walked Pat Gariepy from Eugene—"Hey, stranger!" I said—with a suitcase full of his World War II memorabilia: John's field jacket, a helmet, a musette bag, a flashlight, and a Red Cross shoulder wrap. I put the soundtrack from *Pearl Harbor* in the CD player—how many hundreds of times had I listened to that as I wrote the book?—and we stepped back to drink it all in.

An hour later, excited but too tired to be nervous, Sally and I were dressed and back in the room, awaiting the arrival of the guests. Slowly, they trickled in: white- and gray-haired men and women, some using canes, accompanied by their adult children in their forties and fifties, members of "the Greatest Generation" with looks on their faces of anticipation and a slight touch of uncertainty. Sixty years is a long time.

"Captain Shoham!" I said as Joseph, his wife Ethel, son Michael, and daughter-in-law Andrea walked in.

"Mr. Welch!" His eyes were brighter than I'd ever seen them.

"Yes," I said. "All the way from *Ara-gawn!*"

He laughed. We shook hands. He was wearing a blueish-gray suit, a World War II hat and, as the Forty-fifth's unofficial entomologist, a brightly colored butterfly tie. He pulled a wrapped present out of a bag and handed it to me: a butterfly carefully mounted in a showcase frame.

"It's beautiful," I said. "Thanks."

The evening began like microwave popcorn—a few "pops" here and there giving way to a spirited cacophony of greetings, hugs, handshakes, and photos. Betty Belanger Quinn arrived, soon followed by Dorothy Richter Lewis, and Mae Montague Bowen. All the nurses had arrived. All except Sallylou Bonzer.

Nathan Fendrich, the man whose phone call to me had started all this, chatted with Shoham, who, when that conversation ended, signed a copy of *American Nightingale* for Tom Penix's daughter, Maggie. Retired Major General Kicklighter went from nurse to nurse, presenting pins to them on behalf of the U.S. government. Irwin Sidman met, for the first time, men and women who had known his Aunt Frances. Jim Michalove, whose dad, Fred, had died the year after I'd interviewed him, met people who had served with his father.

"Monty!" said Betty Belanger when seeing Mae Montague. They hugged.

I wanted to put everything in slow motion, so busy was I trying to greet people, take photos, and savor the moments. Ron Palmer arrived with his wife Linda and daughter Kirsten, an Air Force captain stationed in Germany who had come in her service-dress blues.

Sally caught my eye in the crowd. "Where are Sallylou and John?" she asked.

I, too, was getting worried; dinner would begin soon. "Don't know," I said, looking toward the door.

Major Jennifer Petersen of the U.S. Army Nurse Corps spoke enthusiastically with Dottie Richter, two women separated by a half-century in age but bound by service to the same military outfit. Our West Coast contingent chatted with the Northeasterners. The adult "children" of one honoree met similarly aged "children" of another. *Thank you so much for writing this book*, they told me time and again. *I had no idea my mother was such a hero. She never talked about it.*

None of them did. In two years of my doing research, it was among the most consistent patterns I noticed: adult children who knew little more than that their mothers had been nurses in the war. Not women sometimes saving lives and sleeping in fox holes and pulling blankets over the eyes of a soldier's death stare. But tonight was a night to tuck such gruesome memories away and remember the good times.

"Did I ever tell you how I once extracted a tooth using only two match sticks?" Shoham said to Fendrich.

Forty-four people were packing the room. As if this were a high-school yearbook party, Betty and Mae and Dorothy signed their photos in *Nightingale's* mid-section. Shoham pointed to the life-size photograph of him at twenty-nine and laughed. Betty Belanger politely showed off the medal she'd been given by the French government in a ceremony just days ago in Normandy. It was as if the nurses were all Cinderellas; for at least one night, queens of the ball. Waiters began bringing in salads.

"Bobby."

I turned. Sally nodded toward the door. There, bending over a cane, was white-haired Dr. John Bonzer with Sallylou at his side. Their two daughters, Lexie and Laura, walked next to them. I instinctively looked for Shoham, Bonzer's former tent mate. The chatter in the room gradually quieted. Shoham looked toward Bonzer, Bonzer toward Shoham. Their eyes met. And as much as two nearly ninety-year-old men can fly into each other's arms, they flew. They hugged. They wept. And like part of a movie dance scene in which one couple shines so brightly that the others feel privileged to simply stop and watch, we did the same. I think we were all thinking the same thing, that we were in the midst of something special.

"TONIGHT," I SAID in my opening remarks, "we reunite these heroes who, exactly sixty years ago, with nervous stomachs, waited on the *William N. Pendleton* to go ashore at Normandy, among the first nurses in France. Heroes who served our country so nobly. Heroes who raised families, many members of whom we're honored to have here with us tonight ... ."

I recognized that in this room were four generations of Americans from West Coast to East. "All bound by one woman," I said, "Frances Slanger."

Retired Major General Drees then stepped to the microphone, a last-minute substitute for Kicklighter, who had already left. I had no idea who this man was or what he might say, only that Foth believed in him. He began by mentioning the historic event happening across the Potomac River; people had already begun lining up to view the casket of Ronald Reagan in the capitol rotunda the next day. "What's happening over there is historic," he said. "What's happening here is historic as well."

I breathed a sigh of relief. He obviously knew, and appreciated, who these people were and what they had done. He thanked God for the food, for the bond we all shared, for this time to gather, and the festivities began.

After dinner, we showed the DVD. By this point, I'd been with the Bonzers half a dozen times when it had been shown, and each time, at the same point—the mention of Slanger's death—John's eye began glistening. This night was no different.

We honored the fourteen nurses, Slanger among them, who had passed on. We honored Slanger's nephews, Irwin and Jerry, and Frank, who, despite my constant prodding, couldn't make the event. We honored Dr. John Bonzer, Joseph Shoham, and Charles Willin. And, finally, we honored the four nurses still alive: Sallylou Bonzer, Betty Belanger, Mae Montague, and Dottie Richter. The U.S. Army Nurse Corps officers who presented them with medals, Lieutenant Colonel Christine Johnson and Major Jennifer Petersen, were almost more emotional than the women whom they were honoring. "What an amazing contribution they made," Petersen would tell me afterward.

In my final remarks, I read the poem by James W. Foley I'd found in Frances Slanger's scrapbook:

> *Drop a pebble in the water; just a splash and it is gone;*
> *But there's a half-a-hundred ripples circling on and on,*
> *Spreading, spreading, from the center,*
> *   flowing on out to the sea*
> *And there's no way of telling where the end is going to be.*

I told about Betty Belanger sending me the check for $200 and me sending it back, saying she and the others had already given. And how a few days later the people at the retirement organization in Eugene had donated $1,450, unsolicited, to help make this evening possible.

"The message in that money," I said, "is this: You are appreciated. You have served well. And you are leaving the world a better place because of the sacrifices you made sixty years ago."

We then passed the microphone and let people make comments. As people did so it was as if I finally put all this in perspective. At its deepest, this experience wasn't about book sales and national TV and clawing to somehow prove my worth as an author. It was about the people in this room and the people of the Forty-fifth no longer with us. Not the material things, but the deeper things that mattered to Slanger herself. Things I had known but had lost sight of along the way.

In that moment, it was as if it all came clear to me, as if I'd been so busy trying to get to the finish line, trying to win some race of my mind's own making, that I'd missed the simple joy of running. As if my unwritten definition of success had become, in my blindness, all about me instead of about giving myself to something greater than myself. About only what I, in my impatience, could see now, instead of those ripples that were rolling to the future's distant shores. "Waiting for the vision that tarries is the test of our loyalty to God," Oswald Chambers has written. "It is at the peril at our soul's welfare that we get caught up in practical work and miss the fulfillment of the vision."

The banquet concluded, though many lingered to talk before heading for their rooms. I overheard Shoham chatting with Bonzer. "These memories will have to be with us the rest of our lives, Johnny," he said, "because I don't think we're coming back for another reunion." It was as if the tribute was one of the monarch butterflies he used to watch fluttering across Staten Island each year as a kid—beautiful, but fleeting.

Afterward, after we'd cleaned up, Sally and I returned to our room, exhausted but in the best of ways. I turned to this woman who, on New Year's Eve day more than three years ago, had dared me to dream. Had stuck with me. Had rolled up her sleeves for all sorts of behind-the-scenes jobs, from slapping hundreds of labels on packages of books we sent out to letting her house be turned into a television studio. "Thank you," I said, "for everything."

As I lay in bed, the events of the evening racing through my mind, I reflected even more on the *Nightingale* experience. On this one day, despite only a "partial airing," millions had been introduced to Slanger on *Good Morning America*. The book's amazon.com rank had leapt from five digits to three digits: 287th place out of millions of books.

But that wasn't, and wouldn't be, my deepest fulfillment on this journey. The deepest fulfillment had just occurred downstairs at that banquet: unsung heroes, after six decades, finally getting the honor they deserved.

How strange, I thought, that the day began with me and my book being on national television and ended in the obscurity of a banquet that few, beyond those who attended, even knew about. Nobody from the media showed. And yet if I had to choose which moment to relive—Diane Sawyer introducing my book on national TV or Shoham and Bonzer wrapped in each other's arms—I would, without hesitation, choose the hug.

I thought of all the people who blew on the embers that would ultimately spark *American Nightingale* to life: Nathan Fendrich's encouragement—OK, insistence—that I write about Slanger. Sallylou Bonzer's phone call to Nathan after seeing that column. John Greenwood's phone call about Emory Massman's book on hospital ships, which led to the discovery of the "two suitcases" at the Boston University archives. Milton Zola answering a *Boston Globe* classified ad and, ultimately, unlocking Slanger's childhood for me. Richard Boylan of the National Archives taking time to lead me directly to dozens of letters from soldiers whose lives had been touched by Slanger. Erich Dahmen, a stranger who barely spoke English, helping me understand 1940s Belgium. And others who stepped forward with pieces of the puzzle I needed but did not have, from Pat Gariepy in Eugene to Rivka Freudenstein in Israel.

We tend to forget how *necessary* we are to one another. How our choices effect the world around us and each other. Consider, for example, that *American Nightingale* might never have been written had *Register-Guard* newspaper carrier Don Kahle overslept on the morning of December 14, 2000, and not gotten the paper, which included my Slanger column, on the Bonzer's doorstep. Without the Bonzer connection, I had no impetus to write the book, no starting place, no connection to the past. How far-reaching can the ripples of a pebble be. Because what all these people had in common, I realized in my late-night reflections, was this: they took action for the benefit of someone else. Me.

Milton Zola didn't need to write me a letter after seeing that classified ad; he was on his way out the door to watch the Red Sox in *Flawida*. John Greenwood didn't need to fax me that chapter on the Frances Y. Slanger ship; he certainly had more important things to do. Erich Dahmen didn't need to invite in two strangers who knocked on his closed-for-the-season hotel that rainy Saturday morning; we didn't even speak his language. Dick Foth didn't need to hook me up with Dr. Timothy Johnson; Dick is a guy who routinely rubs shoulders with foreign dignitaries and I was just a guy he'd met at a writers conference. But all four took small risks that yielded big results, at least in my eyes. In the end, the book's Acknowledgments included 197 people who, in some way, helped *American Nightingale* be written. And the sum of their efforts had been, in essence, this evening: A tribute to those who might otherwise have died without having been properly thanked.

THE NEXT MORNING, we toured the memorials. The traffic wasn't nearly the nightmare my ye-of-little-faith mind had imagined. The weather was fine, not the unbearable heat I'd feared. We visited the new World War II Memorial on the National Mall first. Fendrich, wearing an old army cap from his service during the Korean War in the fifties, morphed into a sort of unofficial public relations director for the group. "You are amid greatness today," he'd say to a group of other visitors. "These people here are from the Forty-fifth Field Hospital, the first nurses to step ashore in France during World War II."

The $174 million circular monument was a far cry from most tacky memorials. Wrapped around a large pool, it framed a majestic view of the Lincoln Memorial to the west and the Washington Monument to the east, a fitting location to pay tribute to an event, World War II, that changed the Twentieth Century. I found it reverent, sobering—416,800 U.S. soldiers died in battle—and yet somehow hopeful, tiny stars representing war deaths and the fountains representing the continuum of life.

Pat Gariepy and Sallylou Bonzer stopped to be photographed beyond the words of Dwight Eisenhower etched in stone: "You are about to embark upon the great crusade toward which we have striven these many months. The eyes of the world are upon you. I have full confidence in your courage, devotion to duty and skill in battle."

"Nice," said Nathan Fendrich, "but those words should have been Frances Slanger's words. Her entire letter should be chiseled in this stone."

I just smiled to myself. John Bonzer's daughters took turns pushing their father in a wheelchair. Shoham stayed at his old tent mate's side, walking slowly beside Bonzer, sometimes pushing his friend's wheelchair.

"Did you see Betty's medal from the French government?" said Sallylou, who also had been invited by the French to receive the award but had opted out because of John's health. "I could have had one had I gone."

People took photos and videos, took time to sit and reflect, took stock of a meaning that went deeper for them than it probably did for most others who perused the memorial.

Soon we headed for the Women in Military Service for America Memorial at the entrance to Arlington National Cemetery. I had arranged red-carpet treatment; the bus, for example, was to take us to the memorial's front doors so our people wouldn't have to do any more walking than necessary. But a quarter-mile from the entrance, a guard in a blue uniform halted us in front of a wooden barricade. The bus driver and I got out. I felt like some sort of scout leader with forty people counting on me.

"Sorry, you'll need to park back here in the lots," said the guard.

"But we arranged to have our group be brought right to the front," I said.

"All buses park in the lots."

I was surprised at his stubbornness. "This is the Forty-fifth Field Hospital, the first World War II nurses to—"

"Sir, all buses park in the lots."

I glanced back at the bus, then back at the guard. This just wasn't right. I reached in my pocket for my cell phone. Finding a number on my notepad, I called the director and explained our situation. "It's the director," I said to the guard. "She wants to talk to you."

The young guard reluctantly took the phone. "Uh-huh," he said. I glanced at the bus driver, then back at the guard. "Uh-huh, yes, ma'm. Yes. Understood."

He handed me the phone. "Right this way, sir," he said, waving us forward, then dragging the barricade to the side. I returned to the bus and couldn't resist. "The Forty-fifth Field Hospital," I said, pumping my fist in the air, "will not be denied!" Those on board—heroes and their sons and daughters—broke into raucous cheers as if on a high school rally bus.

The WIMSA memorial is impressive and, rather than tucked in some cranny of Arlington's sprawling grounds, anchors the entrance with a sweeping semicircular wall of stone, surrounding a large reflective pool. Built in 1997, it includes a theater, hall of honor, computer registry, and quotations from women etched in glass, including one from Beatrice Hood Stroup, a major in the Women's Army Corps during World War II: "It isn't just my brother's country or my husband's country, it's my country as well," she wrote. "And so the war wasn't just their war. It was my war, and I needed to serve in it."

We toured the memorial, watched movies of women in the war, saw *American Nightingale* in the gift shop. "This book," Fendrich said to a total stranger, "is about these women right here, the Forty-fifth Hospital, women who climbed down rope ladders and jumped out of landing crafts at Normandy."

Later, we gathered out front to wait for the bus. "Pictures! Pictures!" I said. In front of the pool, I posed with the nurses, with Slanger's two nephews, then with the whole gang of honorees. Dozens of cameras clicked, pointed by admiring sons and daughters, by museum staffers, by people like Fendrich who understood so well what these people had done.

We loaded up—slowly, of course—and returned to the hotel. As each person got off that bus, we knew this was it. Most of us would never see each other again. That thought suddenly struck me when I helped Joseph Shoham down from the last step. I had been so caught up in the arrangements, the planning, the logistics of the event, that I'd left little time to contemplate the deeper stuff. To *feel*.

But as I shook Shoham's hand and looked him in the eyes, I was no longer a tour guide or an events manager or, for that matter, an author. I was a fifty-year-old guy from the West Coast, a Christian who had never known war firsthand. Shoham was an eighty-nine year-old guy from the East Coast, a Jew who had been wounded in the same artillery barrage that had killed Slanger. In some ways, he had become like some long-lost grandfather to me. Shoham's words to Bonzer the previous night stirred somewhere deep inside me: *These memories will have to be with us the rest of our lives, Johnny, because I don't think we're coming back for another reunion.*

I started to say goodbye but it seemed too little, too late. I wrapped my arms around Shoham and he did the same to me. I blinked back tears, as if this were a moment that I hadn't stopped to consider would come, and was surprised—though not embarrassed—how difficult it was once it did.

Shoham looked at me. "You brought her back to life, Bob."

"What?"

"Frances. You kept her story alive. Thank you."

"No," I said. "Thank you. *We* kept her story alive. All of us."

All of us who were now pebbles in Frances Slanger's pond.

SALLY AND I left on different flights that night, she to return home, me to go to New Orleans to speak on Slanger at the National Society of Newspaper Columnists conference and at the national Uniformed Nurses Practitioners Conference.

Three days later, I was on the final leg home—Denver-to-Eugene—and thinking what a long, strange trip it had been, from a phone call to the Hotel Buckminster to Normandy on 9/11 to a sleepless night on an airport skywalk to the on-again-off-again *Good Morning America* to the unforgettable banquet.

From beginning to end, I'd been guided, inspired, and encouraged by so much: my faith, my friends, my family. And by a two-inch by three-inch quote I had taped above my writing area: "The greatest risk is not taking one."

Look what had happened because Nathan Fendrich had first

taken a risk, then Sallylou, then me, then dozens of others. A book was written. A hero remembered. A group of nurses honored.

After all the hopes and letdowns, twists and turns, the journey had left me changed from the person I had been at the start. My world had gotten larger; at times, I found myself at Sidman gatherings in Boston where I was the only non-Jewish person in the room. My faith had grown deeper. And my resiliency had grown stronger. Still a flawed human being, yes, pulled, too often by greed and selfishness, but with a better understanding that what really matters aren't the things that the world values—power, money, beauty, and fame. But the God things of the heart.

Would such insight had come to me had I not followed the Slanger trail into the darkness? Perhaps. Would the people on that bus have felt the pride of being honored for something that most people around them had forgotten? Perhaps. Would Slanger's story have been told by another writer at another time? Perhaps. But, looking back, *American Nightingale* seemed to have been like a dramatic production that each of us had been hand-picked to play parts in, as if Jane Kirkpatrick's words had proven prophetic: *You didn't find this story, it found you.*

Was it God's plan that I write this story? I can't say that for sure. I'm not God. What I can say is this: when we catch a vision to infuse the world with even a tiny touch of goodness, I believe the love and grace of God work through us in grand and mysterious ways.

I leaned my head on a pillow and shut my eyes. Life was good. Never mind that the Red Sox had fallen out of first place and were struggling, the ghost of Babe Ruth still vexing Boston. We'd pulled off the banquet. I was going home. The light thrum of the engines lulled me to sleep.

After awakening, probably someplace over Idaho, I went to the restroom and was coming back up the aisle when I saw her. She was on the right hand side of the the plane, a gray-haired woman, aisle seat. No, not Connie Frances, but a woman reading a book. But not just any book. She was reading *American Nightingale*. Just like Sally's experience a week ago.

I couldn't resist. "Excuse me," I said, "are you enjoying that book?"

"Oh, very much so."

"Glad to hear it," I said. "I wrote it."

The woman looked at me, then at the back-cover photo.

"Why—why, you're Bob Welch. I met your wife on the Eugene-to-Denver leg on my flight out east. She asked me the same question when she saw me reading it."

I was stunned. "Sally mentioned seeing you," I said. "So, you're from Eugene, too?"

"Yes," she said. "Read your column all the time. Would you sign the book for me?"

"Gladly."

I signed my name, said goodbye, then slid back into my seat. The poem in Slanger's scrapbook had been right about those ripples. There's no telling where the end is going to be.

Epilogue

Where your treasure is, there your heart will be also.
—Luke 12:34

During the meaningless late innings, three customers walked into the souvenir store on Yawkey Way and switched allegiances. They bought Yankees caps.
—Dan Shaughnessy in *Reversing the Curse*, after Boston was ripped by New York 19-8 to fall behind the Yankees 3-0 in the best-of-seven 2004 American League Championship Series

Hell Freezes Over
—Headline in the *New York Daily News* on October 21, 2004

IN THE LAST half of 2004, I spoke ninety-seven times on *American Nightingale*, often to service clubs, nursing organizations, and military groups, mainly in the Northwest. I sold the book at an array of events, including assisted-living gatherings where some residents would shuffle off to their rooms to get checks to buy books and I'd wonder if they'd ever return. (Most did.) I spoke to Jewish nurses at a national Hadassah conference in Washington, D.C., and at book clubs with a handful of women in a living room. In Chelsea, Massachusetts, on a rainy Friday night, I even found myself in the back of a compact car, en route to selling books after a sabbath service, a Barnes & Noble bookseller next to me, a twenty-pound pull cart sideways across our laps.

American Nightingale was featured in *Los Angeles Times* magazine. It got a smattering of publicity here and there, mostly small reviews in the backs of magazines and on book Web sites. But despite the *Good Morning America* spark and going into a paperback printing, the book never did burst into wild promotional flames and spread across the country. By mid-2008, it had sold about 7,200 hardback and 3,800 softcover books.

The banquet and tour of the memorials wound up costing $3,200, not the $750 I had originally planned on, back when it was going to be a cookies-and-punch gathering for twelve. But I never asked for a cent from anyone and I never spent a cent of my own money on the event. It was paid for by dozens of people who heard me tell Slanger's story, caught the vision, and wanted to be part of it.

From 2001 through 2004, I spent $67,364 on researching, writing, promoting, and marketing *American Nightingale*. Much of that was for a trip to France, three trips to the East Coast, and buying copies of my book from Simon & Schuster to sell at events. But as of May 2008, I had yet to see a royalty check, the book still $947.90 short of earning back its $20,000 advance. Figuring in roughly $35,000 in book sales at events at which I'd spoken—and honorariums paid to me for the speeches themselves—I figured that, seven years after I jotted those notes on a Wendy's napkin, I'd almost broken even.

IN JUNE 2004, I learned that the Massachusetts State Legislature had passed the bill to have a plaque honoring Slanger placed in the State House. I was asked by its sponsors to give the keynote speech at the Massachusetts State House in October. I eagerly accepted.

By early August, the Red Sox had fallen 10½ games behind the Yankees in the AL East, and two games behind the Texas Rangers for a wildcard spot in the playoffs. On August 31, at Fenway Park, sixteen-year-old Lee Gavin was hit in the face by a foul ball and lost two teeth. Gavin lived at 558 Dutton Road in suburban Sudbury, Massachusetts, in the same house where Babe Ruth had lived while playing for the Red Sox. (And, interestingly, only a half mile from the Fort Devens Military Reservation, where Frances Slanger had first reported for duty after enlisting.) On this night, not only would the Sox win but the Yankees would lose 22-0 to Cleveland to tie the record for the most lopsided shutout in modern major league baseball history. Boston fans were forever looking for some sort of sign that the curse might be reversed.

This, said some, was it. For whatever reason, Boston went on a 40-15 run late in the season to qualify for post-season play as a wildcard team. I was thrilled.

In October, I flew to Boston for the dedication of the Slanger plaque. As I dined out with Irwin and Joan Sidman, the Red Sox, who had beaten the Anaheim Angels in the American League Division Series, were at Fenway Park getting shellacked 19-8 by the Yankees. New York now led the best-of-seven American League Championship Series, 3-0. Boston's anguished past suggested that the next night's game would be the final humiliation in the team's attempt to win its first World Series title since Ruth was traded away in 1920. No major league baseball team had come back from a 3-0 deficit in a championship series to win four straight. Ever.

But, in 2004, the Boston Red Sox defied history. They did it. I was there. I saw it. I was sitting high up on the right-field line at Fenway Park, having bought a $90 ticket from a scalper on that cold Sunday evening. Going into the bottom of the ninth, Boston trailed 4-3 and the Yankees had Mariano Rivera, the best closer in post-season major league history, on the mound. But the Red Sox tied the game to send it into extra innings. And in the bottom of the 12th, David Ortiz hit a two-run homer to give Boston a 6-4 victory. Bedlam broke out at Fenway. Strangers hugged each other. I snapped photograph after photograph so I would always remember that extraordinary moment in sports history.

In New York, the Red Sox went on to win two more games against the Yankees, setting up a seventh-game decider. I was in the Fenway Park neighborhood that night, watching the game on TV in a restaurant packed with Red Sox fans. Boston led 10-3 in the bottom of the ninth inning, needing just one out to win the series. It was just before midnight on October 20, a day before the sixty-year anniversary of Frances Slanger's death. Too bad, I thought, the game couldn't drift past midnight and end on the twenty-first.

Suddenly, inexplicably, despite having a virtually insurmountable lead, Boston made a pitching change that prolonged the game. When the next batter grounded out, it was, officially, 12:01 a.m. The game had ended on October 21, Slanger's anniversary. Not that I believed there was some metaphysical connection between her death and Boston's reverse of the curse, mind you. But as I wandered the Fenway neighborhoods and watched thousands of fans screaming, hugging, drinking, and snapping cell phone pictures, I thought it was wonderfully odd that a totally unnecessary pitching change had sealed Slanger and the Red Sox onto the same date in history.

Amid the throng, I walked back to the Buckminster after buying a souvenir Red Sox shirt for $5 from a guy on the street corner whose left hand held a bouquet of bills. I opened the door, assured that if the Babe's ghost had actually lurked behind Mechanical Room No. 3, it had now been sent to the proverbial showers, never again to haunt Red Sox fans. Assuming, of course, Boston went on to beat St. Louis in the World Series.

THE NEXT DAY, as Bostonians continued to celebrate their vanquishing of the Yankees, I gave the keynote speech at the State House event in honor of Slanger. For nearly two decades, attempts had been made to establish the plaque but, every time, the effort died of neglect. State Representatives William C. Galvin and Louis L. Kafka were behind the renewed effort to pass the bill. "Welch's book is what allowed us to push the bill through," Galvin said in a press release. "Suddenly, here was this book showing who this amazing woman really was. People took notice."

Back in Oregon, I watched on TV as the Red Sox swept the St. Louis Cardinals 4-0 in the World Series, never trailing for even a single inning, to officially end the Curse of the Bambino after eighty-six years. When the final out came, I was speaking to a book club in Eugene about *American Nightingale*. Baseball writers would call Boston's comeback the greatest post-season performance in the century-plus history of major league baseball, the tipping point coming that night I was at Fenway when, one out away from elimination, the Red Sox refused to die.

IN ELSENBORN, BELGIUM, Erich Dahmen, after reading *American Nightingale*, talked city officials into having a plaque placed in the town square in honor of Frances Slanger. In Eugene, a World War II Prisoner of War who'd read the book called me and said he wanted to have a tree in the city's memorial garden planted in Slanger's honor; would I write the inscription for the plaque? The tree wasn't cheap—$750. But Bob Mangers reminded me that neither was freedom. "Frances Slanger's boots stepped foot on the same Utah Beach sand mine had," he said. "She can't be forgotten."

As I was boxing up *American Nightingale* files to store in my carport library annex, I came across the copies from Emory Massman's book about the hospital ships. And lamented that I never had been able to track down the man who'd pointed me to a goldmine of Slanger information.

Nathan Fendrich, who turned seventy the year the book came out, continued to do what he could to promote *Nightingale* but found himself increasingly despondent that no movie deal had been struck and that schools weren't welcoming his Holocaust and World War II presentations. Occasionally, he'd travel to Europe to satiate his culinary bent. Back home, for health reasons, his doctor recommended he begin walking while carrying weight on his back. He stuffed a backpack with out-of-date French restaurant guides, 800 World War II photos used for making his slide presentations, and old clothes. And, each day, he walked.

AMERICAN NIGHTINGALE, in the fall of 2005, emerged as a finalist for the Oregon Book Awards, but did not win. Sallylou Bonzer got her medal from the French government like the one Betty Belanger had gotten. It was presented to her at a special ceremony in Portland by a French ambassador. She wore it proudly whenever she'd go with me to some *Nightingale*-related presentation we'd make, the audience always amazed at the zest of this almost-ninety-year-old woman who still played golf once a week.

Meanwhile, though a handful of people at least explored the possibilities of optioning the book as a movie, almost all were inexperienced movie-deal makers. One such person got serious enough to place an option on *American Nightingale*. He paid $7,500—Ted, my agent, would get 15 percent of that—to put an eighteen-month hold on the book while trying to put a deal together. I began imagining a sort of rabbit-out-of-the-hat movie deal that would right the disappointing wrong of my father's *Trout in the High Country* movie having never hit the big time. But with only a month left on the option, no deal had been made.

I flew to Los Angeles and met with the head of this upstart company. My passion for the project seemed to fuel his passion. He sounded cautiously optimistic that he could make something happen. The deadline, however, came and went with no word back from him. Finally, I got an e-mail. This is it, I figured. This is the e-mail telling me he pulled an eleventh-hour deal; *American Nightingale* was going to be made into a movie, which would re-ignite interest in the book, spread the story of Frances Slanger, and even me up with Uncle Visa.

Instead, the e-mail was a "group-send" informing all his regular contacts—and, for some reason, me—that he was frustrated with his old Internet provider and was going with a new company. "Here's my new address," he wrote.

A FEW MONTHS later, I was walking on my lunch hour with a friend and colleague, Paul Neville, who had listened to more book talk since 2001 than any one man should have to. I was worn down. Still in debt. And if not spiritually shaking an angry fist at God, at least feeling—if, intellectually, knowing otherwise—that He'd somehow let me down.

"I somehow thought the end of the story was going to be a movie," I told Paul. "In some ways, I suppose I felt that I needed to make up for what my dad had failed to accomplish."

He pondered what I'd said for a moment. "Do you really think your father failed?" he asked. "Because I don't think he did. He had a dream. He took a risk. He made a movie. Did it fly? No. But that's not failing. He made a movie."

I loved my father, but, deep down, I suppose I was disappointed that he had apparently given up. Paul's words hurt in a painful but good way, like C.S. Lewis's "blows of His chisel." Because, I realized, that to believe my father had failed was to believe I had failed, too.

"I remember—what, four years ago?—you and I making this same walk," Paul said, "and you were wondering if you could write a book about this dead World War II nurse. Months later, you wondered if there was enough info. Then, whether you could find an agent. Then, whether your agent could find a publisher. Then, whether you could pull off that tribute in D.C. And look what happened. You did it, man. You did it. Can you accept that?"

I looked at him and half-smiled. I walked on, then nodded. "Yes, I can accept that." I needed to accept that. Needed to remember that, time and again, when I'd found myself seemingly trapped in a search for something I needed for the book, it was my mother's voice I would hear—*What would you do if you were the last person on earth?*—but it was my father's example—his improvisation—I would see: fashioning me a set of goal posts for my electric football set out of a couple of coat hangers or using a fan to turn our bath tub into the Atlantic Ocean for a movie scene. And I had done the same in the research, writing, and marketing of this book. Improvising. Imagining. Finding a way. I needed to stop blaming my father for his shortcomings and honor him for the gifts he'd passed on to me.

Finally, I needed to stop feeling as if God hadn't made good on some IOU I'd subconsciously thought was due me. And realize I had been blessed with life and grace and extraordinary people around me. Needed to quit playing this game of thinking that my actions deserved some sort of reward. "If we try to prove to God how much we love Him," writes Oswald Chambers, "it is a sure sign that we do not love Him. The evidence of our love for Him is the absolute spontaneity of our love, it comes naturally."

I needed to practice the very lesson Slanger herself had taught me: that our worth should not be defined in dollars and lists and awards and whatever else the world creates to distract us from the deeper things. Instead, it should be defined by whatever boot prints we make in the sand, regardless of whether anyone sees them before they've washed away.

AFTER THE BOOK was published, I received letters and e-mails from people who had read *American Nightingale*. But I was too busy waiting for that "something bigger"—the call from Oprah, the movie deal, The New York Times Bestseller list—to appreciate them. In hindsight, I was the living epitome of a line from that John Lennon song, "Beautiful Boy (Wonderful Boy)": "Life is what happens to you while you're busy making other plans."

Eventually, I slowed down enough to read the letters. Really read them. It was as if seeing them for the first time—letters from nurses, teachers, and sons and daughters of those who had served in World War II. A nurse serving in Iraq. A Florida woman who had, while reading of Slanger's death, cried on a plane home from Newark. Even a ninety-year-old World War II vet from nearby Salem who was sure it was Frances Slanger who had kept him alive when he was wounded in Aachen, near Elsenborn, in early October 1944. (It may well have been.)

"In your afterword," wrote a woman from Baxter, Minnesota, "you so eloquently answer your own question of why we should pursue such things: 'Evil, I was reminded, never goes away. It simply lurks in the shadows of time, morphs to fit the technological advances, and springs on another generation. We must remember the atrocities of the past to prevent such atrocities in the future.' I am inspired by both your book and Frances Slanger's life."

A former newspaper colleague of mine, Eric Mortenson, now a reporter with *The Oregonian*, wrote:

> Our job is to tell other people's stories. By doing that, we help people make connections. We can help them figure out the world around them, or just think about it a little harder. Sometimes we can just make someone laugh, or just nod in understanding, and that's enough. Sometimes we can make someone put a hand to his mouth and say, 'Oh my gosh.' You made me say 'Oh my gosh' with your last line about Frances. Now that's a ripple effect.

Among those ripples: A man who attended the same Grace Community Fellowship church I did rushed up to me one Sunday morning, having read the book: "Bob, I've sailed on the *Frances Y. Slanger!*" Allen Boyden said, "and my father was a surgeon in the Third Auxiliary Surgical Unit that was attached to the Forty-fifth Field Hospital at times. I wonder if the Bonzers knew him."

The ship story was implausible enough, though, after he explained, I realized it was true: he had, as a small boy in New York during the 1950s, taken a family cruise aboard the *Saturnia*, the Italian ship that had been confiscated by the U.S. government during the war, refitted, and turned into the *Slanger*, then released to its Italian owners in 1946. But though the Third Auxiliary had worked with the Forty-fifth, the chances of his late father having worked alongside the Bonzers were miniscule. "It was a big war," I told him. "I kind of doubt it."

I was wrong. "Sure, we remember Allen Boyden," said Sallylou Bonzer when I asked the question. "Good man. Good doctor." Sallylou and I had lunch with Allen Jr. and his mother. How wonderful for them, I thought, to get such out-of-the-blue affirmation about a man they loved but was no longer alive.

A granddaughter of John and Sallylou Bonzer, twenty-four, wrote: "They used to tell stories when I was younger and I had no comprehension of what they meant. This has all been so fascinating to me and I feel another level of appreciation for both of my grandparents." The son of a Forty-fifth Field Hospital man said *Nightingale* "scratched an itch I've had for some time now" about knowing more about his father's war experiences. At an event involving Jewish retirees, a woman with my book in her hand shuffled up to me afterwards, looked me in the eye, and said: "The angels walk with you."

DR. JOHN BONZER died in April 2007 at age eighty-nine. I spoke at his funeral, telling the story of his reunion with Joseph Shoham. At the reception, Sallylou reminded me that John's memory had faded considerably in the last few years of his life. "But for some reason he never forgot the night he and Joe saw each other for the first time since the war," she said.

Four months later, the *New Hampshire Union Leader* reported that Betty Belanger (Quinn), the nurse who had sent me the $200 check to help defray expenses for the tribute, "killed herself Saturday night by jumping from the fifth-floor balcony of her home at Carisbrooke condominiums, according to police." The next day, the newspaper retracted the report, saying "the police now say they don't know how the incident happened."

With Belanger's tragic death, only three of the original eighteen nurses remained alive. Beyond Sallylou, Mae Montague, eighty-seven, lives in Dover, Delaware and Dottie Ritchter, ninety-two, in Lewes, Delaware. Joseph Shoham, ninety-three, lost his wife, Ethel. He and I still talk by phone every few months.

OUR FAMILY grew by three. Jason graduated from the University of Oregon and married a wonderful young woman named Deena Hanson. Sally and I became grandparents, twice, thanks to Ryan and Susan. I bought a satellite radio so I could listen to every Red Sox game, home or away.

In the spring of 2008, as I was polishing the rough draft of *Pebble in the Water*, the Red Sox did something that surprised more than a few people: before their home opener, they honored Bill Buckner, whose error had long been blamed for Boston not winning the 1986 World Series. It was a rare act of forgiveness, rooted in perhaps a bit of shame, given how many fans had persecuted the guy for more than two decades.

A few days later, my laptop computer's hard drive crashed. I had thought I'd backed up nearly all of my files but discovered I had lost everything pertaining to *American Nightingale*. Hundreds of files. Gone.

I haven't figured out the meaning of that one, though I'm wondering if it's that the things we carry forward are best carried in the heart and not on hard drives. (Especially hard drives that haven't been backed up.)

Even if I'm right, I still believe in the value of remembering the past. Recently, Ryan, an amateur movie-maker whose DVD got us on *Good Morning America*, asked if I still had a copy of my father's *Trout in the High Country* movie, that he would love to see it.

I decided to explore the possibilities of having it transferred into DVD format, if for no other reason than to someday say to my grandchildren: *Look what your great-grandfather did. He had a dream and he followed it.*

IN JANUARY 2008, while doing research for *Pebble in the Water,* I stumbled onto a Web trail that led me to an amazing discovery: Emory Massman, the author of the *Hospital Ships of World War II* book that had led to my finding the Slanger "suitcases" at Boston University, was alive and well. I was able to send him the book he had never seen but might not have been written without his key piece in the puzzle.

Sometimes we don't realize the difference we make to others, the ways we play little parts in larger dramas. From time to time, I will see Nathan Fendrich walking beneath the weight of his backpack. Others probably see him as just this odd neighborhood regular who lugs around this weight on his back. But to me, he's far more. He's the man who, with a single phone call, started a chain of events that, if even in a small way, changed the world.

Acknowledgments

To Karen Zacharias and Ann Petersen, who edited the initial draft; Dean Rea, who copyedited the final draft; Tom Penix, who designed the cover; Jeff Wright and Paul Neville, who listened to considerable "Pebble babble" on noon-time walks; Peter Hoffmeister, who wrote a note of encouragement that's still stuck to my bulletin board; Beachside Writers students, who insisted I quit talking about the book and write it; and, above all, to Sally Jean, who loves me, and sticks by me, even though writers are so much more complicated than the farmer she wanted me to be: thank you all.

Also by Bob Welch

American Nightingale

The Story of Francis Slanger,
Forgotten heroine of Normandy

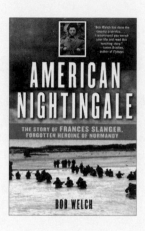

"A stirring story of intense personal devotion."
— **Publishers Weekly**

"Enrich your life and read this touching story."
— **James Bradley, author of "Flags of Our Fathers"**

"Has the golden cast of 'Saving Private Ryan.'"
—**Book Babes**

"A heartwarming story for all ages."
—**Booklist**

Published by Atria, a division of Simon & Schuster
Hardcover $22.
Softcover $14.
Available at bookstores and at www.amazon.com

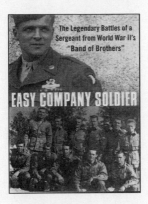
231

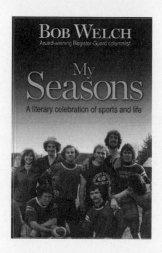

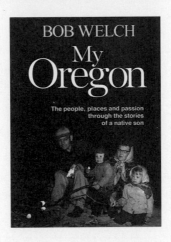

Speaking

BOB WELCH is a seasoned national speaker who uses heart and humor to inspire audiences. He has appeared on ABC's *Good Morning America*, spoken at the Massachusetts State House, and keynoted conferences from coast to coast. Welch reminds audiences that, like a pebble in the water, we often leave ripples that go farther than we'll ever realize. Among his many topics: feeling valued in the workplace, making communities work, leaving legacies of honor, appreciating sports beyond the scoreboard, and writing stories that can change the world.

"Absolutely superb! Mesmerizing, motivating, challenging."
— Clara Richardson, director, Purdue University School of Nursing

"Hands down, the most impressive speaker we have heard in years. The response was nothing short of remarkable."
— Alex Rankin, archivist, Boston University, Boston, Massachusetts

"Forget the hyperbole. Our 261 participants scored Welch a 4.81 on a 5.0-scale. Fantastic!"
— Julie Zander, director, Association of Personal Historians national conference, Portland, Oregon

CONTACT INFO

Phone: 541-517-3936
Email: info@bobwelch.net
Web-site: www.bobwelch.net
Mail: P.O. Box 70785, Eugene, OR 97401

Beachside Writers
Workshops

Yachats, Oregon

BEACHSIDE WRITERS Workshops are for people who love to write. Who want to write better. And who, while on a workshop break, prefer watching waves instead of standing in a 20-person bathroom line at some airport hotel. People who attend our workshops enjoy learning in a relaxed, lighthearted, non-threatening atmosphere. People of all writing abilities are welcome. Founded by Bob Welch in 2005, the workshops are offered on three levels:

Beachside 101. Inspiration on writing and 10 ways to make yours shine. Friday night and Saturday.

Beachside 201. Inspiration on writing, in-class writing and small-group sessions. Friday night and Saturday.

Beachside 301. Inspiration on writing, more in-class writing and more small-group discussions. Special guest: Jane Kirkpatrick. Friday night through mid-day Sunday.

Workshops are held at the Yachats Commons, generally in the fall and spring.

> "One of the most meaningful, memorable weekends in my entire life. Bob gave me one of the most precious gifts anyone has ever given me: validation as a writer!"
>
> **— Cara Zane McKenzie, Eugene**

CONTACT INFO

Phone: 541-517-3936
Email: info@bobwelch.net
Web-site: www.bobwelch.net
Mail: P.O. Box 70785, Eugene, OR 97401